Chicken Soup for the Soul.

Mothers & Daughters

Chicken Soup for the Soul: Mothers & Daughters
Amy Newmark

Published by Chicken Soup for the Soul, LLC www.chickensoup.com
Copyright ©2024 by Chicken Soup for the Soul, LLC. All Rights Reserved.

The publisher gratefully acknowledges the many publishers and individuals who granted Chicken Soup for the Soul permission to reprint the cited material.

Front cover photo courtesy of iStockphoto.com (©tatyana_tomsickova)
Back cover and interior photos: mother with two children courtesy of iStockphoto.com (©aldomurillo), photo of Asian mother and daughter courtesy of iStockphoto.com (©imtmphoto), photo of African American mother and daughter courtesy of iStockphoto.com (©kali9)
Photo of Amy Newmark courtesy of Susan Morrow at SwickPix

Cover and Interior by Daniel Zaccari

Publisher's Cataloging-in-Publication data

Names: Newmark, Amy, editor.
Title: Chicken soup for the soul : mothers & daughters / Amy Newmark.
Description: Cos Cob, CT: Chicken Soup for the Soul, LLC, 2024.
Identifiers: ISBN: 978-1-61159-112-5 (print) | 978-1-61159-347-1 (ebook)
Subjects: LCSH Mothers and daughters--Conduct of life--Literary collections. | Mothers
    -Conduct of life--Literary collections. | Daughters--Conduct of life--Literary collections. |
    BISAC SELF-HELP / Motivational & Inspirational | SELF-HELP / Personal Growth / Self-
    Esteem | FAMILY & RELATIONSHIPS / Parenting / Motherhood
Classification: LCC PN6071.M7 C4885 2024 | DDC 810.8/02--dc23

Library of Congress Control Number: 2023949946

PRINTED IN THE UNITED STATES OF AMERICA
on acid∞free paper

30 29 28 27 26 25 24   01 02 03 04 05 06 07 08 09

Mothers & Daughters

Amy Newmark

CSS

Chicken Soup for the Soul, LLC
Cos Cob, CT

Changing the world one story at a time®
www.chickensoup.com

Table of Contents

❶
~Mom to the Rescue~

1. It Won't Rain, *Tracy Crump* 1
2. More than a Medical Kit, *Jaclyn S. Miller* 4
3. The Pool Party, *Keeana Saxon* 6
4. My Black Friday Lesson, *Carole Brody Fleet* 9
5. Not My Child! *Sara Nolt* 12
6. Dry Her Tears, *Jean Ferratier* 15
7. Acceptance, *Erin Miller as told to Marie-Therese Miller* 19
8. Christmas Vacation, *Jill Burns* 22
9. Our First Christmas Tree, *Ferida Wolff* 25
10. Stranded, *Miriam Hill* 28
11. Leading the Fire Drill, *Judy Lee Green* 31

❷
~You Just Have to Laugh~

12. Umbrella Chairs, *Felice Prager* 36
13. Dressed to Impress, *Annie* 39
14. One-Pot Favorites, *Judy DeCarlo* 42
15. The Cut-Rate Poinsettia, *Denise Flint* 45
16. Queen of the Porcelain Throne, *Vera Frances* 48
17. The Holiday Merger, *Dawn Turzio* 51
18. Never Tell Anyone, *Gina Farella Howley* 54
19. Who Me? *Erika Tremper* 57
20. Breaking the Rules, *Suzanne Garner Payne* 60

3
~Role Models~

21. Super Strong Mom, *Brenda Barajas*......................65
22. A Man's Profession, *Kathy Ashby* 67
23. In My Mother's Kitchen, *Madeline Clapps* 69
24. She Did It Herself, *Marsha Henry Goff* 73
25. The Ice Cream Truck, *Samantha LaBarbera* 75
26. Can't Take My Smile, *Sarah E. Morin* 78
27. Like Daughter, Like Mother, *Courtney Conover* 82
28. Everything We Need, *Diane Morrow-Kondos* 86
29. Burned, *Lisa Wright-Dixon*...........................88
30. A Certain Samaritan, *Jeannie Lancaster*............92
31. Singing in the Rain, *Marla H. Thurman* 95

4
~Across the Generations~

32. The Re-Gift, *Erica McGee* 100
33. Tasting My Past, *Sandy McPherson Carrubba*...........102
34. The First Birthday, *Betsy Alderman Lewis* 106
35. Stronger, *Valerie Dyer* 110
36. The Grinch Came to Visit, *Lynn Gilliland* 113
37. The Latke Legacy, *Deborah Shouse* 116
38. Ma Tovu, *Alison Singer* 119
39. What If It Had Been Me? *Leslie Calderoni* 122

5
~Isn't Life Grand?~

40. The Gift, *Johanna Richardson*...........................126
41. Naughty Granny, *Catherine A. MacKenzie*...........129
42. Reserved for Seniors, *Donna Volkenannt* 132
43. Grandma Lillie's Red Cadillac, *Melanie Adams Hardy*.........134

44. Just Press Play, *Kelly Sullivan Walden*..............................138
45. Mammie's Meatloaf, *Melissa Face*.................................141
46. My Two Grandmas, *Sarah Foster* 144
47. The Barbie Christmas, *Gloria Hudson Fortner*....................148

❻

~Mom Knows Best~

48. Christmas with a New Family, *Bonnie Jean Feldkamp* 151
49. Rich Is Better, *Linda Baten Johnson* 155
50. A Mother Knows, *Crystal Duffy*....................................158
51. Is Everybody Smiling? *Andrea Langworthy*......................162
52. Dream Date, *Heidi Gaul* 166
53. ThanksChristGivingMas, *Lil Blosfield* 170
54. The Christmas of My Dreams, *Victoria Fedden* 173
55. The Bird, *Jean Salisbury Campbell* 178
56. Life Is for the Living, *Nancy Julien Kopp* 182
57. Third Time's the Charm, *Jodi Renee Thomas* 186
58. The Question, *Haylie Smart*...189
59. Listen to Your Mother, *Debbie Acklin* 192

❼

~In-laws and Outlaws!~

60. My First Hanukkah, *Crescent LoMonaco* 197
61. Backseat Driver, *Barbara LoMonaco* 200
62. Kiss the Cook, *Connie K. Pombo* 203
63. Bad Tidings to You, *T. Powell Pryce*................................207
64. Mom's Sneaky Tree, *Gabrielle Harbowy* 210
65. Outspoken and Outright Outrageous,
    Janet Lynn Mitchell 213
66. The Tide-Turning Whisper, *Annmarie B. Tait* 216
67. My Geriatric Vacation, *Diane Stark* 220

8

~Mother-Daughter Adventures~

68. A Heart Full of Memories, *Kaitlin Murray* 224
69. The Great Family Cook-Off, *Pauline Hylton* 227
70. Sidewalks, *Mary-Lane Kamberg* 230
71. Surfing at Sixty, *Jane Cassie* 233
72. Birthday Balloon, *Phyllis Nordstrom* 236
73. Saturdays with Jill, *Bobbi Silva* 238
74. The Gift that Keeps on Giving, *Kristine Byron* 241
75. Better than Prince Charming, *Stephanie McKellar* 243
76. Starbuck, *Jeanne Blandford* 246
77. Hair Raising, *Jennifer Quasha Deinard* 250
78. Running on Empty, *Heidi Kling-Newnam* 253
79. But I Can't Touch Bottom, *Geneva Cobb Iijima* 256

9

~Like Mother, Like Daughter~

80. Should Today Be a Pajama Day? *Marlys Johnson-Lawry* 260
81. My Dearest Friends, *Karla Brown* 263
82. Mom's New Home, *Audra Easley* 266
83. She Tricked Me! *Caitlin Q. Bailey O'Neill* 269
84. How I Survived, *Alice Muschany* 272
85. A Magical Conversation, *Marie MacNeill* 276
86. The Potato Salad Rule, *Carrie Malinowski* 280
87. Going Where You Look, *Lorri Carpenter* 285
88. Resolving to Honor Memories, *Sally Friedman* 289
89. Eight Thousand Miles, *Carol Strazer* 292
90. No Silver Platter, *Tina Haapala* 295
91. Grab Bag, *Cathi LaMarche* 299

92. A Little Nudge, *Pat Wahler* 304

93. The Garden, *Kathryn A. Beres* 307

94. An Unbreakable Bond, *Kristi Blakeway* 309

95. A Grand Visitor, *Val Muller* 313

96. Heaven's Mail, *Joanne Kraft* 317

97. The Accident, *Connie Kaseweter Pullen* 320

98. A Note from Heaven, *Cathy Stenquist* 322

99. The Pull of the Magnet, *Teresa Otto* 325

100. Thanks, Mom, *Suzanne Baginskie* 327

101. Dragonflies, *Celeste Bergeron Ewan* 330

Meet Our Contributors 333

Meet Amy Newmark 347

Thank You 349

About Chicken Soup for the Soul 350

Chapter
1

Mom to
the Rescue

It Won't Rain

The best thing one can do when
it's raining is to let it rain.
~Henry Wadsworth Longfellow

The six-acre park next to the city hall couldn't have been a more picturesque spot for a wedding. Impeccably manicured lawns rolled gently down to a shimmering lake. Paths wound through azalea bushes, and a pavilion overlooked the entire scene.

"What do you think?" My future daughter-in-law, Lindsey, could barely contain her excitement. "Won't this be perfect for an outdoor wedding?"

"It's beautiful," I agreed.

"We'll set up the guests' chairs here." She pointed to an area under a stand of oak trees. "Reverend Spencer will stand with his back to the lake, and Jeremy and I will be married under the archway my dad is building for us."

I smiled as I pictured the charming wedding Lindsey described. Then my practical side stepped in. "Where will you dress? And what if someone has to use the bathroom?"

"The mayor's office said they would give us a key to City Hall so we could use their facilities."

"Sounds like everything is falling into place." I glanced up as a cloud passed over the sun. "What will we do if it rains? After all, it is springtime."

"It won't rain," Lindsey said with certainty.

"Okay, but..."

"It won't rain."

We worked out the rest of the details. Then Lindsey left to run errands while I stayed behind to find out about getting a key for the building. The receptionist directed me to the mayor's office where I told his secretary, Connie, what I needed. After signing the necessary papers, I turned to go and then hesitated. While I loved Lindsey's indomitable spirit, I somehow doubted she could control the weather by sheer force of will.

"Is there a room here we could use just in case it rains the day of the wedding?" I asked. "I'd hate to try to notify guests of a change in location at the last minute."

"Sure," Connie said. "You can use the boardroom. I'll show it to you."

Connie unlocked the door to a large room with high ceilings. Over a hundred chairs faced a dais ringed by a semi-circular desk that held microphones for the city council members. The rich walnut paneling and rails were beautiful but not very romantic. As Connie and I talked, I pondered how to convert the stiff, courtroom-like surroundings into a backdrop suitable for a wedding.

Then I turned around.

Twenty-foot glass walls framed two sides of the "back" of the room. "Can we open those blinds?" I asked.

"Certainly."

As we drew back the long, vertical blinds, sunlight streamed in. One window faced the parking lot, but azaleas lined the front and hid most of the asphalt from view. Water spurted merrily from a fountain in the center of the oval drive. Oaks and birches lined the parking area and side of the building.

Perfect.

Later, I told Lindsey about the boardroom. "At least now we have a contingency plan in case it rains."

"It won't rain," she said.

"But..."

"It won't rain."

The weekend before the wedding, it began to rain. And I don't mean gentle April showers. By Tuesday, it had rained nonstop. We weathered tornado warnings and heard reports of cars being swept away by floodwaters in a nearby city.

On Thursday, Lindsey called. "It's still raining!" she wailed. "Even if it stops now, everything will be too soaked to have the wedding outside."

I tried to reassure her. "I know. We can use the boardroom. It'll be all right."

On Saturday, my sister and niece helped me decorate the boardroom while Lindsey's mom prepared for the reception dinner to be held at her house. As thunder crashed outside, we ironed tablecloths and hung paper bells. My husband and some of Jeremy's friends set up a truckload of white folding chairs and dried the seats. The caterer hurried the wedding cake inside before rain could destroy the icing. Almost everything was in place.

Then the archway arrived. Lindsey's dad had carved it of 150-year-old cedar from a barn on her grandfather's farm. Double wedding rings crowned the top. We wound ivy through the latticework sides, hung white silk bouquets on the corners, and placed potted plants on either side. It looked like an archway fit for royalty.

When we pulled back the blinds, the room was transformed. Branches brushed the tall windows, giving the illusion of trees swaying overhead. Flowers bloomed throughout the grounds. We looked upon a world that was fresh and green and inviting — and dripping rain, of course. It was as close to being outdoors as we could get.

Later that day, as Lindsey and Jeremy exchanged vows before a background of gray clouds, love filled the room. Even torrential rains could do nothing to dampen the beautiful event we had come to celebrate.

I now have a daughter-in-law who still looks upon the world with a can-do spirit, and Lindsey is blessed — or cursed — with a pragmatic mother-in-law who is not a last-minute person. When Lindsey's "can-do" turns into "Oh, no! What now?" I hope I'll always be there to help her see that contingency plans can be a beautiful thing.

— Tracy Crump —

Chicken Soup for the Soul

More than a Medical Kit

Luck can often mean simply taking advantage of a
situation at the right moment. It is possible to
"make" your luck by always being prepared.
~Michael Korda

"Anybody have a bandage?" a voice echoed down the dorm hallway.

It was our first week at college and we were all experiencing "forgot-it-itis." I had neglected to bring snacks for late-night munchies. Some poor girl on the wing had apparently forgotten bandages. We all felt a little displaced.

Several months before, I sat at my high school graduation party admiring my gifts and battling waves of post-high school sentimentality. The usual and beloved inspirational books were scattered around my feet, silently proclaiming the wealth of wisdom they wished to share. A small pile of personal checks lay nearby. Laundry items, desk supplies, sewing miscellany—all well-intentioned and well-received. They would demonstrate their givers' thoughtfulness over and over during my college career.

But one gift struck me as strange. I frowned when I opened it. Medicine? A small packet of pills and creams, ointments and lozenges lay within the wrappings. Who would give that as a gift?

"You'll need that once you're at school," Mom pointed out. "You won't have to chase down the campus nurse for every cough."

Good point.

Not long after, in August, I packed my life into a borrowed truck and slipped the bag of medicine in with my toiletries. I barely thought about it once I reached campus, caught in the whirlwind of unpacking, book-buying, scheduling and meeting new friends.

When "anybody have a bandage?" rang out in the dormitory hall that day, I remembered my little medicinal package.

I swallowed self-consciously. "Actually," I gave a little wave, "I have one."

"Great," my new wing-mate chimed.

As I dug out the kit, we began to chat.

Soon, many of the other girls on the wing heard of my little kit and paid me a visit. One had bug bites — anti-itch cream popped out of my supply. The wing-mate with the headache nearly kissed my hands when I passed her simple painkillers. As cold season approached, many needed cough drops. Each girl stayed to chat for a few moments.

The little gift I had questioned now led me toward new friendships. As it broke fevers, it also broke the ice, allowing me to meet and befriend many on the wing.

Gradually, the others purchased their own supplies and my kit rarely left the closet.

Eventually, I graduated and threw the dangerously outdated bottles into the garbage, along with stacks of papers and trash — all items now unnecessary. I began my adult life, forgetting the simple medical kit and how it helped me befriend others.

Then one day, I received a party invitation. A young friend was graduating from high school. "Come celebrate with Sarah!" read the cheerful type. Memories of my own party rushed back to me, and I smiled at the opportunity presenting itself.

As I drove to the pharmacy, I knew exactly what gift I would give her. The chance to be a friend.

— Jaclyn S. Miller —

The Pool Party

*If you're having fun, that's when
the best memories are built.*
~Simone Biles

My mom and I woke up early the day of Hannah's pool party to do my hair. It needed to look "right," not only for the social event, but also for church the next day.

I was about to withstand seventeen minutes of the creamy chemical to relax my hair. My mom worked quickly to make sure my strands were smoothed out and evenly saturated. The noxious odor of the relaxer permeated the entire kitchen.

Mom then carefully set my hair with big hard plastic rollers so that it would come out straight. She set me under an old beautician's dryer that she bought at a yard sale. The neck of the dryer could not be lowered, so I sat on a couple of phone books. Those old-fashioned dryers had one setting: High. I sat sweating under there for an hour and twenty minutes. By the time my mom lifted the hood, my back was moist and stuck to the chair.

She took the rollers out slowly, quietly praying for a "miracle." She gently combed out the parts, smoothed out the roller lines, and sat back to admire her work with a smile.

Thanks to my mom, I felt ready for the pool party.

"Don't get your hair wet. I don't know what that chlorine will do."

"Okay."

"Keeana, I'm serious now. Don't get it wet."

"Okay!"

My dad drove me to Hannah's house, and we chatted cheerfully during the quick trip. He let me wear his T-shirt over my bathing suit because I didn't have a cover up.

When we got there, I surprisingly found the rest of the kids already in the pool. Hannah was fully soaked and immersed in a water game.

I sat comfortably at the shallow end of the pool's edge, an obedient observer. My shirt remained dry as I baked in the sun. The water lapped quietly against the side of the pool. It seemed angelically harmless. I dipped my right foot in and felt a jolt of joy.

I looked longingly at Hannah, who seemed to be having so much fun in the pool. I wished I knew how to swim like that.

"Keeana, why don't you come in?" she asked.

"Oh, um, I don't know how to swim that well."

"We'll teach you! You can't sit at the edge of the pool the whole time. Come down here!"

"Well, I don't want my hair to get wet."

"I have a swimming cap. Your hair will be fine. Trust me!"

Problem solved! The cap would protect my hair. And how much damage could chlorine really do to relaxed hair anyway?

Getting the cap on was a team effort. I wondered if my curls would get flattened by the tight rubber. My mom wouldn't like that. But it was time to have fun!

I took off my dad's T-shirt and jumped in. I splashed. I laughed. I felt included in the crowd. I had a blast.

My dad came to pick me up four hours later. My heart had begun to pound sometime before he arrived because, in all my splashing, the devilishly sneaky water had seeped under the cap. I knew when it had happened: the cannonball. When I felt it, my heart skipped a beat, but I calmed down when I concluded, nay, declared, that it was my day — a great day to be reckless.

"Wow… It looks like Keeana had fun," Dad said slowly as he raised an eyebrow in my direction.

"Yes, your daughter is a delight! She picked up quite a few pointers in a short amount of time. You know, George, your daughter should really learn how to swim!"

"Yes... Thanks... Bye now."

Hannah gave me a quick hug and waved as my dad and I got into the car.

The entire car ride was silent. I knew I was in trouble. My chlorine-soaked hair was limp and plastered to my head. Worst of all, it was air drying into straw.

When my mom saw me, she gasped. "George! What about church tomorrow?"

"I know, Tina... but she did have fun at least."

"FUN? You call ruining one's hair fun?"

I spent the rest of the evening under my mom's wrath, under the faucet, under her exasperated hands, and under that blasted old-fashioned hair dryer again.

That night, as I tossed and turned trying to find a comfortable spot on my head full of rollers, I relived that cannonball. It was worth it.

— Keeana Saxon —

My Black Friday Lesson

The Christmas spirit whispers softly in my ear
to be of good cheer.
~Richelle E. Goodrich, *Being Bold*

I had never participated in the Black Friday phenomenon. I was always recovering from hosting our big Thanksgiving dinner. But one year there was a sale on an item that I badly wanted to get my husband for Christmas.

And so it was that I arose at 4 a.m., donned yoga pants and an oversized sweatshirt, threw my hair into a ponytail, and set off into the cold November pre-dawn on my quest. I was sure that this most special gift would be worth the effort — and cause a declaration of undying love.

When I arrived at the store I was stunned by the full parking lot. I had to park a quarter-mile away. Once inside, I was greeted by what I would call, at best, "organized chaos." Wooden pallets stood stacked to unsafe heights in overly crowded aisles. Crowds of frighteningly determined shoppers surrounded pallets that were still shrink-wrapped, hands firmly placed upon coveted treasures that would not be available for purchase for several hours. Families scurried about — parents with overflowing shopping carts accompanied by children in pajamas. Groups of teenagers carrying energy drinks happily roamed as if this mayhem was the social event of the season.

Not only was I unable to locate the precious gold at the end of my personal rainbow, but even if I had found it, I would not have had a prayer of getting near it without GPS and two really large bodyguards.

I hiked the quarter-mile back to my car (fulfilling the cardio portion of my day) and proceeded to another store, where I was greeted by an almost identical scene. I actually witnessed a woman arguing with an armed security guard over her place in line. Now, I had always thought that "They who wear small artillery automatically win the debate," but no, apparently there were customers desperate enough to do battle over line placement anyway.

I left.

I drove around looking for the now-impossible Christmas gift at other stores. As I continued to find long lines of people outside the stores, I realized that despite my valiant efforts, I was not going to return home with my precious gift. All of my wee-hour efforts had been for naught.

And then I remembered…

My daughter Kendall was starting her career in fashion at that time, and that included preparing for and working on Black Friday. Kendall was due to arrive at her store at 6:30 a.m. While I would be heading home to climb back into pajamas with a hot, soothing cup of sanity and the TV remote, she would be on her feet for the next fourteen hours.

I hurriedly drove to a coffee house and purchased the largest latte I've ever seen, along with Kendall's favorite pastry. I drove to her store where there, too, a throng of people who had been sitting in the cold for hours awaited the store's opening.

I parked and waited.

When Kendall pulled into the parking lot, I jumped out of my car and hid behind another parked car, praying that no one whose name began with the word "Officer" caught a peculiar-looking, ponytailed blonde skulking behind a parked car with a gigantic latte, while simultaneously stalking a young woman.

Kendall emerged from her car and strode purposefully toward her store. I was immediately struck by her beauty at that early hour — hair softly coaxed into chocolate-brown waves, gorgeous smoky-eyed make-up, bright red lipstick that popped against porcelain skin. She was the personification of "street chic" in a black mini dress, a red scarf that perfectly matched the lipstick, black tights and high-heeled ankle boots.

Quickly, I fell into step alongside and intentionally bumped into her.

Not immediately realizing with whom she had gently collided, Kendall started to politely say, "Excuse me, I'm sor…." Then, realizing who had bumped her, she finished the sentence with an expletive, presumably because she hadn't seen her mother awake at that hour since a long-ago vacation in Las Vegas. I quickly gave her the latte and the pastry, kissed her on the cheek and wished her a good day. The smile that crossed her grateful face made the fruitless odyssey preceding that moment fade into nothingness.

As I made my way home through the now-sunlit streets, I felt just as good as if I had successfully found that precious gift. No holiday magic comes from a store, no matter the gift or the deal-busting, door-smashing, ceiling-caving sale price that comes with it.

It really is about the little things. It's about putting a smile on the face of someone who badly needs to smile. It's about lifting a spirit that may be bruised. It's about putting spare change into a charity collection instead of the glove compartment. It's about something as simple as a surprise latte and a kiss on the cheek.

I have reverted to what works for me — spending the day after Thanksgiving curled up in a warm bed with hot coffee and a purring cat.

— Carole Brody Fleet —

Not My Child!

*There is an instinct in a woman to love most
her own child — and an instinct to make
any child who needs her love, her own.*
~Robert Brault, rbrault.blogspot.com

My friend Alice should have been sleeping. In fact, she had been sleeping, but her breathing had quickened until it came in gasps as though she was running. Suddenly she was awake, crying. Her dream had been so real, so vivid she stumbled out of bed and walked to the room beside the one she shared with her husband, Dan, just to check. Yes, all four children were there. It had been a dream.

But what a terrible one! Alice climbed back into bed, wide-awake now, and gripped with a heavy fear. Her mind replayed the dream: Their little family was walking over a footbridge crossing a busy city street. Dan was walking ten feet ahead of Alice with Evan by his side and little Joseph on his shoulders. Alice had the baby in her arm and Ellie by the hand. The baby slipped lower on her hip and, letting go of Ellie's hand for a second, Alice readjusted the baby. In that moment, a strange woman ran beside her, grabbed Ellie, and ran to a black getaway car that sat in a nearby alley. Ellie was gone!

The pain… the horror… the desperation… the futility of running after the car… it gripped Alice all over again until she felt tears raining onto her pillow.

"Please, God," she whispered. "Please lift this fear. It was only a dream."

Or was it? The days passed but the heaviness and guardedness Alice felt refused to lift. She told Dan about her dream and the nagging fears and together the two of them prayed over their children. They hadn't known that child trafficking was an issue in this Asian city until the dream alerted them and research confirmed that it was a major problem. "Oh, God," they prayed, "protect our children! Let this dream pass unfulfilled!"

Only when each child was thoroughly bathed in prayer did peace come. In fact, peace came so completely that Alice forgot about her dream until the day their family was restocking supplies in a large city miles away from the little outpost they lived in.

The city was crowded as usual and the footbridge they were crossing was clogged with people. Horns honked below them. Bicycle bells rang. Exhaust choked them. The children's tired feet were dragging, causing a little crowd to collect behind them on the narrow bridge.

"Let's stand to the side and let the people behind us go past," Dan suggested. "We're blocking the walkway."

The children, grateful for a brief rest, plastered themselves against the side of the bridge to let an equally grateful crowd pass them by. And then at the pace of the tired children, the little family made their way toward the bus stop. Dan, with Joseph on his shoulders, walked on ahead with Evan by his side. Alice followed them with the baby on her hip and Ellie holding her hand. Ellie's feet slowed and the distance between Dan and Alice widened.

Suddenly Alice felt uneasy. She glanced over her shoulder to see a lone woman still following them. It was the woman from her dream.

As if on cue, the baby slipped lower on Alice's hip. But Alice remembered the dream and there was no way she was going to readjust the baby now. Clamping her arm tightly across the baby's back in lieu of a readjustment, Alice picked up her pace, hurrying Ellie along. Ellie's small hand was clenched in her mother's iron grip. That woman wasn't going to get this child!

At the end of the footbridge was the alley from the dream. Alice stole a quick glance down the alley. Would it be there? It was. The black getaway car was there idling. Waiting.

Miracle of miracles, a rare taxi chanced past and was flagged by Dan, who had no idea of the drama unfolding behind him. As he opened the door of the taxi to lift the boys into it, Dan was startled as an ashen-faced Alice raced past him, leaped into the car, and pulled Ellie into it behind her.

The taxi doors slammed shut. Bus horns honked, the taxi horn responded in protest, and the little car carrying a family of six pulled away from the curb. The woman from the dream scowled. Her prey gone, she turned and disappeared into the crowd.

— Sara Nolt —

Chicken Soup for the Soul

Dry Her Tears

Tears are the safety valve of the heart
when too much pressure is laid on it.
~Albert Smith

Dani could not dry her own tears as she walked off the airplane trailed by the flight attendant carrying her backpack. I was allowed to go to the gate, which is unusual in this day and age, to pick up my 23-year-old daughter.

There she was, wearing flip-flops, gym pants, and a tank top. Never mind that in Springfield, Illinois, it was winter; she was coming from balmy Florida. These were the clothes her friend found that fit over her two broken arms, heavily encased in casts.

Sometimes small slips have large consequences. In Dani's case, it was literally true. Dani was an event planner. While helping a caterer bring in trays, she slipped on wet pavement and fell backwards. Both of her arms were fractured.

I helped her into the car and covered her with blankets. The ride home, after hours of flying, was excruciating. Looking in my rearview mirror, my mind raced with panicked thoughts of "How are we going to do this?" as I calmly told her how glad we were that she was home and that we would take good care of her.

The "we" in this case was an exceptional word. Thankfully, I was on very amicable terms with Louis, my ex-husband. It meant that we would work as a team.

Once home, I helped her to the couch and really started assessing the situation. Her left arm was cast from above the elbow, hanging straight down the side of her body. The other arm was cast at an angle toward her right shoulder, but she could not reach her mouth.

I thought, "Straws are the first thing on the shopping list." It took about two seconds to realize that Dani was as helpless as a baby. She would not be able to feed, wash, or dress herself.

We found a routine that worked for us, but those first days were filled with adaptations. Solutions had to be found to the challenges we all faced in caring for a handicapped person. Fortunately, Dani was instrumental in being able to help us learn how to help her. What a reminder for me that survival issues do not apply just to the sick and elderly! I salute people who care for those with physical and mental disabilities day in and day out.

It was obvious to her father and me that Dani could not be left alone for any length of time after she awoke in the morning. I sent substitute plans to school for the first few days, while Louis arranged to take vacation time from work. He would come to the house around 10:00 and leave soon after I came home. What a relief it was that he was able to feed her lunch, take her to appointments, and keep her company. We joked that television with Dad was watching the Food Network. Television with Mom was catching up on past seasons of *Grey's Anatomy*.

It was very difficult to dress Dani. The lower body was easy. Her arms, however, were at strange angles. Like a contortionist, Dani moved this way and that so I could get a sleeveless tank top on her. Ponchos that slipped over her head were our clothing salvation.

Soon after arriving home, we braved the cold, snow, and ice to get her to an orthopedist. I took one of my winter jackets and made cuts in the sleeves so she would have something warm to wear. The orthopedist recast one arm into a more comfortable position. She could wiggle her fingers, but not enough to hold a food utensil.

Dani had abdominal muscles made of steel. Hours of ballet had really paid off in developing core strength. She could lift herself up from a seated position without using her arms. What most impressed (and scared) me was that after a bath, when the water flowed down the drain, she would rock back and forth and stand up. Her first bath felt so awkward to me. My daughter accepted that I had to help her, but I was very self-conscious bathing and drying her the first few times. Together, we adjusted to an uninhibited manner of dressing and undressing. At night, instead of getting her ready for bed, I would dress her for the next morning so all she would need was shoes and socks when her dad came. We made arrangements with a hairdresser to have her hair washed every two days.

It was a very difficult time for Dani. She was in physical and mental pain. Thankfully, she could walk, talk, and think, but could do very little for herself physically. She could use her fingertips to dial an oversized speakerphone and to slowly tap out keys on the computer. She tried to be very brave through it all, but it was an ugly day when her boyfriend sent her a computer message breaking off their relationship. I was in the kitchen hearing the tap-tap of the keys and sobbing. My heart ached because I wanted to give her privacy, but I knew even in her misery she could not blow her runny nose.

After that event, she was in such a state of nausea, pain and anxiety that she lay on the bathroom floor and could hardly get up. It was as though a portion of her soul had splintered apart. After what seemed to be a long time (but was actually less than an hour), I took her to the emergency room. Once there, she was given medicine that dulled some of the physical pain, nausea, and anxiety.

It was very late when we got home, and I put my daughter to bed. As I gazed at her face, her eyes spoke volumes of silent communication. I knew I could not leave her room. Dani's raw vulnerability brought out a depth of tenderness and love that had been dormant in me since she was very small. I sat next to her on the bed so I could stroke her hair. I have no words to describe the energetic bond that took place as I held my vigil until she fell asleep.

A month passed, but Dani was not yet physically ready to return to her job as originally anticipated. As time passed, shorter casts were applied to her arms. She wanted to be able to brush her teeth and comb her hair before she returned to Miami. After a few weeks, she had to go back to Florida to coordinate a work project that was due. She could brush her teeth, but not her hair. When she flew back, she was able to stay with very close friends whom we all trusted to see her through the rest of her convalescence.

When people hear stories about the time Dani broke her arms, they ask how we managed it. I say it was difficult, but I think to myself that this experience was one of the most sacred, healing times that we had ever shared as a family.

—Jean Ferratier—

Acceptance

The greatest oak was once a little nut
who held its ground.
~Author Unknown

"Eighth graders rule," my friend Dee yelled to me as I left the school bus. "Yeah, we do," I shouted back. I turned to make sure the bus had rounded the corner and was out of sight, and I did a little conga step of celebration down my driveway.

I burst through the back door. "Mom," I said. "I've been nominated for the National Junior Honor Society."

My mother gave my shoulders a squeeze. "I'm so proud of you," she told me.

Mom and I sat together in the family room as I filled out the honor society application. I had to prove that I had all the characteristics required in a candidate: scholarship, leadership, service, character, and citizenship. I wrote that I worked hard at my honors math and science classes; I made the high honor roll most quarters. I listed my baking cookies for prison inmates and my singing with the District Select Chorus to raise money for the community. My mom had me put in that I was first chair in orchestra, to show leadership, and she also told me to include that I sold hand-beaded bracelets and crocheted purses to benefit St. Jude Children's Research Hospital and the ASPCA. Moms make you put everything on these applications!

The next day, I turned the paperwork into the advisor and didn't think any more about it.

Months went by, and I received a letter from the school about the honor society. As soon as the bus let me off that afternoon, I raced into the house. My mother was typing at the computer. "Mom," I said, "I didn't make the honor society."

She smiled and held up her hand to give me a high five. "You jokester."

I felt tears seep from my eyes. "No, really, they didn't pick me," I said and handed her the letter.

"Oh, honey, I'm sorry. I thought you were kidding," my mother said. "There must be some mistake." She grabbed the phone from the charger and dialed the honor society advisor.

He told her that no mistake was made, but he couldn't disclose the reason for my non-selection. The decisions of the faculty committee were final. There was no appeals process. However, when my mother perceives an injustice, she is like a German Shepherd with a tug toy; she contacted the principal. His answers were the same.

"It's not fair," I said that night at supper. My mother agreed. She proceeded to tell me a story about a high school friend of hers. "He was intelligent and had a good heart, but for some reason he wasn't chosen for the National Honor Society. He was hurt and angry." She paused for effect. "Do you know what he does for a living?" she asked. "He is a world renowned lung cancer specialist, and he saves lives every day."

I understood what my mom was trying to say. Not being a member of the honor society wasn't going to ruin my future, but it was hurting me now.

Nearly all of my friends were chosen for the honor society. One day, they went to a rehearsal for the ceremony. Afterwards, I heard that the teacher in charge called my name during attendance. "Oops! I forgot to skip the names of the non-selected students," she told everyone. On the night of the induction, Facebook was filled with posts about what dresses my friends wore and photos of the event.

I told my parents how difficult those weeks were for me. "This shouldn't happen to anyone else," I said. We discussed ways that the selection process might be improved. "I wish that teachers who knew me well could have shared their input with the committee," I said.

My dad, the engineer, was all about the process. "They should set up a concrete set of requirements for selection. For example, each candidate must have five hours a month of community service."

"It bothers me that I don't know why I wasn't chosen," I said. "The committee should give a reason, so the student can do better."

Not surprisingly, my mother wanted an appeals process put in place.

We arranged a meeting with the school principal to share our ideas. A few days later, he telephoned to say that the committee was going to use some of our suggestions. I felt proud that I had helped future students, like my younger sister.

As the weeks went by, I began to feel happier. Finally, the night of my graduation arrived. I wore a new dress. My older sister helped me do my hair, and I thought I looked somewhat sophisticated.

Everything was going well. Then, the principal announced the names of the honor society members — alphabetically. When he skipped my name, I felt a stab of sadness return.

When the applause quieted, the principal said, "One of our teachers nominated a student for a special New York State award in recognition of her scholarship and civic involvement. This award is given to Erin Miller."

I was so excited and surprised. I jumped up and ran onto the stage. I couldn't stop grinning. As soon as I sat down, I heard the principal say, "The award for the best German language student is Erin Miller." I popped out of my seat again, like a whack-a-mole.

This was turning into the best night of my life. After the ceremony, my friends gathered around to congratulate me. Dee was smiling, yet behind her glasses, her eyes looked sad. I knew just how she felt. She hadn't won any awards.

I rushed over to her and gave her my tightest hug. "Freshmen rule," I told her. "Yeah, we do," she said, and her eyes were smiling.

— Erin Miller as told to Marie-Therese Miller —

Christmas Vacation

Good instincts usually tell you what to do
long before your head has figured it out.
~Michael Burke

Whatever they had slipped in my ginger ale had taken its toll. I couldn't believe someone would invite me to a party and do something so cruel — even dangerous. My insides burned, and my head was spinning. I could hardly see, let alone think.

"What's the matter?" he asked. I didn't think I could feel any colder, but his tone chilled my blood. "Think you're too good for me? You thought you'd be with my friend tonight, didn't you?" I staggered to the side of the road and vomited over a snowbank.

University had let out for Christmas vacation. The holiday break had left my boss shorthanded, so I'd offered to stay in town and work at the bank until the day before Christmas Eve.

Only a few students remained in the dorms, none of them on my floor. When I had volunteered to work, I had no idea that I'd spend my nights with no front-desk security and the main entrance unlocked. Anyone could come and go, and no one would ever know. So far, I'd spent several nervous nights locked in my room with my dresser pushed against it for added protection.

Hours before the party, my mother had called. I lied and told her my girlfriend and I had dinner plans and might go see a movie after that. Mom would not have approved of me going to a party with men

I didn't know, and I didn't want her to worry about me.

Ever since accepting the party invitation, I'd had a powerful feeling I shouldn't go, but I didn't want to appear rude. After all, they were new customers of the bank. How dangerous could they be? As I stood there shivering in the night air, I kept thinking of my mother and desperately wished I'd heeded my disquiet.

After leaving the party, I'd asked my so-called date to take me back to my dorm. Instead, he'd headed to a desolate area in the countryside and driven the car into a snowbank. Sick as I felt, I'd had to help push the car back on the road. Now, I had no choice but to get back in the car or freeze. Again, I pleaded with him to take me to my dorm, which made him so angry he floored the gas pedal, causing the car to slide back and forth over the snowy road, scaring me to death. At least we were going the right way. During the drive, my mother weighed heavy on my mind.

When we pulled into the dorm parking lot, I thought about screaming but knew no one would hear me. I slid out of the car and staggered inside, hoping he might stay behind. Instead, he followed me up to my room.

Unable to see clearly, I fumbled with the lock, which ticked him off. The second the door opened, he followed behind me, shut the door, and blocked it. I asked him to leave, but he refused. At that moment, I wished I'd been honest with my mother in case the worst now happened.

Then the phone rang.

"Don't answer it!" he said, but I'd already picked it up.

"Jill?"

"Mom?" It was 1:30 a.m. My parents had always gone to bed after the ten o'clock news. A fresh wave of panic swept through me. "What's wrong?" I asked, suddenly aware that I'd thought about my mother all night because I'd probably sensed that something horrific had happened back home. What if a family member had died? As I waited for her answer, my date's threatening eyes remained glued to me.

"I couldn't sleep," she said. "I had an urgent feeling you needed me to call you. Let's talk."

I could hear it in her voice. Mom knew something had gone awry and that I wasn't alone. Throughout the early hours of that morning, my mother stayed on the phone with me. We talked about cooking, sewing, vacations, relatives, and everything under the sun until my intruder became so enraged that he finally left, slamming my door behind him. Once I locked my door, I peeked out my window to make sure he'd driven away. After that, my mother hung on while I left to use the restroom. Once I returned, Mom waited until I'd secured and barricaded my door before hanging up.

I'd been foolish to ignore my uneasiness about attending that party. Thankfully, my mother acted on hers, most likely saving me from harm. It's possible that nothing would have happened to me, but I'm grateful I never had to find out.

—Jill Burns—

Our First Christmas Tree

The best of all gifts around any Christmas tree:
the presence of a happy family
all wrapped up in each other.
~Burton Hillis

As Christmas approaches each year, our house becomes a stop for our young grandsons on their way to visit their other grandparents. Our daughter and her husband unpack just enough for a night or two with us and then they are all on their way. Since we are Jewish, our house isn't set up for Christmas, so it is understandable that, in their mixed family, they would want to be where the holiday is celebrated. We don't mind. It is a chance for my husband and me to see them for a few days as they travel back and forth.

Only this year was different. The family came, as usual, a couple of days before Christmas Eve, but it was obvious as they exited the car that something was going on. One of our grandsons was coughing and the other was sniffling.

By the afternoon they were both cranky and in need of a nap. When they awoke, my daughter said both boys felt feverish. They had planned to leave the next day but, not wanting to travel with sick kids, asked if they could stay a little longer.

Of course they could.

In the morning there was no fever but the coughing was worse and both boys had drippy noses. My daughter and I were constantly washing the dishes the boys used, the clothes they wore, the toys they played with — just to keep the germs at bay. I was fast running out of disinfecting wipes. It was not the time for them to leave.

Another day passed and things were pretty much the same. Was it just a cold affecting both boys or was it something more serious? Should we call a doctor? And which one? I hadn't needed a pediatrician in forever so I wasn't up on who was available. We decided to wait one more day and see how things were going.

Now it was the day before Christmas. The boys seemed better but they were still coughing. It still didn't seem like a good idea to travel with sick kids. Could they stay one more day?

They were certainly welcome to stay as long as they liked but the boys were disappointed that there was no Christmas tree.

It wouldn't feel like Christmas Eve without a tree. It was time to make the house holiday friendly. We had a small Norway pine in a planter in a corner of our living room. It wasn't a traditional Christmas tree but I suggested that we decorate it.

Our daughter set up a decoration-making station on our coffee table. Our older grandson made long, colored-paper chains while our younger grandson decorated paper circles to use as ornaments. I found some small, carved wooden birds, which I attached to twine and hung on the tree. We sang as we worked. The whole house came to life. My husband took photos for posterity.

Our son-in-law laid woolen scarves at the bottom of the tree for the blanket where the presents would be placed when the boys were asleep. After such a busy day, they trotted off to bed, happy.

Before I retired for the night, I looked at what we had all created. It was our first Christmas tree, transformed from an ordinary evergreen into something grand, and it graced our house with its simple beauty. I smiled at the thought of how excited our grandsons would be in the morning.

And excited they were. They reached under the tree and eagerly opened their presents. My present was that the boys were feeling much better. They left the next day, finally on their way to their other grandparents, who were eagerly awaiting their visit.

When the holidays were over, I removed the decorations. The tree reverted to its former self — though not quite. I left a little bird on one of the branches for a while longer as a reminder of the joy our impromptu Christmas tree had brought. I later put it in a special place, easily accessible, just in case we decide to do it all again next year, but this time, with healthy grandchildren.

— Ferida Wolff —

10

Chicken Soup for the Soul

Stranded

Semper Paratus (Always Ready)
~Coast Guard motto

I stood at my window and squinted through binoculars as I brought the small island into focus and searched for my daughter and her husband on the sliver of beach. Waves churned into white caps, and the knot in my stomach tightened.

"Do you think I should call the Coast Guard?" I asked my husband.

"Naw, they'll be fine," Jim grunted from behind his newspaper.

"But they could be in danger," I persisted. "We are the only ones who know that Laura and Geoff took the canoe and are camping on the island. What if they can't paddle back in this storm?"

"You're overreacting," Jim mumbled as he turned to the sports page.

Was I being a drama queen? What if they were in danger? Should I call for help?

The day before, when the couple arrived for the weekend, Laura proposed a plan to Geoff. "Let's take advantage of Florida's sunny weather and paddle the canoe to that spoil island in the distance. We can take a tent and sleeping bags and stay overnight." Her eyes twinkled with excitement as seagulls squawked and lazy sailboats moved along the calm Intracoastal Waterway. Within the hour, they were on their way, and before long the green canoe was a speck on the beach.

By morning, the weather had changed. Dark clouds hung low in the gray sky, and stiff winds stirred the water.

"Something is wrong. They should have returned by now," I said.

Jim lowered his newspaper. "Look, they'll be fine. But if it will make you feel better, give the Coast Guard a call."

Feeling foolish, I looked up the number and dialed.

"Hello. My daughter and her husband took a canoe to a spoil island yesterday, and they're camping there. The water looks too rough for them to paddle back."

"Well, ma'am, there is evidence of a front moving in. Keep an eye on them, and if conditions worsen, give us another call."

I squinted through the field glasses again and suddenly spied Geoff as he pulled the canoe away from the surging surf. He paused, massaged his chin, and looked toward the binoculars.

Notify the Coast Guard again, urged my inner voice.

"Hello, I just called about the couple stranded on the island closest to the Causeway Bridge. You told me to call back if things got worse. They're worse."

"Yes, ma'am, the wind has increased several knots during the last hour. We'll dispatch a rescue boat and arrive at the island in about twenty minutes."

"Thanks… and hurry!"

I watched four men in a small orange and black boat land on the beach. Minutes later, they loaded Laura and Geoff and their camping gear, lashed the canoe to the side of the boat, and then scrambled into the craft.

The boat thrashed about in the choppy seas. Waves crashed over the bow and drenched the huddled passengers. The experienced rescuers fought stiff winds as they maneuvered the boat to our dock and secured it.

"I was worried about you!" I yelled over the storm as I rushed to my daughter with outstretched arms.

"We were worried, too!" said Laura as she shivered inside my hug.

The officer in charge staggered against a violent gust of wind and approached us.

"Are you the lady who called us?" he shouted.

"I hope you don't think I over reacted," I yelled into his ear.

"You didn't overreact! There is no way that couple could have paddled the canoe upwind, against those waves. If you hadn't called, and they had tried to get back, they would have capsized and died of hypothermia within minutes. You did the right thing by calling the Coast Guard!"

The blood drained from my face as I listened to his solemn words.

After a hot shower, Laura snuggled in her pink robe and sipped hot chocolate. "Thanks for keeping an eye on us, Mom. We never would have made it back alive if you hadn't used your good judgment and called for help."

As I put away the binoculars, I was overcome with gratitude for the brave men and women in the Coast Guard who risk their lives daily to rescue others.

— Miriam Hill —

11

Leading the Fire Drill

And though she be but little, she is fierce.
~William Shakespeare

My six-year-old daughter came home from school and asked, "Why do boys get to do everything and girls don't?" Fire drills were held at the school on a regular basis and they had just had one. Each room had a plastic fireman's hat, and a boy was always picked to lead the class safely away from the building. "Why can't a girl be the leader?" my little girl asked.

Girls were not reared to be independent women when I grew up in the 1950s. At the age of eighteen, I married and went from my parents' home to living with my husband. I had never spent the night alone. When my husband was drafted a short time later, my two younger brothers thought it was great fun to spend the night with me, make fudge and popcorn, watch TV, stay up late, and sleep on my sofa. But the fun soon wore off, and I was left alone for the first time in my life.

I was alone when the electricity went off in the middle of the night, and I had no flashlight. I was alone when the water heater blew up, and water covered my kitchen floor. I was alone when the fuel line froze. I had no heat, and the temperature was below freezing. I was alone when the car wouldn't start and I had no way to get to work. I was alone when a Peeping Tom was caught looking in my window, and when there was not enough money to pay the bills and only enough food to keep from starving. And I was alone during the first seven months of my pregnancy, through morning sickness and doctors' visits.

When my daughter was born, I resolved that she would not be like me. I would raise her to be a self-confident, independent woman. From the very beginning, I encouraged her potential, praised her efforts, and exposed her to ideas and dreams. I was determined that I would help her explore the possibilities that were available.

She showed leadership in kindergarten. Her first-grade teacher said she was a born leader. A move shortly thereafter didn't faze her. As we registered at the new school, I was told that my daughter could attend that day in the stylish little pantsuit that I had made for her, but that pants thereafter were inappropriate. She had to wear a dress or be sent home. The principal believed that children behaved better when they wore their Sunday clothes.

The boys, however, did not have to wear suits, shirts and ties because they liked to hang upside down from the monkey bars on the playground. I suggested that perhaps little girls might like to hang upside down as well without their underwear showing. "My daughter will wear Sunday dresses to school when the boys wear suits and ties," I said. Within a week, every little girl at school was wearing pants.

When my daughter mentioned that she might like to be a nurse when she grew up, I agreed that nursing was a wonderful profession. "But if you want to go into the medical field, you might also think about becoming a doctor," I said.

When she said she wanted to be a teacher, I praised her choice, but I suggested that if she wanted to go into education, she should think about administration, too. She could be the principal of an entire school or the head of a college or university.

When she said she wanted to be a flight attendant and travel all over the world, I agreed that flying would be an exciting career. "But if you want to fly," I said, "think about becoming the pilot. The pilot gets to fly the plane."

Neil Armstrong walked on the moon. When my little girl took exaggerated steps like she saw him do on television, she said she wanted to be an astronaut. I told her that she could be the first woman to walk on the moon if that was what she wanted.

Of course, little girls change their minds often, but whatever she thought she wanted to be at any given time, I supported and then challenged her to dream even bigger and to think outside traditional gender roles.

After my daughter asked why a girl couldn't lead the fire drill, I spoke to the teacher. She said, "It's never been done by a girl, but I suppose if she really wants to..." My daughter wore the red plastic firefighter's hat and led the class safely away from the building during the next fire drill.

The school my six-year-old attended was innovative in encouraging the children to work independently at their own speed. Assignments were given, and as each child finished, she or he could go to various stations around the room for stimulating activities. There were puzzles to work, books to read, and games to play.

At one station, a tape recorder held a tape of *Casey at the Bat*. My little daughter saw the excitement of her male classmates as they donned headphones and listened to the classic baseball tale. They were having fun. She finished her work and made a beeline for the vacant play station, only to be directed by the teacher to an activity she deemed more suited for girls. My daughter came home and asked me why she could not hear the story of *Casey at the Bat*.

After I made another trip to the school, the teacher agreed there was no reason why the stations should be designated by gender. She never thought that little girls might want to hear about baseball or play with building materials or that little boys might want to put on a boa and read *Cinderella* or string necklaces from fruit-flavored cereal and macaroni. When my daughter finished her assignment the next day, she headed straight for the play station, put on the headphones and heard *Casey at the Bat* for the first time.

Times were changing. Each time I went to school, I wanted equal opportunity for my daughter — nothing more and nothing less. I never confronted a teacher in front of anyone else. I handled each situation pleasantly. I was never critical or angry.

I simply wanted my child to be exposed to possibilities and opportunities. She could then decide what she liked or did not like. I wanted her to study academics based on interests and not gender, to have dreams and a non-traditional career if she chose one.

And I wanted her and the other girls to lead the fire drill just as often as the boys.

—Judy Lee Green—

Chapter 2

You Just Have
to Laugh

Umbrella Chairs

The best advice is this: Don't take advice
and don't give advice.
~Author Unknown

She wanted large; I wanted small. She wanted an event to remember; I wanted intimate with only close friends. She wanted country club; I wanted backyard. She wanted a six-course meal; I wanted chocolate cake and champagne. It went on like this until she suggested umbrella chairs, and I said I wasn't coming to my own wedding. In retrospect, what my mother wanted was very generous and done with tons of love. However, what my mother wanted wasn't me. Sam and I had been living together for several years. We were just going through a formality. My mother was the one who wanted a party. We would have been happy making it formal with just a handful of our closest relatives and friends.

The "discussion" came to a head on an unusually warm Sunday in April. After several phone calls from Mom, I told her we were going out. This was before cell phones, so the ongoing stressful wedding conversation would have to wait until I got back. That's when Mom started calling the machine. I was sitting by the answering machine with Sam, listening to my mother's messages as they came through.

"It's Mom. I'm sitting in the backyard. It's about noon. Since you're insisting on doing YOUR WEDDING in the backyard, I just wanted you to know that it is already very hot out here. In August, it will be sweltering. This isn't a good idea." That was the first message.

A few minutes later, she called again. "I'm still in the backyard. It's 12:05. We need a tent. We need a large tent with some kind of air conditioning pumped in. People will melt if they have to be out here in the heat of the summer. That's how hot it is. You'll have to have ambulances on call."

Continuing her one-sided dialogue, she left a third message. "It's Mom again. Are you sure you don't want to just do this at a country club? CALL ME BACK!"

I told Sam I wanted to elope.

The messages continued.

"It's Mom. I don't think the backyard is large enough for a tent."

"It's Mom. I don't know why you have to be so stubborn. A country club would be so nice. All you would have to do is SHOW UP. We can tell the orchestra that you don't want to do a first dance and the caterer that you don't want to make a fuss about cutting a cake."

"It's your mother. I was thinking. If I cut all my second cousins and friends I haven't seen in over two years off the list, I can get it down to 150."

"It's Mom. In August, it's also very humid. This backyard wedding idea of yours is inhumane. People will die, and then we'll be planning funerals."

"It's Mom. I've got it! This is brilliant: UMBRELLA CHAIRS!"

On that, Sam looked at me and asked, "What's an umbrella chair?"

"It's Mom, the one who carried you for almost ten months and was in horrible labor for a week before you decided to make your entrance. Umbrella chairs will solve all the problems."

I picked up the phone before she hung up. "What's an umbrella chair?"

"So you were home."

"We just walked in. What's an umbrella chair?"

"You know. Chairs with umbrellas on them to block the sun. I'll bet we can get them to match whatever color you choose for your wedding. We can even have cup holders on the chairs so people who are prone to heat stroke can have a glass of water. We can have the umbrellas removable so the guests can carry them around when they're not sitting."

"And if it rains, Mom, they won't get wet!" I added, with a definite tone of sarcasm.

Sam scribbled on a pad and put it in front of my face. "Your mother has lost it," I read. Then, "Don't fight!"

There was a long pause from my mom. Then she said, "You're making fun of me, aren't you?"

"No," I said. "But umbrella chairs are stupid. If you order umbrella chairs, I'm not coming."

"Then how will we keep everyone comfortable?" she asked, in all sincerity.

"We won't, Mom. If they're too hot, they'll eat fast, leave a present, congratulate us, and go home early. Then Sam and I can get back to our apartment and start making babies."

"Making babies?" my mother asked.

"Sure. Why else do you think we're getting married?"

At that, my mom sighed, "Babies…"

I got my small backyard wedding on one of the hottest days recorded for that day in August. People came dressed comfortably and commented on the heat, but no one complained. We handed out "Sam and Felice, August 1, 1982" spray bottles and champagne as each person arrived in case anyone needed to cool down. It was a wonderful wedding. My mother did hire a caterer because "You can't just serve chocolate cake and champagne, Felice."

And Sam and I went home… to make babies.

— Felice Prager —

13

Dressed to Impress

What a strange power there is in clothing.
~Isaac Bashevis Singer

My future mother-in-law. She was a tough nut, all right. My mother could only repeat, "Thank goodness, there's only one of her," whenever my fiancé Phil's mother, Helga, was mentioned. As a result of her "commanding" personality, Helga's niece called her aunt "The General" when she was safely out of earshot. And when my godmother met Helga at Phil's and my engagement party, she leaned toward me, kissed me on the cheek, and whispered into my ear, "Good luck with that one."

In the years leading up to Phil's and my engagement, his mother made her assessment of my appearance perfectly clear: my nails were too long and too brightly polished; my heels were too high; my jeans were too tight. Once, despite having no training as a beautician, she even offered to cut my hair, commenting, "Why don't you let me fix that style up for you?"

So when I learned that Phil's father, my future father-in-law, was to be honored at a party hosted by his genealogy club, I had my share of concerns. As outgoing president, he, my future mother-in-law, and the balance of their family, including me, would be seated at the head table on a raised dais for all to see. This was to be my first introduction to my father-in-law's friends and associates. Certainly, I wanted to look my best. More than that, however, I wanted to avoid any further criticism at the hands of Helga. So I embarked on a citywide search for the perfect outfit.

For weeks, I made my way through malls, badgered boutique owners, and ransacked racks of evening wear in search of the appropriate garment. Finally, my insecurities brought me home with not one, but two possibilities. The night of the party, as I readied for the big event, I held up the two outfits for Phil to inspect: one, a fashionable silk suit with a black skirt complemented by a simple white jacket; the other, a form-fitting little black number accented by a floral scarf.

"Which one?" I asked. Phil chose the suit.

I must admit that Phil's choice surprised me. Of the two, the suit was more no-nonsense, while the little black dress with its bright scarf was more frivolous, sexy even. I would have thought Phil would have preferred for me to wear that one. However, I accepted his advice willingly. Certainly, he was a better barometer of his mother's likes and dislikes than I was. Still, as I stood before the mirror adjusting my jacket, my lungs tightened and my stomach rumbled.

"Well," I thought, "if Helga has anything to say about the way I look tonight, I'll just tell her that her son chose my outfit."

Bolstered by my false confidence, I walked tall out of the house and into Phil's car. Yet as we drove toward the venue, my anxiety only worsened. I twisted my hands and made the annoying throat-clearing sound I always made when I was nervous. Recognizing my tension, Phil quickly put me at ease with a good-natured impersonation of his mother's heavily accented speech. "I vill cut your hair und you vill like it," he said, reminding me of one of his mother's more over-the-top comments.

By the time we reached the parking lot, Phil and I had both succumbed to a bad case of the giggles. As we approached the building, though, I quickly sobered. After a deep, cleansing breath, I entered through the ballroom's elegant glass double doors. Then, from way across the room, my mother-in-law and I spotted each other. Even at several paces, I could see her jaw drop. When she regained her composure, I watched as she turned to her husband, pointed toward me, and howled out, "She's wearing the same dress as me!"

With shaking knees, I approached her. "We're wearing the same dress," she repeated. I stood there, speechless, the air sucked from my lungs by the sight of my fashion-twin. Then she lifted her hand above her head and brought it down on my shoulder.

"That's all right," she said. "At least people will see we have good taste in common."

Silently, I prayed that good taste was the only thing people would think we had in common. Yet, as my fiancé sat at the dais flanked by two women wearing identical outfits that night, I realized that my mother-in-law and I had something else in common: we both loved her son very much. And that one fact, and that fact alone, has kept my mother-in-law and me at peaceful odds for well over twenty years.

— Annie —

14

One-Pot Favorites

I have not failed. I've just found 10,000
ways that won't work.
~Thomas Edison

I sure didn't buy it for the love of cooking. Meal planning and preparation were things I did more out of duty than pleasure. At the time, our daughters Christine and Mary were about nine and seven. They needed healthy, homemade meals, while I wanted them fast and easy. I was also in the throes of a mild addiction to televised home shopping.

So when I saw a "one-pot" cookbook offered on TV, I grabbed the phone and ordered one. The book had recipes for seemingly luscious meals with creative names that I was sure my family would love.

Three days later, the cookbook arrived. My supportive and consistently hungry husband, Frank, was enthusiastic that I give the recipes a try. Since his own father often worked the second shift, most of Frank's childhood meals came in the form of TV dinners.

"Mom, what's for dinner? I'm starving!" Christine, my older daughter, was right at my heels, practically climbing into the pot.

"Give me some space, here. I'm trying to cook this new recipe from that cookbook I bought on TV. Call your dad and sister, will you? It's almost ready."

"But what is it? And how can you buy a book from TV, anyway? There's no one to pay."

I caught the edge of disapproval in my daughter's questions. The girls weren't overly fond of my television shopping habit, especially when it interrupted their favorite cartoons.

"Since you're not calling them, I will. Come and get it!"

In waddled Mary, clutching "Bearie" to her chest.

"No stuffed animals at the table," I admonished. "Everybody wash their hands?"

"Yes," three voices responded.

"Good." Nearly preening with delight, I set a steaming casserole on the table. Three pairs of eyes stared at it.

"What have we here?" my husband asked. I noted his smile looked forced.

"A one pot favorite," I quipped, poking a soup ladle into its mushy center. "It's a layered macaroni casserole. Everything's in here. There's pasta and hamburger, vegetables and seasoning—all in one pot!"

"But I don't like my food touching!" Mary squealed.

"Me either, Mom. You know that," Christine complained.

"When I was a kid, I didn't like my food to touch either, but it doesn't matter," Frank said.

I smiled, thinking of those compartmentalized TV dinners.

"It doesn't matter because it all goes to the same place, anyway," he continued.

"Ew, Daddy. Gross."

After spooning out portions onto everyone's plates, we began to eat. It might not have been the most appetizing-looking dish, but it tasted fine, though the elbows were a little overdone.

"There are so many good recipes," I enthused, my fork in mid-air.

"What kind, Mommy? Could you let us know before you try any more?" Mary asked, intent at the task at hand. She had succeeded in separating her peas, carrots, and elbows into tiny piles on her plate.

"How does Continental-style country ham and noodle casserole sound? You girls like ham."

"Ham's okay, but not continental country stuff," Christine said.

Ignoring them, I dipped in the ladle for another serving.

Later that night, taking out a bag of trash, I spotted something red and shiny in the garbage can. I plucked it out and charged angrily into the girls' bedroom, not caring if they were asleep.

"What's the meaning of this? I found my new cookbook in the garbage! You never throw a book away, especially not one of mine."

Under the covers, Mary's little voice squeaked. "We don't like one-pot favorites, Mommy."

Christine piped up. "You can keep the book. Just don't make anything from it. We like it when you use lots of pots."

"We're sorry," came the chorus.

I couldn't be mad, not when they looked nearly angelic lying there. Bending over to kiss them good night, their hair smelled of grass and spring air.

Now both girls are grown and on their own, strapped for time, just like me all those years ago. I often ask them what they're eating, hoping they're not living on cereal and pizza.

Christine's go-to dish is stir-fry, using chicken, vegetables and rice. Mary simmers vegetables and sauce, and then adds them to boiled pasta. How ironic — both dishes are made in one pot.

— Judy DeCarlo —

15

The Cut-Rate Poinsettia

Christmas isn't a season. It's a feeling.
~Edna Ferber

As Christmas approached one year, my mother exclaimed out of the blue, "Why is it that other women are given beautiful flowers by their so-called loved ones for no reason whatsoever, and I don't even warrant a poinsettia at Christmas? It doesn't seem like a lot to ask. I don't want some fancy plant from the florist. Any broken-stemmed reject from a discount department store would do."

I may or may not have rolled my eyes at her. *Fine,* I thought, with all the disdain that only a teenage daughter can command. *If that's what she wants, that's what she'll get.* That evening, I trotted off to the local cut-rate emporium and picked out the most disreputable specimen of seasonal flora I could find.

"Here," I said when I got home, slamming down the plastic bag triumphantly before her. "You asked for it, you got it."

My mother opened it, saw the woebegone little plant inside and promptly burst into tears.

"It's lovely," she cried, hugging me (and the plant) to her ample bosom. The poor thing, with its single red leaf, was placed in the most coveted spot on the mantel. Throughout the season, she pointed the gift out to all as if it were a diamond tiara.

Somehow a tradition had been started, and every year after that it became a point of honour for me to present her with the most bedraggled little plant I could find. She never failed to exclaim over it or express her disdain for what she referred to as the soulless pots of perfection with which her friends were forced to decorate their homes.

As time passed, the yearly poinsettia seemed to become a kind of surrogate daughter. She was able to lavish the attention on it that my prickly nature refused to accept. I remember the Christmas Day my husband and I endured a nasty eight-hour drive home from the distant city we had moved to. That was another year she cried when I gave her the plant I'd brought along with me, confessing how worried she'd been all day that "it" wouldn't survive the trip.

The situation was reversed a few years later when my parents flew out to spend Christmas with us in our new home even farther away. I picked them up at the airport late at night and brought them home to a house that was almost fully decorated. The next morning, I went out to buy the poinsettia and gave it to my mother's adored eighteen-month-old granddaughter to present when she came down for breakfast. Again, there were tears.

My mother was obviously unwell that Christmas, but I didn't realize how ill. Nor did I realize that it would be the last poinsettia I would ever give her. She died the following June.

The next year, my father flew out alone to spend Christmas with us. We knew it would be difficult, but enough time had passed since my mother's death to take the edge off our grief. He came quite early in December, so he was able to get involved with all the decorating and preparation for the season. We baked cookies, shopped, cut down the tree and generally threw ourselves determinedly into the trappings of the season.

One day, the three of them — my father, husband and daughter — came home from shopping with tentative smiles and a carefully protected package held in front of them. Inside was a poinsettia. It was large and showy, and that difference was the only thing that kept the tears in check as I gave it a place of honour on the mantel.

That was many Christmases ago. My father has been gone for several years, and we have moved once again. Many other things have changed as well. But every Christmas, my husband and long-suffering teenage daughter come home with the most disreputable looking poinsettia they can find. Sometimes, its only stem is bent. When we were living out in the country, it often needed first aid for frostbite after enduring a forty-minute drive in our inadequately heated pickup truck. But its arrival is as much a tradition as any other ceremony of the season.

— Denise Flint —

Queen of the Porcelain Throne

Some are born mad, some achieve madness,
and some have madness thrust upon 'em.
~Emilie Autumn

I'd finally done it. I'd confessed all to my father. Unfortunately, he suggested that I spill the beans to my mom. "I'll tell her if you don't want to," he said, "but I think it's only fair that she knows what's going on with you."

I took a deep breath and shuddered. Mom was such a goody-two-shoes that she'd never handle this kind of news with ease. "Where is she?" I asked.

"On the toilet," Dad said. "Go on in."

"Great," I grumbled. Unfortunately, Mom's bathroom habits had an unusual twist: she always left the door open and allowed family to visit her while she relieved herself.

And while growing up, almost every serious talk I'd ever had with Mom had taken place while she nestled on her white, porcelain throne, royal scepter (book) in hand. Even during my grand moment of starting my first period, my mother had sat like a queen, gathering me a sanitary belt from the medicine cabinet with one hand and a pad from the box on the floor, while keeping her cheeks planted firmly on her seat.

My parents' tiny half-bathroom had its own sliding door, with the commode almost perfectly centered in the doorway, facing out so that Mom could sit comfortably and hold court. And hold court she did. Our family could come and go and it never bothered her in the least. I've always loved my mom, but is that normal?

As a young mother, I thought that maybe she'd kept the door open so that she could keep an eye and ear out for us kids. Actually, I'd done that when my children were little, until two neighborhood girls walked into our house without knocking and entered the bathroom while I was in there. That ended that experiment.

Although Mom kept herself covered, I couldn't understand how a woman who never let us watch R-rated movies, even in our teens, and who insisted my sister and I dress modestly (no miniskirts), felt comfortable with her potty habits, especially as the years progressed.

My stomach felt queasy as I entered my parents' bedroom and even though I'd seen this sight a million times, I couldn't believe my eyes. The queen of the porcelain throne didn't glance my way, but continued reading her book. The absurdity of it all me made me feel as if I'd jumped headfirst into a Monty Python movie, and I suddenly relaxed as my fears washed away. This was insanity at its finest. Who makes announcements such as mine while her mother is using a toilet?

My husband and I had been separated for a year at that time. While he still used our home as a base of operation, he worked out of state where he had a steady girlfriend, and he was rarely back.

My father already knew the details of my new relationship, but learned of the pregnancy while I was visiting them. While my mother knew that my husband and I had basically separated, she knew nothing about the new man in my life. And now, the unthinkable had accidentally happened.

"Mom," I said quietly. "I've got something to tell you." I'll admit I almost started giggling.

"What is it honey?" she asked, eyes fixed on her book.

"I'm pregnant and it's NOT my husband's baby."

"Oh that's wonderful news!" she said. "I'm so happy. I'll have to start on a baby blanket."

I can still picture my mom's reaction that day. With the coolness of a cucumber, my mother had concentrated on the baby part of my announcement and let the rest slide, and I remembered that while we argued a lot, most of our past toilet talks had ended peacefully. Perhaps there was magic in her throne.

— Vera Frances —

The Holiday Merger

Love is no assignment for cowards.
~Ovid

Mom jumped up from the dinner table and said, "I have an announcement to make!" My petite Italian mother hovered over the yams, part of the first holiday meal that I was hosting to introduce my fiancé Jim's conservative Catholic parents to one-half of my non-practicing kind.

Mom glanced at me and then at Jim, excited about something neither of us knew about. As her smile widened, I squeezed the stem of my wineglass. Mom, who'd been divorced for seventeen years, turned to the rest of the people she'd just met: my future in-laws who had recently celebrated forty years of marriage.

"I'm married again!" she proclaimed, hugging her chest.

I'd spent my twenties dating one toad after another and had resigned myself to the fact that I was going to be a thirty-something cat lady. Then, on St. Patrick's Day in 2008, I met Jim. It was chaos, hardly a time to meet someone worthwhile, but we quickly connected as we stood outside an overcrowded bar in Manhattan and started talking, realizing we went to the same high school in the neighboring borough of Staten Island.

Jim, thirty-one, was divorced with no kids, and yet he understood the repercussions of coming from a divorced home. He mentioned, however, that his church-going family rarely spoke of the "D-word,"

You Just Have to Laugh | 51

even when he was in the midst of his own.

Despite his solid upbringing, Jim was pretty rebellious. He forfeited a scholarship after high school to join the military, and later bought a motorcycle — both decisions made against his parents' wishes. After a yearlong relationship, Jim proposed to me in Las Vegas, and we planned a wedding that didn't include the Catholic Church. Although I wasn't a favorite of theirs, his parents did like that I had a successful career, owned my condo, and was thriving on my own. I didn't need their son's money, car or townhouse. They were formal yet friendly when we visited them and gradually grew comfortable with our arrangement. That's when Jim and I decided to host this holiday meal where both families would finally break bread over our engagement.

Because my mother lived in Florida, she had to travel by plane to the event. Everyone else was within driving distance. And because this was my first time playing Martha Stewart for real — stressing about menus (who had a food allergy?), the ambiance (should I stick with traditional harvest colors or spice up the theme?), seating arrangements (if I put my family on one side of the table and his on the other, was that insinuating "us versus them"?) — I became neurotic, and Mom knew it. She had arrived a few days early to help me prep.

So when her outburst came on the heels of a "Welcome to our family!" toast to me from Jim's father, I was stunned. I presume she thought the evening was going well, which it was, up until her proclamation. Picture a reserved senior standing proper and talking calmly when a rather vocal woman who was enjoying her wine suddenly interrupted him.

I glanced down at my full plate as everyone else sat around the table nervously smiling and blinking at one another. Not sure what to do, I immediately took a swig of the Cabernet Sauvignon. I wasn't upset over Mom's announcement, but rather the timing of it.

"That's wonderful news!" Jim said, jumping up and wrapping his arms around her. He saw the corners of my mouth do a funny dip, so he reached out and patted my knee. Right away, I knew that my soon-to-be-hubby, a full-time firefighter with the FDNY, was going to somehow save us from these smoldering embers.

Jim's mother slowly stood and straightened her perfectly pressed slacks.

"Congratulations on your nuptials," she said, and motioned for a hug.

Jim's dad, ever the gentleman, got to his feet and raised his cup.

"It's an honor to have learned that our family is growing already," he said, and winked at me.

I smiled and turned to Mom. "We're both brides! Who woulda thunk it?"

She gave me a firm squeeze. "Sometimes it takes another shot at finding true love. Jim gets it."

I, too, knew what she was getting at. I think we all did. What matters most is our happiness, regardless of the path we have to travel to get there.

— Dawn Turzio —

Never Tell Anyone

*A secret remains a secret until you make
someone promise never to reveal it.*
~Fausto Cercignani

Monday night! I've had a pretty awful day at work and a worse forty-five-minute-turned-seventy-minute commute home. After eating something cold out of the fridge, showering and getting in my jammies, I'm just in time to watch *Everybody Loves Raymond*. Feet up on my couch, I'm in for the night. The phone rings.

"Yes?" I answer, barely taking interest.

"You need to come over." It's my dad.

"I'll be right there."

"It's nothing bad," he adds.

"Then I'm not coming; my show's on." Raymond and Robert argue in the background. Yes, I'm recording it, but I intend to stay planted.

"You've got to come. It's good news. And don't tell anyone that you're coming."

"Dad, I'm not going anywhere. I'm already showered and in my pajamas."

"You have to come."

My very cute, very Italian parents, who reside six minutes from the first condo of their only daughter, frequently have insignificant emergencies. Today they have caught me on strike from the world. "You're going to have to tell me what's up or I'm not budging."

A sigh... "Your mom won the lottery."

"A lot of money?"

"A lot! But don't tell anyone!"

"Okay," I say, "I'll get dressed. And who am I going to tell?"

Driving the six minutes to my parents' house, I contemplate getting rich before my soul mate materializes. How will I know if he's interested in my money or me?

Getting to the house, I find my grandmother on the stairs with her walker, my uncle and aunt flanking her. "I'm so happy!" she says when she gets to the top, grabbing my hand and hugging me. This was the grandmother who never hugged.

A party is starting before my eyes. Everyone greets each other warmly like it's been so long since Sunday dinner at Grandma's house yesterday. All the liquor in the house is now on the kitchen counter. Most of the bottles, some still in boxes, have a layer of dust on them. My brother Jim grabs my hands and tries to lead me in a weird jig.

At the kitchen table, Mom writes a list. She has been allocating her lottery winnings. First on the list are the retired nuns. *Retired Nuns? Where did that come from?* Second, she intends to pay off Jim's car and my own; that's fair, I think sarcastically. Jim's car is a new sports car that he rolled off the lot last week; I've made about 180 of 350 payments on my far more practical used car, but whatever.

Suddenly, I remember a friend who said a prayer for my mom in Rome. Prior to his trip, he had collected everyone's intentions and was praying throughout his sabbatical. He'd told my mom that when he'd actually seen the pope waving from a distance, all he could think of was "Marie Farella's special intention." She'd beamed when he'd told her that.

"Mom," I ask, "was this the special intention you'd asked Ron to pray for you in Rome?"

She looks down, blushing and smiling. Guilty as charged.

"Well, I'm happy for you!"

I hear my father announce that he has called the state lottery number, but they don't know that there's a winner yet. That doesn't sound right. I walk over to look at the ticket on the counter. Next to it is the newspaper, open to yesterday's winning numbers.

Uncle John is leaning over it, matching the numbers. I hear his brain wheels turning. Looking over his shoulder, I stare at the newspaper and the ticket in turn. Stupidly, I hear myself ask, "Wait, could she have won more than one lottery? These *all* seem to match yesterday's. All the winning numbers match for *each* type of lottery."

He snaps out of it. Grabbing the ticket, he looks to my mom. "Wait! This is the slip from the gas station! The one they print out when you ask for yesterday's winning numbers. Where's your lottery ticket from yesterday, Marie?"

Mom looks like she's been slapped. Reality hits the entire room. Mom looks for her purse. When she returns with the actual lottery ticket that she'd purchased, it has only three matching numbers. Everyone has been reveling in the winning numbers on the print-out given to her *today* by the cashier at the gas station, which displays the winning numbers from yesterday and looks very much like a lottery ticket. We all look at her dumbfounded. Ours for only minutes, the treasure is gone.

"You ruin everything!" my brother yells at me. All of this is suddenly my fault. New dust gathers on the champagne and the other bottles. The celebration ends. No nuns, no car payments, no special intention prayer to the pope answered. We are middle-class-broke once again.

We all look to my mother. She sits at the kitchen table, completely deflated. "Promise me," she calls to us all, "you will never, ever tell anyone about this."

— Gina Farella Howley —

Who Me?

Mothers are the only ones that think
nothing is beyond their control
when it comes to their children.
~Ali Fazal

The letter from the principal couldn't have been clearer: The bus will pick up your new kindergartner at the designated bus stop. Parents are not to ride with children on the bus, and under no circumstances are parents to come to the school, whether to drop off their children or to take pictures. Parking is tight, even for teachers, staff, and buses, and additional cars are strictly forbidden at the beginning or end of the school day.

That was all understandable but they didn't know my five-year-old twins. Shy and sensitive, they hid whenever the doorbell rang. They couldn't be coaxed out of their hiding places with ice cream, candy, or new toys. Their paternal grandparents didn't get a good look at them until they were about seven. They clung to me whenever we ventured out in public — one girl per leg. And while my Frankenstein-monster walk was not graceful or elegant, it did have the advantage of providing a combination of resistance training and aerobics for a busy mom.

My fear on that first day of school was that my girls would hide under a bus seat, or somehow get lost or stolen. The first day of school wouldn't be easy for them (me).

The day came, and it was sunny and beautiful. The girls were adorable in their new dresses and light-up sneakers. Each wore a nametag on a construction-paper cutout of a school bus around her neck.

The bus was late, and they were nervous, but they smiled for the camera. I sat on the front lawn under a shady tree for a minute, and their father finally took his eye off the camera lens and took in what I was wearing.

"Oh, no, you're not," he said.

I had on my running gear and favorite long-distance running shoes. The school was a few miles away.

"I am not going to run after the bus, if that's what you're thinking," I said, insulted.

Our conversation was cut short when the bus approached. I watched Morgan and Chloe get on (how could human beings be so impossibly cute?), turn and wave on the top step, and then...

Okay, then I ran like hell. But I ran *before* the bus, not *after* the bus, so I wasn't lying to the husband. Can't a woman go for a run? I ran faster than I ever ran before.

The bus finally overtook me a few hundred yards before the school building. Panting, I made my way to the front entrance by sprinting from behind one car to another until, hidden safely behind a large SUV, I had a bird's-eye view of every child that climbed down the bus steps and walked into the school doors. As each bus emptied, it would pull away, and the next bus in the row would pull up to the spot directly in front of the school entrance. I willed my breath to quiet down, the blood in my temples to slow its pulse. My legs felt like jelly, and I concentrated hard on just being still because getting caught would be beyond embarrassing, even for me. Sweat dripped down my forehead and mixed with the sunblock I had thoughtfully applied hours before, stinging my eyes and making them tear up.

A few minutes went by. Two more buses emptied and left, and then there they were! Chloe smiled shyly as the principal gave her a big smile and "Welcome!" Morgan stayed tightly behind, chin down, but she was smiling and holding her sister's hand.

I said it was the sweat and the sunblock that made me tear up. I was lying about that part.

— Erika Tremper —

Chicken Soup
for the Soul.

Breaking the Rules

List, list, O, list!
~William Shakespeare, Hamlet

om and I had our arms up to our elbows in warm, sudsy water, washing dishes from our Thanksgiving dinner. Mom had just shared how much she liked my boyfriend, John. It was the first time my family had met him, and Mom had beamed when John presented her with a bouquet of freshly cut flowers. Dad had taken such an instant liking that he asked John to help carve the golden brown roast turkey. All had gone better than expected, but now my mom had a puzzled look on her face because I had just told her that I had to break up with him.

"But why?"

"He's six years older than me, and your rule is no more than five."

My mom had a list of rules for how to find the right marriage partner, and the rule of no more than five years' difference was on the list. After carefully studying successful and failed marriages, Mom had determined an age difference larger than five years could well lead to incompatibility later in life.

I had already ignored Rule #1: "A relative or close friend should introduce you." Mom felt that my family and friends would know if the guy had good character and would be a good match. How could I explain that John and I had met in a bar on Singles Wednesday? He smiled and introduced himself, and we started talking every Wednesday after that until he finally asked for my phone number. Mom hadn't asked how we met, and I wasn't volunteering.

While my former boyfriends had been from North Carolina, and my parents often knew the boyfriend's family, John had been born and raised in Los Angeles. His favorite foods included sweet corn tamales and chicken enchiladas with mole verde sauce. He needed me to explain Southern sayings like "if the creek don't rise." As a Duke professor, he traveled all over the U.S. and Europe to attend conferences, while I explored the East Coast.

I was my parents' only daughter, born and raised in Greensboro, North Carolina, a graduate of East Carolina University, and an elementary-school teacher. I had moved an hour away to Durham, but in many ways it was a world away. I lived near two major universities — UNC-Chapel Hill and Duke. UNC has always been our state's pride and joy, and one brother, two uncles, and several cousins were UNC grads. We all cheered for the Carolina Tarheels. Dean Smith, the UNC men's basketball coach, was often quoted in our home. Barely ten miles from UNC, that other university, Duke, with its impressive gothic architecture, was a nice place to visit, but we Tarheels considered Duke to be the devil, just like its mascot. Every year when the UNC men's basketball team played the Duke Blue Devils, the rivalry between the two teams and their fans became even more intense.

"What religion is he?" my dad asked. Yes, another rule for a spouse. My parents felt that marriages worked best when both persons worshipped alike, and both my mom and dad came from a long line of Methodists, including several ministers. John, however, did not identify with one denomination, and he felt no need to go to any church — an answer that did not sit well with my parents. How could I get them to see that he lived life in the way that churches hoped their parishioners would? I saw the way he treated others with respect, taking the time to thank a person for a job well done — from the short-order cook who prepared his omelet to the volunteer firefighters at their annual fundraiser. I knew that he spoke well of a person or said nothing at all, just like my dad had taught me. I knew that he was as good as his word. I knew, without a doubt, that he was a good man with a strong moral compass.

I loved John with all my heart, even if he didn't fit Mom's list of rules. I noticed the way he listened to opposing viewpoints, stating that he had definite opinions, but that good evidence could convince him to reconsider. He seldom offered his opinions unless asked, but when he spoke, I never second-guessed what he meant. Underneath his quiet reserve, he had a passion for his research, and when I asked a question, he would draw diagrams and explain the concept, without ever making me feel less intelligent.

He worked long hours, and his research was often cited, but he always acknowledged that his work built on the ideas and research of his mentors. He appreciated my passion for teaching remedial reading to kids who needed successful school experiences. He understood the importance of my family and friends in my life. Most of all, I loved the way he made me feel about myself. With John, I could be myself — my *best* self.

My parents wanted to get to know him better. John joined our family for Christmas, several Sunday dinners, and Mom's family reunion the following June. John and I visited his California family in July, and I enjoyed getting to know his mom, sisters, aunt and uncle, cousins, and best friends from high school. The two of us drove north on the Pacific Coast Highway from Los Angeles to San Francisco, and John showed me places he loved in his home state.

In late July, we visited my family to announce our engagement. My brothers and dad welcomed John with firm handshakes, and one niece gave him a bear hug, but I could tell that Mom still had reservations behind her smile. Which rule still worried her?

"Mom, I thought you'd be thrilled. I'm in love with him, and he is with me."

Still trying to understand Mom's hesitation, I added, "And you said that the six years didn't make a difference, that he looks young for his age."

As I held my breath, waiting for her answer, I realized how desperately I wanted my mother's blessing. I wanted more than an acceptance of John as my future husband. My hope was that John would be welcomed with open hearts as a member of our family.

"I'm not worried about his age, or that he's from California. I love how he looks at you, the way he treats you. I love the way he laughs when you are sharing your stories. He loves you for who you are, just as you are. You two should be married. But my team is UNC, and John's team is Duke. All I ask is that I never have to watch the UNC-Duke basketball game in the same room with him."

For the man of my dreams, love of my life, the one who didn't fit Mom's checklist of rules for how to select the right mate, this was Mom's only concern? No problem.

— Suzanne Garner Payne —

Chapter
3

Role Models

21

Super Strong Mom

Mother love is the fuel that enables a normal
human being to do the impossible.
~Marion C. Garretty

My mom is the greatest mom ever! As I grew up, I saw her as my hero for all the things she would do for me. I remember when she would fix my baby dolls or when she helped me color pretty pictures when I started elementary school. I remember in middle school, I would see her do things that fathers were supposed to do, like fix the car without caring how greasy her hands would get. Now that I'm in high school, I see how she is strong but sensitive at the same time. She looks at life with a positive attitude no matter what the situation is.

One day I came home from school and saw papers on the kitchen table and my mom sitting with a worried face looking at my dad. My dad wasn't working at the time because he had broken his arm. I had heard my parents talk about money issues a couple of times before but I never asked about the situation.

"What's going on?" I asked.

"We have to be out of the house in two weeks," my mom said. She had her elbows on the table and one hand over her forehead. Then I realized this was a serious problem. That very day, she made phone calls and started to look for a place to rent.

We had no money and no idea what we were going to do. I read the papers on the table; it said we had lost the house because we hadn't been paying rent. I was surprised that all this was going on and my dad seemed to be doing nothing about it and my mom never said anything about it. It seemed like everything was falling apart, but my mom seemed as if this was making her stronger.

That whole week she tried her best to find a place for rent. Besides the fact that we had no place to move to, we also had nothing to eat since the food my dad had bought the month before had run out. Even though she didn't show it, I felt my mom's pain and how much it hurt her to not be able to provide a good shelter and food for us.

After that whole week of seeing her struggle, I came home and she had a smile on her face and was cooking, which was really weird because she doesn't like to cook. I assumed there was good news and asked her, "So what's new?"

"We are starting to move today," she said with a smile on her face. "There's a place near your school and thank God they allowed all of us even though the place is pretty small." I could tell she was relieved and happy. At that moment, I admired her so much.

My mom is the greatest mom ever. I would not know what to do without her. Times like these are moments that make me admire my mom's strength. Some people might give up in bad situations. My mom looks at bad moments in life as a test, or a chance to make her stronger. When things seem to be the worst, she makes everything seem so easy to fix. I want to be like my mom when I have children of my own. I thank God for giving me such a wonderful mother like her.

— Brenda Barajas, age 16 —

22

A Man's Profession

A girl should be two things: who and what she wants.
~Coco Chanel

My granddaughter follows me into my old glass studio. Her eyes scan the shelves, empty of glass. All the packed-up boxes and equipment are covered up and leaning against the walls. I have retired from glassblowing and lampworking. She was very young when I stopped, so she never had the opportunity to watch a demonstration. I feel sad about this, sad about giving up my occupation and passion. I had worked hard to be accepted as a woman glassblower, but I can no longer do it. Alas, my body has aged.

When I started in the 1970s, glassblowing was traditionally a man's profession. This viewpoint stemmed from the era of glassblowing in Europe, mostly in Italy, a time when glassmaking was revered, and secrets were handed down to sons only. Glassblowing was held in high esteem, admired and respected.

Things changed. A "new-art glass movement" started first in California and then spread east and north. Over a few short years, it expanded throughout North America. I became part of that movement. At art college, I majored in the medium of hot glass. No one told me that I couldn't work the glass. However, the real world awaited me when I finished my training.

I married another glassblower. My husband and I worked hard to establish our artistic reputations and make a living. At least with a husband, the path was partway clear in the outside world. Signatures for contracts, for things like oxygen and propane delivery, were done by my "man." Job propositions and commissions were acceptable at first because of him. Since my husband's name was on any documents required, no one questioned whether my husband or I had made the glass.

Tired of not being accepted in my own right, and with my husband's support, I reached out for a position at a theme park. The public loved to watch glassblowing demonstrations. I was now in the public eye — a woman blowing glass.

People did a double take when they saw me work the hot glass. Some of the comments shocked me. One day, I heard a female voice coming from around the corner. She said to her grandchildren, "Let's go watch the man blow glass." I didn't look up from my work. The voice changed, "Oh, it's a woman." The next few moments of silence were awkward. Still, not looking up from my work, with determination and calm on my face, I finished my piece. Then I looked up and stared in defiance. The grandmother gave a little laugh and said, "Oh, nice."

I smiled, especially at the little girls who gazed up at me. I will never forget the looks of wonder and admiration they gave me. I gave them a little nod, imparting the message, "I can do this. You can, too. You can do anything."

At age ten my granddaughter has a different life ahead of her. She can be a doctor, scientist, or astronaut, all now accepted professions for a woman. She can also be a glassblower. Over the years, I have given her small pieces of my work, mostly miniature animals. I can tell by how she displays them in her room that she admires her treasures. She proudly shows them to her friends.

Out in my old studio, I get an idea. "If you're interested," I say, "maybe I can teach you when you are a little older. All this... I can save it for you, when you are ready."

The look of excitement on her face fills me with pride and joy. She has respect for my chosen vocation as a glassblower. She can be one, too. She can be whoever she wants to be.

— Kathy Ashby —

23

In My Mother's Kitchen

*As a restaurateur, my job is to basically control
the chaos and the drama. There's always going
to be chaos in the restaurant business.*
~Rocco DiSpirito

"Pick up!" I hear her scream from the kitchen as the bell chimes. Instinctively, my feet start to move across the tile floor, passing the bar on my left and the other servers moving swiftly, filling glasses and wiping counters. I turn left, into the bright lights of the kitchen.

In front of me is the rack where I pick up one bowl of pasta with pesto, lusciously green on a spotless white plate, and a steak, drizzled with chimichurri sauce and settled on French fries. I pull both plates down, one in each hand, and now I can see her. She is framed by the metal rack. Her hair is pulled back by a red bandana, but her gray roots are evident — unsurprising, since she hardly has time to eat, let alone color her hair. There is moisture on her face, a little sweat, and her eyeliner is smudged. Again, I am not surprised. I heard her put her make-up on at five o'clock this morning. We're well into dinner service now.

"Hot, hot, hot!" she yells, at no one in particular, as she hauls a sizzling pan from one burner to another. She is running on pure adrenaline and kitchen fumes at this point, and I hurry into the dining room, afraid of what exhaustion might bring out of her if I let the food get cold.

This is my mother.

Many peoples' moms cook for them, their families, and occasional guests. They make brownies for school birthdays and banana bread for bake sales. When I was very young, that's how it was. My mom didn't go to cooking school until after her divorce from my dad when I was seven, and so I have memories of broccoli steamed only for me, lasagna made just for our dinner, and Christmas cookies for holiday gifts instead of throngs of customers.

But that wasn't what my mom wanted to do. Cooking, she realized, was her gift, and it was one she wanted to give to more than just our little brood. She opened her first business, a bakery, when I was in high school, and there she made café food — egg sandwiches on fresh-baked croissants, simple salads, and omelets — while her partner handled the baking. I worked for her, enjoying the edges of the brownies and admiring the beautifully crafted pastries. Her partnership with the baker, however, was not so beautifully crafted, and she soon left the business.

Her next venture was her own restaurant — a place that was really hers. I remember spending hours in the space before it opened, watching it take form. The wall sconces, the artwork, the placemats. The glistening red bar with flecks that sparkled — just enough flare for it to belong to my mother. It was a sensuous place, dramatic and well made. It was my mom, in a restaurant.

I worked there too, but not willingly. By the time I was in college, I had realized that though I grew up in the restaurant business, I didn't love it. In fact, I hated it. I hated how my mom was never home and was always exhausted. I hated that our own refrigerator at our house was consistently bare unless she brought home leftovers. I hated the grueling pace of the restaurant, the customers with nothing nice to say, and the feeling that if I failed in the restaurant, then somehow I failed my mother too.

Because my feelings were so conflicted about her restaurant and her choices, and because I subsisted on leftovers and family meals at the café, I never cooked for myself. I didn't really want to. I had no desire to do what she did.

That changed when I moved into my first college apartment with a kitchen. Wanting to save money and make what I considered a move into adulthood, I decided to cook something my mom always made — pasta with sautéed broccoli and sausage. A simple dish I figured I could make.

I boiled some water to blanch the broccoli, and got out my only cutting board. I began chopping the garlic, and something came over me — a strange, instinctual knowledge. I had never really done this before — chopped garlic — but how many times had I watched it done? How many nights had the scent of chopped garlic filled the kitchen while I did my homework? How often had I seen my mom or her employees fill plastic containers with garlic to use for dinner service? The answer was too many to count.

I looked down at my hand. I was holding the knife the proper way, lowering the blade front to back the way my mom always did. Why wouldn't I? Hadn't I sat on my mother's bed, quizzing her with flashcards on knife techniques while she was in cooking school? I was a good student. No matter how hard I had tried to stay away, somehow I had learned.

That night, I made a fine pasta dish. It didn't taste quite like Mom's, but I realized right away that I wasn't culinary-challenged. It came naturally to me to cook, and I did enjoy it. Since that night, I have done a lot of cooking, and especially baking. My mom, enamored with the hot line, didn't have time for slow, pretty decorations. I like to sit and decorate fluffy cupcakes, one by one, for an hour. You might call it a rebellion of sorts.

I tell people that I grew up in Connecticut, but I really grew up in the kitchen. For me, food is intertwined with love, but also loneliness, resentment, and forgiveness — blood, sweat, and tears. Food has made me cry, but food has also forced me to learn. Now, whenever I seem to feel, instinctually, that it is time to let the steak rest or take the chicken out of the oven, I know why and where those instincts come from. I am still learning from my mother. And my mother, of course, is still cooking.

—Madeline Clapps—

24

She Did It Herself

*A woman is like a tea bag — you never know how
strong she is until she gets in hot water.*
~Eleanor Roosevelt

My grandmother was only in her sixties when Grandpa died. She continued to run their junkyard in the small Kansas town of Sabetha, sculpting her biceps with her newly acquired welding and cutting-torch skills, and sorting metals into neat piles. During the Depression and World War II, the A.M. Henry Salvage business had been a major employer that helped the town weather those troubled times. Grams, who had previously handled the bookkeeping, saw no reason to close the business and embraced some of the outdoor work that Grandpa had hired others to do.

She was much older when she ceased doing business, but she never quit working. I well remember the summer day that my husband Ray and I, along with our two young sons, drove the ninety miles to Grams' home and found her up on the roof nailing on shingles. She was then in her early eighties, measured five feet tall, and weighed her age. Ignoring her protests, Ray quickly took over the job for her. When she led the boys and me into the house, I noticed her shiny hardwood floors and realized they were newly refinished. "I did it myself," she said matter-of-factly. "Just stripped off the old varnish and brushed on the new. It wasn't that hard."

She had also painted her kitchen a soft mint-green. Hoping to be of belated assistance, I asked, "Grams, would you like Ray and me to move out your refrigerator and range and paint behind them?"

"Why, honey," she replied, "I already did that."

"How on earth did you move those heavy objects?"

"I just went out to the iron pile, got a steel pipe, hoisted up the appliances and rolled them out. When the paint was dry, I rolled them back."

Back in the living room, I noticed a baseball bat by the door. Grams explained, "Our neighborhood has been having trouble with burglars lately. If one comes here, I'll hit him with the bat." Any burglar who encountered Grams would wish he had taken up a different line of work.

Grams was brave, but never foolhardy. At eighty-six, when she climbed a tall pear tree, she asked my great-aunt, aged ninety-something, to act as spotter. Suddenly, Grams plummeted about fifteen feet, landing with a thump at Aunt May's feet. When Aunt May could not revive her, she presumed the worst and went into Grams' house to call the mortuary. She was talking to the funeral director when Grams—shaken but otherwise unhurt—walked in the back door.

When we were alerted to the accident, we drove to Sabetha and insisted on taking Grams to the doctor. He lectured her sternly, "I don't want you climbing any more trees."

"I won't climb any more *pear* trees," Grams promised. And until her productive life ended at almost ninety-one years of age, Ruth Moriarty Henry was true to her word.

—Marsha Henry Goff—

25

The Ice Cream Truck

Winners never quit, and quitters never win.
~Vince Lombardi

"**N**ever give up! Never give up!" chanted my two young children, Max and Charley, as they marched barefoot behind their grandmother Mimi. My mother was clad in her favorite faded-denim, button-down shirt thrown casually over her swimsuit. Wild tufts of her short, auburn hair peeked out from a wide-brimmed, yellow straw hat.

Mimi was leading Max and Charley on yet another adventure, straight off the beach where they had spent the day building sand castles and splashing in the waves. This time, they were seeking the elusive ice-cream truck. As always, shoes were optional.

Over the years, Mimi had become our family's beacon of positivity. It was not a title she earned without concerted effort, however. Having been widowed at only forty years old and left to raise me and my ten-year-old brother alone, she faced heart-wrenching tragedy powerful enough to cloud just about anyone's upbeat outlook. She had been the one who had to make the decision to remove our dad from life support fourteen days after he was in a car accident.

My mom could have lived under a black cloud. Instead, she challenged herself to find joy every day. She was always up for a new challenge, whether that was hiking across the steep, rocky terrain of a mountaintop in Austria to get a better view of the breathtaking landscape while my brother and I looked on terrified, parasailing over the Gulf of Mexico, or signing up for tap-dancing classes at fifty. Leading by example, Mom taught us just how much one could accomplish with a positive attitude.

She has taken the same approach in her relationship with her grandchildren. Prior to starting her adventure with Max and Charley on that hot July afternoon, Mimi heard the familiar clang of the ice-cream man's bell from her beach chair. She turned and saw him briefly, spotting his fluorescent green shirt and catching the gleam of his waving bell before he turned and disappeared over the dunes. Happily, the ice-cream man's visit is a daily occurrence at the beach, although the lag time between the sound of his bell and the departure of his truck is not long. One must be quick to catch him.

Max and Charley were disappointed when they didn't catch him in time that day. That was until Mimi's eyes sparkled and she said, "Never give up!" She explained that the truck might be gone, but they could hustle off to find it at its next stop.

They walked block after block. Not knowing which direction the truck had taken, they had to make their best guess about where to search. My kids' tiny legs were tired, but they forged on, continuing to chant their mantra, "Never give up!"

After about twenty minutes of walking, Max's faith in the mission began to waver. He wondered out loud, "Maybe we should give up. We have been walking pretty far and haven't seen the truck yet." Charley squealed a quick, "No way! Never give up!" and resumed her chant with Mimi. Somewhat skeptically, Max acquiesced.

Just two blocks later, they found it. Mimi threw a triumphant fist in the air, and Max and Charley screamed with excitement, "Never give up!" In that moment, my mom had done for my children what she had done for me countless times. Simple though it was, that phrase has become our battle cry for the challenges we face. Whether studying for a difficult test, pushing through a challenging cross-country practice, or practicing lines to audition for a school play, I know I can always look at Max and Charley and say, "Never give up!" Upon hearing those words, they are instantly transported to a positive state of mind — where the next ice-cream truck is just around the corner.

— Samantha LaBarbera —

26

Can't Take My Smile

Mothers and daughters together are a
powerful force to be reckoned with.
~Melia Keeton-Digby

Mom said the unforgettable words, "I have cancer," and clasped me in a tight hug. I could feel her chest shaking as she tried not to cry but failed.

If adulthood is bestowed in a moment, that was it. For all of my twenty-four years, my mom had been sturdy, supportive, and an unchanging presence. For a moment, I was the adult, and she the child. Strength and compassion had always flowed from her to me. Now I knew it would have to flow the other way. I felt a wave of protectiveness I had never felt before, and I promised her with a smile I would help her through anything.

But Mom didn't stay down for long. After the initial shock of the breast-cancer diagnosis, she armed herself with a purple spiral notebook and pen and a thousand questions for the doctors. She took notes on white blood cell counts and medications with eight-syllable names as though she were studying for entrance exams into medical school. "The not-knowing is the worst," she said.

Almost before we could blink, she was waking up from surgery that claimed her lymph nodes and dictated she would need both chemo and radiation. She couldn't use a towel on her tender, bruised chest, so she took to air-drying the area with a blow dryer on the cool setting. Dad offered to get the job done more efficiently with the leaf blower. Mom laughed until it hurt.

We knew chemo would take her hair, so before it fell out, Mom and I went wig shopping together at a tiny salon that catered to cancer patients. You would have thought we were picking out outfits for a costume party. We tried on everything from Betty Boop-style brunette bobs to electric-pink, rock-star locks like a pair of middle-school girls squealing at a makeover. Other customers stared. Was it sacrilegious to belly laugh at a cancer shop?

Trying on new hairdos in the mirror was a chance to reinvent ourselves. As a new adult, I was in the habit of reinventing myself anyway: new clothes, new diets, new jobs. But Mom had been loyal to the same short perm for over two decades. I had never seen her with any other hairstyle. When she put on a shoulder-length wig, straight and banged, I paused the festivities and stared. Honestly, I had to double-check to be sure it was her before I spoke. I didn't recognize my own mother. But then she grinned, and I saw the same sweet smile as in black-and-white pictures I had seen of her as a twelve-year-old with the same hairstyle.

Mom was one of my closest friends, but I realized there were still parts of her I didn't fully know. She held stories inside she hadn't told me. Neither of us knew the end of her cancer story that day in the wig shop. It might turn out to be an inspirational story, or a tragedy, or even both. It was still being written. I had never considered that mothers, too, are still growing into their most adult selves.

I went with Mom to every chemo treatment and watched as soft-shoed nurses hung bags of her chemo cocktail over her head. "Cocktail? Sounds like a party!" I said. So we called her bi-weekly treatments "chemo parties" and made an event out of them. During the two-hour IV drips, she joked about life, medical issues and even the pain. We celebrated with hot grinder sandwiches afterward. Mom hasn't been able to stomach one since, but back then they tasted like a victory meal after a sports championship. We spoke on the phone almost daily. She rarely complained, though I heard far more about my mother's toenails and fingernails than I ever wanted to as they fell out one by one. We joked that she could save money on nail polish and put it toward the doctor bills, even though she never wore nail polish. Fear became a guest at our party. It was the guest no one wanted to come, but we invited it in on our own terms.

"Cancer can take my hair, my nails, my health, my very life. But it can't take my smile," Mom said.

Mom learned to share her fears with me, and it formed an even deeper bond between us. Yet I am certain there were fears she didn't share because she was still protecting me — worries she only shared with Dad, or maybe even refused to give voice to. My mom, who never played sports and demurred when she won a hand of rummy, was a warrior determined to defeat breast cancer. Defeat it, and even joke about it. When you look your greatest fear in the eye and laugh at it, you take away some of its power.

I made Mom a survivor's box from a purple and pink shoebox. Every time I visited, I left behind a small gift, like some kind of cancer tooth fairy. Lotion for skin chapped by treatment. (It was called Udder Butter, which we found hilarious for a breast-cancer patient.) A mirror labeled "The Most Courageous Woman in the World." A lock of my hair left over from the eleven inches I had donated to a wig-making organization. A huge hat I had crocheted — somehow I had made a nine-sided octagon even though I had read the pattern. And a whole bunch of silly quotes and puns.

Mom was the most sociable patient the cancer center ever had. She made homemade noodles for the medical staff. She chose to be grateful to the hands that tried to heal her, instead of resentful when fatigue kept her from the job and social life she loved. Each morning, she chose to thank God for the day He gave her, instead of being angry that He allowed her to have cancer.

One day when I went to visit I found Mom sitting at the table doing her crossword puzzle without her wig. The morning light shone on her vulnerable, bald scalp. Her fingertips, raw and nail-less, grasped a pencil over the newspaper. She looked up and smiled, not self-conscious at all. I had never seen a stronger or more beautiful woman.

Months later, after the final radiation treatment, we held a graduation ceremony for Mom. I made a mortarboard out of pink foam sheets and a curtain tassel. She placed it on her hairless head like a crown and paraded around the dining room as Dad played "Pomp and Circumstance" on his baritone horn. We presented her with a teacup to remind her that the finest porcelain only grows strong after it goes through the fire.

Mom was one of the lucky ones. She did beat her cancer, though not without scars. To this day, she wears a compression sleeve to control the swelling from lymphedema, a result of the removal of her lymph nodes. But she lived, and whenever she can, she encourages others in those first scary weeks of diagnosis.

Most of all, I saw a change in Mom. Nothing afterward seemed to worry her quite as much. She was more patient and resilient. Cancer was her fire, and it refined her. From her, I learned I may not get to choose what I face, but I do get to choose how I face it.

— Sarah E. Morin —

27

Like Daughter, Like Mother

*One woman filled with self-love and self-acceptance
is a model more super than any cover girl.*
~Amy Leigh Mercree

She was unlike anyone I had ever seen. I watched her while lying on the beach in Hollywood, Florida. And I didn't know what illuminated her more — her wind-blown, tightly spiraled curls or her radiant happiness.

But what struck me — even more than her presence — was the fact that I was able to conflate the two.

Some background: I was thirty-three years old, and I literally had no idea how to style or maintain my natural hair. I had spent my life trying desperately to make my curly hair something it wasn't, and I worshipped my flatiron like it was my religion.

I would sooner gouge out my eye with the nearest blunt object than be seen in public with my hair in its natural state. But there I was, mesmerized by a complete stranger with the kind of hair I had previously despised.

I wanted to talk to her.

Looking back, I now see that my desire to approach her was driven less by curiosity and more by a primal need for understanding.

When the man she was sitting with rose from his Adirondack chair and walked off, I made my way to her and asked blatantly, "How do you wear your hair like that?"

As soon as the words escaped my lips, I cringed. I knew she didn't do anything to her hair — my question wasn't literal, no. What I really wanted to know was how she was able to experience such apparent joy in the wake of vulnerability. I likened wearing my hair curly in real life to one of those bad dreams when you're inexplicably walking down the street naked and embarrassed, and everyone's laughing at you.

But, somehow, she had deciphered my intended context. She chuckled and responded, "How do I *not* wear my hair like this? These curls are mine. And I love them. How can I deny who I am?"

I heard her words, but I still didn't understand. I unleashed on her my feelings about hair, identity, and unrealistic beauty ideals — topics better suited for a therapist's couch. Again, I asked, "But how do you do it?"

"Oh, honey, you just do!" the woman said, laughing. She was so carefree. "Embrace your curls. Don't think about it. Just do it. It's a heck of a lot easier than you think. One day, it will be clear, and you will understand," she said.

That was in September 2010.

Fast-forward to a Saturday in November 2015.

Despite my best intentions to evade the massive raincloud looming over the parking lot, an all-out monsoon had broken out by the time I had exited the market with my two small kids in tow. (Scotty was four then, and Kennedy was two.) I sprinted to my minivan, soaking my hair and nearly pulling a hamstring in the process. Then I drove home as fast as I legally could and immediately commenced flatironing my hair in my bathroom. Only after I had finished did I realize that I had neglected to put the kids' frozen treats — a hard-earned reward for good behavior — in the freezer.

The bag was a pile of mush on the kitchen counter.

Frustration and shame washed over me.

I couldn't function like this anymore.

One might dismiss my mishap as simply what women do in the name of beauty. But the lengths I have gone to — to make my curly hair straight — are no laughing matter.

There is nothing funny about spending my entire life shunning my natural hair texture. And there's certainly nothing pleasurable about enduring scalp burns — and the subsequent scabbing — that result from the use of chemical hair straighteners, which I had put up with for years.

To be clear, straight hair isn't the enemy; it's lovely, in fact.

The problem, though, is when the pursuit of straight hair rules your life. There is a difference between straightening your hair because you want to, and doing it because you feel it's mandatory or, worse yet, you know no alternative.

From the time I was knee-high to a grasshopper, Sunday afternoons were spent sitting still as my mother blow-dried and then braided my hair. When I hit the teenage years, I wanted my hair even straighter, so she used a hot pressing comb, too. And, before long, that didn't get my hair straight enough — enter chemical relaxers.

As the late poet Maya Angelou stated so beautifully, "When you know better, do better." But there were few alternatives back then. In the eighties and nineties, drugstores didn't have entire aisles dedicated to serving the natural-hair community — there *was* no natural-hair community. YouTube didn't exist, and no one had any idea what a hair tutorial vlog was.

But the birth of my daughter sparked a change in direction for me.

Kennedy was born with thick, dark, perfectly clumped spiral curls, and from day one I instilled in her that her curls were beautiful. And she agreed. I prided myself in caring for — and never straightening — her curls, despite my need to straighten mine incessantly.

And herein lies the problem.

When I straightened my strands during my lengthy blowout sessions, I noticed how Kennedy studied my every move. I could see the wheels in her head beginning to churn: *If you think my curls are so pretty, why do you straighten yours?* The day Kennedy would call me hypocritical was heading toward me like a freight train.

The image of the gorgeous woman on the beach began appearing in my head more frequently, poking my conscience; her words were more poignant than ever.

I decided, at age thirty-eight, that I would stop straightening my hair.

But imagine the horror I experienced when I washed my hair... and it wouldn't curl.

Come to find, all the years of applying excessive direct heat in the form of blow dryers and flatirons had permanently altered my curl pattern.

Instead of "big chopping" — cutting off all my hair at once — I chose to trim my hair over the course of several months until the last of my damaged ends were cut off on my fortieth birthday.

Although I've been on this journey for nearly three years now, I feel in some ways that I've only just begun. But, make no mistake, the woman on the beach was right: That day had come, it is now clear, and I do understand.

Here's what I've since learned: I should have done this sooner, and that chance encounter on a Florida beach many years ago was a clarion call.

And here's what I'm most grateful for: In an effort to teach my young daughter to love her wildly curly hair, I've finally learned to do the same.

— Courtney Conover —

28

Everything We Need

While we try to teach our children all about life,
our children teach us what life is all about.
~Angela Schwindt

I knew I had it easier than most single mothers. We had a roof over our heads, I managed to pay the electric bill each month, and there was always food on the table.

After my divorce, I had returned to graduate school and finished my master's degree. I had a job I loved as a case manager for medically frail and low-income elder adults. My duties involved arranging home services to enable the elderly to stay in their homes as long as possible, a service I believed was vitally important. Yet, as with most social-service jobs, it barely paid a living wage. One day as I was filling out forms for one of my clients to receive food stamps, I realized that if I didn't receive child support, my salary would have qualified us for the same entitlements! I was fortunate I didn't need the supplemental government assistance, but I was aware that many single-parent families relied on the help, and I was grateful it was available for them.

I was fortunate to have the basics covered for my daughters and me, but it was the unexpected costs that kept me up at night. If something broke in our home, it was probably going to stay broken. What if we needed a new roof? What if the air conditioner went out in the 100-degree Oklahoma summer? What if the car needed repairs? My children's father provided health insurance for them, but I couldn't afford insurance for myself. I was very healthy, but I knew one medical catastrophe would financially destroy me.

Then there were all the things I wished I could do for my children. Their friends were usually off on exotic vacations in the summer while I scrambled to make a picnic and trip to the zoo feel like a real vacation. I wished my children could have new furniture and cute clothes and all the latest gadgets.

I thought I was doing a good job keeping my worries from my children, but I wasn't. Children are very sensitive to their parents' moods, and they are often listening when we're not aware. A neighbor had been pressuring me to share the cost of a new fence, and I was talking about it with my sister on the phone, wondering how I would magically make money appear to cover the cost. After I got off the phone, my six-year-old daughter approached me and said, "Mom, please don't worry. We may not have everything we want, but we have everything we need."

That statement, made by an innocent but very wise child, forever changed my perspective. Whenever I found myself giving into my anxieties concerning finances, I would remember her words. I would focus on being grateful for shelter over our heads and food on our table. I'm so thankful to my little girl who was smart enough to remind me that we often confuse wants with needs. Listen closely to children; it is from their hearts we may learn great wisdom. We had shelter, food, clothing, and love for one another — we did, indeed, have everything we needed!

— Diane Morrow-Kondos —

29

Burned

*Every day may not be good, but there's
something good in every day.*
~Author Unknown

I had just finished watching the twentieth anniversary of *The Oprah Winfrey Show*. Previous guests appeared and picked their own favorite guests who inspired them, and in some cases, changed their lives.

I will never forget the woman who had face cancer. She said she used to feel sorry for herself, until she saw the show with a beautiful young girl who was hit by a drunk driver. The girl had caught on fire. Her face had literally melted away. The story really hit home.

My mother had been burned over seventy percent of her body in a house fire two years before. I'll never forget the phone call that I received at work that cold January morning.

"Is this Ms. Dixon?" The voice on the other end of the line sounded distant. "I'm calling from the Vineland Police Department." I lived in South Carolina. My mom and brother lived in Vineland, New Jersey. I knew it was something tragic.

"Your mother is Naomi Cook? I'm sorry to have to tell you this, but your mother has been flown by helicopter to Philadelphia... there was a fire in her house. She is critical."

The drive to New Jersey was the longest of my life. The whole way there it seemed that every memory of my childhood came back. Warm cookies and loads of love is the only way I could describe my childhood. I recalled how my mom walked me to school when I was very young. Once, there was this little boy who was taunting me. When she heard him calling me names, she went right up to his mother and in no uncertain terms told her that her son better knock it off. That's how she was. She didn't put up with any guff, not from anyone. She was tough, and she taught me how to be the same. Yet she had a heart of gold when it came to the ones she loved.

When I arrived at the burn center, I honestly didn't know if I was prepared for what I might see. I was right. My mom was wrapped from head to toe in bandaging. She looked like a mummy. All that was showing were her eyes and nose. I broke down and sobbed most of the night.

The next few months my mother fought her way back from the brink of death. She was kept in a drug-induced coma because of the pain from the burns. During this time, she survived two bouts of pneumonia, the constant infections that plague burn survivors, numerous operations, and skin grafts. The medical teams that kept her alive were incredible, and the fact that she hadn't succumbed to these horrific injuries was nothing short of a miracle.

Four months after the fire, the doctors felt it was time to bring my mother out of the coma. To help bring her around, the doctors suggested playing her favorite music and talking to her. The children from the Sunday School class that she taught all drew her pictures. I had them all over the cabinets in her room and explained each one to her in detail. After one particular long night at her bedside, and two weeks of waiting, I began to lose hope. Would she ever come out of this? Was all of this in vain?

The next morning, as I came down the hospital corridor, one of the nurses from the night crew jumped up when I went past her. "Good Morning!" She was awfully cheerful.

One of the male nurses who especially watched over my mom came up to me. He linked his arm in mine. "Did you have a good night?" He was upbeat too. He pulled back the curtain that protected my mom's room. "She did." My eyes filled with tears. My mom was being helped into a wheelchair by two of the physical therapists. In the course of the night, she had awakened. When she looked up and saw me, her face lit up, and she smiled. Everyone present in the ward started to clap. "Mom! Oh, Mom." The tears streamed down my face.

It would be a long, long journey down the road of recovery. But, my mother did recover. To say it was a lot of hard work on her part would be a gross understatement. She had to re-learn how to walk, talk, eat, dress herself, all the things we take for granted. Not to mention living with the disfigurement of the burns. She did all of it.

I won't lie and say that there weren't times when it would have been easier for that fire to have taken her away from us. It was inhumanely painful dealing with the physical affects as well as the emotional. People often would stare at her. There was a time I took her to the grocery store. An insensitive man outside asked, "What happened to her?" I quickly rushed her inside. I just wanted her to have normalcy. I didn't want anyone to notice that there was anything different about her. I wanted people to only see the inside, to know how much this woman was loved.

While she was resting on a bench near the checkout line, a little girl, maybe five or so, came up to her. She had a Band-Aid on her finger. "What happened to you?" The little girl asked innocently. I was in a panic. I couldn't get to her from the line. Mom had to handle this one on her own. "Oh, I was in a fire, but I'm doing a lot better now." My mom smiled at the girl. Holding her bandaged finger up, the little girl said, "Do you need a Band-Aid? My mommy has more." The sincerity was heartwarming. "I think this boo-boo is too big for a Band-Aid, sweetie," Mom joked. Then she looked over at me and smiled. For a brief moment, she had that familiar twinkle in her eye that I'd missed so much since this whole nightmare started. She was Mom again. It was just a quick glimpse into the past, but all the love and memories poured into that one moment and it has stayed with me and sustained me after all this time.

That fire was never able to take away my mom's willing and determined spirit. In spite of her dire circumstances, Mom touched the heart of everyone she came in contact with. Whether they were young or old, healthy or sick, she would tell them her story of how

God spared her life from the fire.

I have tried, however difficult, to carry my mom's great attitude about the fire throughout these years. No matter what life brings to me, I try to remember to see the glass as half full. I owe it to my mom, who never gave up.

—Lisa Wright-Dixon—

A Certain Samaritan

Have you had a kindness shown?
Pass it on!
Let it travel down the years,
Let it wipe another's tears;
Till in heaven the deed appears —
Pass it on!
~Henry Burton

My parents divorced in 1963, when I was eleven years old. One year later, my father stopped providing any type of financial support for my three sisters and me. My mother was on her own, working to provide for her family of girls, one of whom had severe developmental delays.

Times were definitely challenging then. I remember the threatening calls from bill collectors, the sound of my mother crying late at night, and those few evenings when flour and water pancakes made for a very meager dinner. But the memory that surfaces much more strongly than all of the others is one in which I learned a dear lesson about caring and sharing.

To support our family, my mother worked during the day in a local newspaper office. In addition, several nights a week, she sold women's clothing at home-based parties.

Driving home late one night, she sat stopped at a red light. Weary from her work, she did not see the speeding car racing up behind her, its driver oblivious to the stoplight. The other car crashed into the back of my mother's car at sixty miles per hour.

It may have been her weariness that saved her life that night. Her limp, tired body was propelled from her seat into the back of her station wagon. The car was crushed into an accordion of metal around her.

Amazingly, my mother survived with only bumps and bruises, cushioned by the clothes she had hoped to sell. But her car did not survive, and the driver of the other car was a young man with no insurance. I remember the look of anguish on my mother's face as she worried about how she was going to get the money for another vehicle.

The next day, I saw our neighbors, the Claytons, walking down the hill from their home. They handed my mother an envelope with $500 tucked inside. I remember my proud, tough mother protesting that she couldn't take their money. There was no way she could possibly pay them back.

Mr. Clayton smiled at her protests and then gave her a powerful admonition. "Don't worry about paying us back. When times are better, just help someone else who is in need. That will be payment enough."

My mother took his counsel to heart. A year later, she returned from a long bus trip to a neighboring town where she had been selling advertising for a local publication. As she walked through the door, huddled close beside her was a young woman holding a crying baby. My mother ushered them into our kitchen and proceeded to put together a few simple things for a dinner for our guests.

As the night wore on, the young woman's story unfolded. She had run away from an abusive husband, taking only her young child and a handful of possessions. She had only enough money to get as far as our city. When my mother met them on the bus, she knew what she had to do.

My mother made them a makeshift bed on our living room couch. Later, I saw her open her purse and hand the young woman enough money for the remaining bus trip to the distant city. I knew that was all the money she had, yet I saw such a look of determination and joy upon her face as she handed it freely to the girl. I listened as the young mother tearfully called her parents, telling them she was coming home.

Through the years, times continued to be tough for my mother and our family. In spite of this, again and again, I saw her reach out to help others however she could, whether it was with money, time, or another form of service.

It has been several decades since our neighbors came down the hill with their gift. I try to follow their and my mother's example, helping a little here and there. I'm hoping that my own children will in turn learn the sweet lesson that I did all those years ago from a dear neighbor and mother. I hope that they will see that even when times are tough, acts of kindness and generosity can make such a difference.

— Jeannie Lancaster —

Chicken Soup for the Soul

Singing in the Rain

I don't sing because I'm happy;
I'm happy because I sing.
~William James

It had been months since my dad went to work one night and never came home, but we were nowhere near over the divorce. My siblings didn't talk about it. Kelly went out a lot and my brothers, John and Matthew, just sort of wandered around doing what they always did, but in a kind of fog.

My mother cried night after night. Of course it would affect her differently. She had not had a clue Daddy was leaving. The shock of it alone made her cry. She screamed a lot, too, misdirecting her anger at my dad towards us, mostly me. It was one of the hazards of being the oldest child.

Then our house burned down. Neighbors actually stood outside in the street and chatted and laughed as our house burned one January morning. I stood there, shoeless, watching my mother weep and all I could think was, "We are broken."

We moved into the Ramada Inn, where my mother worked, five of us crammed into one tiny room. In no time, we were on each others' nerves. After four months of not having any of our own air to breathe, we were on the verge of just giving up. We were never going to have a home again. Putting one foot in front of the next felt impossible.

One day Mother stood up, looking frenzied. "Let's go for a ride."

Kelly, John, Matt and I looked at one another warily, not sure we had heard right. There were two issues. One, Mother had just been learning to drive out of necessity since Daddy left. Two, she was very bad at it.

"Come on," she urged. "It'll be fun."

This confused us further. We didn't have fun in our family. We fought and cried. Our mother's anger at our father's abandonment had seeped slowly and surely into each of our lives. Fun was something we might have known about once, but which seemed foreign to us now.

Still, we minded our mother and piled into our 1972 blue Ford Torino, a blue so faded as to appear almost white. As the oldest, I sat in the front seat with our mother, while Kelly, John and Matt sat in the back. Mother started the car and backed out of the parking lot. "I thought we'd go look at all the houses we've lived in."

We had lived in quite a few places. Mother drove us by the house where we'd lived when I was just a kindergartener and then down the road a few houses to where we'd lived when I was in first grade. We even hazarded the main drag to see where my parents had lived when I was born, a tiny one-room apartment over a pharmacy that looked about the size of the motel room we inhabited now.

We talked about everything you could imagine — all the things we had to avoid talking about in that motel room. When there were lulls in the talk, we sang. We had always been a singing family, growing up with two parents who loved music. We started by singing "On Top of Old Smokey" the right way and then we sang every strange variation we could think of. We laughed a lot.

After this first foray, going for a ride in my mother's car became a regular thing. Every night we piled into the car and the world changed. We told jokes and sang and looked at houses we wished we had the money to live in. One night we stopped at the grocery and were having so much fun joking and laughing that we were halfway back to the motel before we realized we had forgotten five-year-old Matthew. We laughed hard all the way back to the Kroger store where Matt was waiting patiently outside on the sidewalk.

I loved riding in the car. As spring turned to summer, the breezes blew through the car and cooled us even on the hottest of nights and we were spared the sticky, humid nights of anger in the motel. The singing allowed us to vent emotions we couldn't face back in that cramped space. It was during one of those nightly car rides that my mother taught me how to harmonize.

We sang "You Are My Sunshine" and "K-k-k Katie" and a million other songs. The hope we seemed to have lost in the rest of our life was real again in the car as we sang.

So was laughter. We sang a Lynyrd Skynyrd song, "What's your name, little girl? What's your name?" at the top of our lungs to a tiny girl in another car at a stoplight and fell into hysterics when the occupants of the other cars pointed and laughed at us.

The hymns were my favorite. Mother didn't go to church. God had become a taboo topic since our dad had left. The hymns we sang — "Amazing Grace" and "How Great Thou Art" and "Shall We Gather at the River" — let us connect on a different level than we'd ever been able to in the past and calmed us down at evening's end for the return to the motel. More often than not, Mother and I ended these nights by carrying our sleeping boys, her sons and my brothers, in to bed, exhausted but happy.

One night as we were singing loudly, "In the pines, in the pines, where the sun never shines and you shiver when the cold wind blows…" Mother suddenly slammed on the brakes. "This is it!" she cried.

"This" was a house, and a for-rent sign in the front yard brought me more joy than I could believe.

"Really?" I asked.

My mother jumped out, excited, and ran to peer in the windows of the house. My siblings soon followed, and when I realized we might really have a house again, I got out, too. "This bedroom is mine!"

I realized that night that my mother was just a person, just like the rest of us. She was no better and no worse and she had been through a lot. And her driving had improved dramatically!

We moved into our new house the following weekend. We were very busy and the nights in the car became a thing of the past. The following summer we tried again with the car, but the times had changed and the car was never the same kind of haven for us again. Better off, we had moved on. New jobs and activities of every kind used up our time now. But we knew that one summer in the blue Torino had saved a vital part of us all. My dad had left, it was true, and we had lost our home, but my mother, whether by accident or design, had found a way to bring us together and keep us that way.

— Marla H. Thurman —

Across the Generations

32

The Re-Gift

Well, if he can re-gift, why can't you de-gift?
~Jerry and George, Seinfeld

Now, since it is Christmastime and thus the season of forgiveness, I must confess, I have a dirty little secret. Before any of you get worked up, you better know that you all probably have one too. I am a closet re-gifter. (Gasp!) I know. Not only am I a closet re-gifter, but I actually have a closet that is just for my gifts to "Re"!

Don't judge me. Re-gifting is a longstanding Southern tradition. I mean, waste not want not, right? Most of you probably have a shelf or a drawer at home that houses some things that are nice but just aren't for you. SO, rather than throw them away, you save them for a rainy day when you realize you need just the right thing for that person you totally forgot about.

My re-gifting is an inherited trait. My mom keeps a cabinet above the washer and dryer filled with goodies to give. And my grandmother? One year she gave my mom this really interesting sweater on Christmas Day. After dinner we pulled the videos and we watched everyone open the gifts from the year before. What did we see? My grandmother receiving the exact same sweater that she had just given my mom! Coincidence? No. Certifiable? Yes. So see? There was no way I was gonna be able to avoid my re-gifting dysfunction.

You would think I would learn my lesson since I have had a re-gift or two backfire on me. Once, I sent my cousin, who lives in

California, a wedding present from my stash... a clock that was given to me on my birthday by my crazy Aunt Nadine. It was... unique. I truly thought she would love it. Weeks later I received a thank you note for my thoughtful gift:

> *Dear Erica,*
> *Thank you so much for the wonderful clock. I was a little confused when I opened it up and there was a card inside that said, "Happy Birthday Erica. Love, Aunt Nadine"*

Busted! But even after all that, my affliction remains. I mean, I promise I'll quit someday. First, I just have to get rid of the whistling key finder, light-up shower mirror, cupcake-scented bath gels and the leopard-print long johns. Any takers?

— Erica McGee —

33

Tasting My Past

Mothers and daughters are closest
when daughters become mothers.
~Author Unknown

irst, I must prepare. At the farmer's market, I select what seem to me the best tomatoes—red and plump and promising. Next, I look over the peppers, choosing eight sweet red ones and a dozen hot red ones. Their shiny skins feel smooth to the touch. Finally, I buy onions, their flavor wrapped loosely in thin brown skin. Eight of them will join the tomatoes and peppers, vinegar, and seasonings as ingredients in my chili sauce.

Before we moved to our smaller, urban property, I grew what I needed myself. It felt right then, standing in my garden, pushing aside foliage and finding the perfect vegetables for this project. Now I buy from farmers who picked their crops hours before.

I remember my mother strolling among the selections at the market and choosing carefully. Like her, I continue to seek the best.

I keep her recipe in a special place. When I take it out, it feels like I greet an old friend. It has been a kind of companion all my life.

At home, I remove the huge silver-colored canner from its basement shelf. Next, I assemble pint jars. Some still wear their gleaming metal bands that will hold the lids. Although I packed them away carefully, I scrub them to ensure their cleanliness.

During more than forty years of marriage, I have assembled count-less boxes of jars and lids as I canned our garden's vegetables and fruit.

Most important, I have that family recipe, given to me to continue the tradition. I must carry out this duty.

The chili sauce I make connects me, with love, to Mother and to others in my family, long gone. I hear them ask my mother, "Where is your chili sauce? I'd prefer that on my hamburger." My father smothered his breakfast eggs with it.

Whenever I prepare to follow the recipe, I remember helping Mother. She did not actually need my assistance, but she must have realized I needed the practice to make the sauce myself some day.

I begin as she did, soaking the tomatoes in hot water to make their skins come off easier. As the red orbs bob in the sink, I hear Mother say, "Go out to the garden and find one more good-sized tomato."

She was always well prepared. The day before she planned to cook her chili sauce, she peeled the tomatoes. That day, the one prior to the actual canning, my father and I anticipated the flavorful result of Mother's efforts. It seems as if it were just yesterday that my mother's inviting chili sauce aroma filled every room of the house, tantalizing and teasing.

When I prepare the onions and the peppers, I grind them in my cast-iron grinder. As I grab the wooden handle and crank it, I see my mother turning into a white-haired woman who continued making chili sauce until the year before she died. Working this way puts me in touch with she who went before me.

Just after I started my chili sauce cooking this day, my youngest child called from her California home. "I am making chili sauce," I told her.

"Oh, wow. I wish I could smell it," she said and reminisced about coming home from school as a young child and smelling the chili sauce from the sidewalk on the corner. "The house smelled so wonderful for a few days," she said. I remembered that was true all during my childhood as well.

Today is not simply the day I fill waiting jars with the taste of summer we will savor all year long; it is the stirring of love and warm memories. My grandmother and her mother before her canned every fall. As a child, I explored their basement food pantries lined with home-canned fruit, tomatoes, and pickles. I knew at some family dinner during the coming winter, I would taste some of those put-away treasures.

Perhaps, my mother's recipe came from one of them. I do not know. Someone perfected that recipe and gave it to the next in line. And we continue to follow it, handing it down in an endless circle of labor and care for our families just as the earth continues to yield its bounty.

I imagine my own daughters may someday follow the same directions I do. My older daughter inherited her grandmother's dark blue canning pan. Perhaps, someday a daughter of one of my daughters will decide to engage in the family tradition. Then, her today will merge with all those yesterdays and her family will taste the past.

And when she stirs the simmering concoction, I hope she thinks of me with love.

Chili Sauce

30 ripe tomatoes
8 medium onions
6 green sweet peppers (Mother preferred a rich red color so she used all red sweet peppers)
12 red hot peppers
1 quart cider vinegar
3 tablespoons salt
4 cups sugar
1 teaspoon allspice
1 teaspoon ginger
1 teaspoon cinnamon

Scald tomatoes in boiling water to loosen skins. Peel and cut into quarters.

Chop fine or coarsely grind onions. Put vinegar and onions in large non-aluminum pan with tomatoes. Bring to a boil, then simmer, uncovered, for 20 minutes.

Seed and chop fine (or coarsely grind) peppers. Add peppers and all other ingredients to pan. Simmer until it is a little thicker than ketchup, four hours or more.

Clean jars thoroughly. (Recipe yields from 6 to 10 pints.) Put jars and lids in hot water. Carefully drain and then fill hot jars with warm chili sauce. (If jars aren't heated enough from the hot water, they will break.) Clean off any drips from jar rim. Place warm lid on jar top and screw on ring to hold lid in place.

Place warm jars in rack in canning pan. Lower jars into water so they are completely covered. Bring to a boil. Boil for 25 minutes. Lift rack. Refrigerate any jars that do not seal.

Use the sauce on fried eggs, hamburgers, hot dogs and sausages. Mix with soy sauce for a marinade for fish or with mayonnaise for salad dressing. Use in any recipes calling for a sweet or spicy sauce. I like to add it to a white sauce to use in a casserole with noodles and clam.

— Sandy McPherson Carrubba —

The First Birthday

The manner of giving is worth more than the gift.
~Pierre Corneille

My courageous and selfless mother, at age seventy-nine, died from breast cancer. Her name was Betty. She asked for one thing only — that she make it to her eightieth birthday. She believed that if she made it to eighty, she could consider her life long and well lived. We focused on that birthday.

When Mom lay dying in July, she was still eight months away from her March birthday. The staff in hospice had kindly offered to throw her a party, but I declined. She was so sick, how could I invite people? And, if I am honest, I didn't think I could bear anything else on my shoulders, especially planning a party, even a small one. Selfish perhaps, but I just couldn't do it. The week my mother entered hospice, we also moved my father to the nearby VA hospital due to his Alzheimer's disease. My heart was breaking. Then mom died. It was like losing both my parents at the same time.

I somehow managed through the holidays. But Mom's upcoming eightieth birthday was weighing on me. The first birthday after Mom's death. What should I do for it? How should it be acknowledged? How would I make this a celebration when my heart was still so sad?

I thought about what my mother would have liked for her birthday. She loved being with her children, grandchildren and great-grandchildren and, in the last few years, not having to cook. That was a start. I would host a dinner with my family and grandchildren at our home. We would sing "Happy Birthday" and have a birthday cake decorated with sugary frosting and bright-colored roses, the colors of spring. She always felt that her birthday announced the arrival of spring, even if it was snowing.

Something was still missing, however, and I couldn't place it. I didn't want the occasion to be gloomy. No, Mom wouldn't have liked that. I didn't know what to do.

That is, until the day before her birthday dinner.

That morning I hung a quilted wall hanging in the dining room that Mom had sewn. My mother called it "The Birthday Quilt." It was white with multi-colored Sunbonnet Sues and exploding fireworks. Perfect.

Next, I realized you couldn't have a birthday celebration without presents. But I couldn't give my mother a birthday present. How would that work? Then it came to me.

Before Mom passed away and Dad went into the nursing home, she had instructed me to distribute all their belongings to family members who wanted items and then donate or sell the rest. That wish was carried out for the most part, but I still had jewelry and several boxes of items that hadn't been distributed for any number of reasons.

Hanging on to those items solved my First Birthday dilemma.

I spent the afternoon going through boxes. I thought about which family members would be at the birthday dinner. They included my husband, son and daughter-in-law, daughter and son-in-law, and four grandchildren — ages eighteen months to six years old, three girls and one boy (the oldest). I went through those boxes with an eye toward any item that might fit as a gift from my mother to that dinner guest. I shed many tears but they were tears of love and remembrance. I also used some of Mom's stationery to write each person a note about the item, how or why my mother had it, and why I connected it to that family member. Then I wrapped the "gifts" in colorful birthday wrap and tied them with fancy curling ribbons. I attached the cards. After singing "Happy Birthday," and after the great-grandchildren blew out the candles, I said, "You can't have a birthday without presents!"

My son looked at his sister and said, "I didn't bring a present, did you?" She had not. It made me chuckle to see their concern. But I said, "No. These are presents from your grandmother."

My daughter received a white gold necklace with an aquamarine stone (my mother's birthstone). I told my daughter it was because the stone reminded me of her eyes, which her grandmother had always loved.

My daughter-in-law received a necklace of silver charms from a designer my mother liked a lot. The style was well suited for my daughter-in-law.

My son received a set of pilsner glasses, as he likes beer. I told him in his note that his grandmother was very fond of having a cold beer on a really hot day and that when he used those glasses he should think of her.

My ice-cream-loving son-in-law received my mother's ice cream scoop. I wrote to him that my mother and father were known to occasionally eat ice cream instead of dinner.

I explained to my grandson that it was hard to find something for a boy in his great-grandma's things but I hoped he liked what I found. He snuggled right up to me. I told him that I didn't know why Grandma Betty had the little toy deer in her belongings, but I thought it should go to him because he was interested in hunting. He also received a masculine-looking sterling silver ring. I told him how it had been created, and that it was made from silver that could be found in the earth. He's a very curious boy and likes to know all about things. He kept it on his finger the rest of the evening.

My oldest granddaughter received a silver bracelet made of connecting porpoises from a trip Grandma Betty had taken to the ocean. Because this little granddaughter had enjoyed her own visit to the ocean, I knew she would like this bracelet.

To the next granddaughter, I gave a blue star sapphire pendant. I told her it was one of Grandma Betty's favorite stones and that if it was held up to the light just right, she could see a white star on it.

The youngest granddaughter received my mother's silver baby cup from the early 1930s. It had been lovingly used and had the dents to prove it.

In every note I told the recipients how much their grandmother or great-grandmother had loved them.

Even though it has been a while since that First Birthday, I have heard different things about the gifts. My granddaughter, now four years old, told me about the necklace she has with the white star on it from Grandma Betty. I heard my son is looking forward to summer parties when he is going to bring out the pilsner glasses, and my son-in-law used the ice cream scoop the night after the party.

But I think the best comment I have heard was the day after the party when my daughter said, "Mom, it was just right."

If you are struggling with how to get through that First Birthday consider having a party with gifts from your loved one. You might find that "it's just right."

— Betsy Alderman Lewis —

Stronger

Here's to strong women. May we know them.
May we be them. May we raise them.
~Author Unknown

I didn't set out to be a single mom. I didn't dream of a life of setting mousetraps, shoveling snow, and stacking wood by myself. But in 2013, all those things became my new reality.

I had been questioning whether I was happy with the path our marriage had taken for several months. I went alone to basketball games to watch our older daughter cheer. I watched gymnastic meets for our younger daughter alone. I went to bed many nights alone, and I spent my days dreaming of a future alone.

Once, after a basketball game, I was standing in the hallway outside the gym waiting for my daughter, and one of the other cheer moms smiled and made a comment about being single moms. I corrected her, "Oh, I'm not a single mom. My husband just works a lot." The interaction left me feeling exposed from a truth I tried to hide from, and even more uncertain of my future than ever before.

I had spent the majority of my adulthood married to this man, and it was shocking to see how fast everything had unraveled when I finally pushed back and tried to even the playing field that our relationship had become. He walked out for the last time in the summer of 2013, leaving a broken family in his wake.

That summer was the turning point, not only in my life but in my girls' lives. Not once in my thirty-six years had I given a thought to the upside of divorce.

The girls and I started to change that summer. Aubrey was thirteen and had amazingly supportive friends. Alli was only ten, and as always, was Mama's little shadow. We spent those summer weeks recovering, creating new routines, and forging the new direction our lives would take. We had sleepovers in the living room, stayed up half the night watching scary movies, and ate chicken wraps until buffalo sauce nearly poured out of our ears. They learned how to do their own laundry and began pitching in around the house. For the first time in my adult life, I was officially responsible for every single decision and obligation, and, most importantly, for the two young girls who counted on me to make it all work.

They slept with me every night for months, and we dried each other's tears until there were no more tears to dry. Over time, we grew and morphed into much stronger versions of ourselves. At the time, the girls didn't know any more than I did that they were witnessing firsthand the power of being a strong, capable, independent woman.

A year later, I surprised them with tickets to a One Direction concert in Boston. I was terrified of driving in city traffic, but I did it nonetheless. It was a concert to remember, from Aubrey holding her sister on her back for over an hour in ninety-degree weather for a chance at seeing "the boys" before the show, to scream/singing along to all the songs we knew and loved so well, to driving for hours after the show with a car full of sleeping girls while trying to find the hotel.

Two years after that, I took the plunge again and married John. He had his own teenage daughter, Olivia, who happened to be nestled right between my two girls in age. The five of us ventured to New York City for a "family-moon" after our backyard wedding. There was a point during the early part of the trip when the five of us, trekking along the unfamiliar sidewalks of the city that never sleeps, found ourselves completely lost. John handed me the map and asked if I could make sense of where we had gone wrong. For the first time in my life, I became the navigator. I had never been asked to take the reins of navigation before, and I found it oddly exhilarating to plot our way around the largest city in the country.

The next few years brought with them driver's education, teaching teenage girls how to pump gas and check tire air pressure, and eventually driver's licenses! The years brought dances, boyfriends, and high-school drama. They brought with them questions of faith and truths and more mother-daughter squabbles than any mom thinks she can survive but somehow does. The years brought fear and anxieties, experiences and wisdom.

We've been seven years in the making, this new family of ours. We've grown and changed and added new people. I don't profess to have anything "figured out." In fact, there are many days when I just want to go back to kindergarten and play with the Letter People rather than face another day of being an adult. But what I do know now is that divorce wasn't the worst thing to happen to Aubrey, Alli, and me. It was the best thing.

In a recent conversation with my girls, we were standing around the kitchen reminiscing about old times when the unthinkable happened. After years of questioning myself and every single parenting move I ever made, I heard the words every mom hopes to hear.

"Mom, you are the strongest person we know," Alli said, and her sister nodded in agreement. "The way you picked up the pieces after the divorce and kept going… Being a single mom and having to raise two daughters by yourself…" Her voice trailed off, and we all started to tear up. "We wouldn't be who we are today without you. You showed us not to settle for less than what we deserve."

I wiped away a tear as we reminisced about that summer, almost seven years ago. "It was the best summer ever." Aubrey agreed, "Remember how we watched *Sleeping with the Enemy*, and we screamed so loud that the neighbors heard us?"

We laughed at the memory, and I felt a pang of nostalgia wash over me. Sometimes, when we think everything is falling apart, it might take a while to realize that everything is actually falling into place, right where it needs to be.

— Valerie Dyer —

36

The Grinch Came to Visit

To us, family means putting your arms
around each other and being there.
~Barbara Bush

L ast December, the Grinch came to visit. We were caught
unaware because from all appearances, it was going to be
a fine Christmas. Our two daughters and their families,
from Wisconsin and Chicago, would be with us in Ohio,
and preparations were mostly finished. The tree was up, the house
decorated, and presents wrapped and under the tree.

The day before the Grinch arrived, Christmas was still five days
away, and we were completing the planning for the nine people who
would be here. By the end of the day, we were ready. That was Tuesday.
On Wednesday, the Grinch was the first of our guests to arrive.

He arrived at 10:00 p.m. when my wife Kathy, heading for bed,
complained of a little bloating and pains in her stomach. An hour
later, she was in the bathroom on her knees for the first of dozens
of visits the rest of the night. It continued all Wednesday night and
into Thursday, when we called our kids to tell them not to come. We
didn't want the little ones catching whatever she had.

Susan, the one farthest away in Wisconsin, decided not to chance
it and kept her family home. It was a wise decision.

Missy, however, still planned to come from Chicago because

her family also had plans for Christmas with her husband's family in Toledo. We reserved a hotel room for them, thinking that staying away from us "most of the time" would be somewhat of a flu-prevention method. On Friday night, I met them at the hotel and took them out to dinner, while Kathy stayed home alone, staring at a paper plate of food she didn't want to eat.

The next day was Christmas Eve. I returned to the hotel in the morning to take them to visit my mother, who was recovering from hip surgery. We arrived home that afternoon to find Kathy was still sick. Missy and I managed to make dinner preparations for our Christmas Eve dinner, and things appeared to be proceeding satisfactorily.

But late in the afternoon, I, too, began feeling pains in my stomach and became bloated. Within an hour, I began my own series of visits to the bathroom. By dinnertime on Christmas Eve, I sat beside Kathy with a few untouched bites on my own paper plate.

Then things deteriorated further. The Grinch launched a second attack, and everyone fell like flies. Throughout Christmas Day, more and more headed for bathrooms or to bed. By the time we tried to serve lunch on the day after Christmas, the only ones still standing were two grandchildren—thoroughly enjoying having access to all the desserts. The rest of us stared at the tiny portions we had put on our plates. Ultimately, the two "well" grandchildren didn't escape either. One of them fell ill on the turnpike halfway back to Chicago the next day, and the other got hit the moment she got home.

In the middle of all this, we managed to sit around the tree and open presents. The Grinch couldn't steal Christmas! We had laughter and joy and somehow enjoyed being miserable together. The joy of Christmas never left, even though we sometimes had to remind ourselves we would enjoy it more later when we'd tell the story year after year.

The Grinch never had a chance. He gave us his best shot, but he couldn't destroy our Christmas.

The only one disgruntled was our daughter Susan who stayed in Wisconsin and missed it all. "Boy! It sounds like you guys had a really good time. I wish we had been there and gotten sick with you!" We had learned, once again, that Christmas has nothing to do with presents and big meals — and everything to do with love and being together.

— Lynn Gilliland —

37

The Latke Legacy

*Real cooking is more about following
your heart than following recipes.*
~Author Unknown

"This is not like Mom used to make," I had to confess. It was my first Hanukkah being the latke lady. My mother's potato pancakes were crisp, flat, and nicely rounded. The texture was smooth but not mushy and they shone with just a glint of leftover oil. I had been a latke apprentice for years, pressed into service by Mom. I was a key cog in the labor pool, peeling the potatoes, then wearing out my arm rubbing them against the stainless steel grater, using the side with the teardrop shaped holes. My mother must have known that enlisting my help would keep me from pestering her to make potato pancakes for other occasions. Only once a year did these delicious patties grace our table, when we lit the first candle of Hanukkah and began the eight-day Festival of Lights.

My debut latkes were pale and greasy, like something carelessly served in a late night diner. I myself was pale and greasy from the stress of trying to coax the patties into cohesion. First they had drifted apart — too little flour. Then they had turned cliquish, glomming into rebellious lumps. When I had finally worked through the potato/flour/ egg ratio, I bumped into the complex dynamic between potatoes, onions, oil and heat. For three hours I had struggled to create what turned out to be a barely edible token of tradition.

Years passed. Every Hanukkah, I faced a different challenge. The oil was too cold, too hot, not enough, too much. The texture was too coarse or too fine. The grated onions were too strong or too weak. The latke mixture was too thin, then too thick. Every year, I hoped for pancakes that tasted like Mom's and got instead gray leaden latkes. My daughters, who peeled and grated potatoes with me, examined my finished product warily, smothering it in the traditional applesauce and often taking only a few bites. I worried that when they grew up, they would forego the holiday tradition and turn to something simpler and more delicious, like frozen hash browns. I felt a sense of failure as a mother and as the guardian of the tradition. My mother had shown me how to make the latkes: why couldn't I measure up and instill the potato pancake protocol in my progeny?

Then my daughter Sarah, fresh from college and a first job, moved back to town and offered to help me prepare the holiday meal. She was a food show devotee and had already orchestrated several dinner parties, creating the menus and cooking all the courses. She understood the relationship between vegetables, oil and heat.

"Mom, I think you need to squeeze more water out of the potato mixture," she advised. "Maybe you could use a food processor to grate the potatoes. What if you used two pans instead of trying to cram so many into one?"

I stepped back and she stepped forward, and under her guidance we prepared the latkes. As I watched my daughter mastermind the cooking, I realized that tradition could be kept alive in many ways. My daughter was starting the tradition of "doing what you're good at," giving me a chance to forget my own culinary challenges and applaud her self-taught abilities.

That Hanukkah night everyone at the table exclaimed at the sight of the latkes. Each one was golden brown and crisp, free of extra oil. I didn't even have to secretly search and pluck out a "good one," like I had been forced to do in previous years.

I looked around the table of friends and family and took a bite of my daughter's latke. My mouth filled with the crunch, flavor and intriguing texture of a well-fried potato pancake. This was the latke I had been waiting for; just like Mom used to make… only better.

— Deborah Shouse —

38

Ma Tovu

God gives us dreams a size too big
so that we can grow in them.
~Author Unknown

The first four times we went to Sharing Shabbat, the weekly children's service at our synagogue, we didn't make it through the opening prayer of Ma Tovu. I cried after the first two weeks, and by week four I was ready to give up. Perhaps it was a mistake to think Jodie could become a Bat Mitzvah.

Jodie was diagnosed with autism when she was two and a half. Many parents of children with autism say the day their child was diagnosed was the worst day, and that after that initial shock, things improved. That hasn't been our experience. Every family celebration and milestone is bittersweet, because it is a reminder of Jodie's constant struggles. Looking at the empty seat at the Thanksgiving table after Jodie has gotten up after two minutes because she can't sit still is just as hard for me as it was to hear the initial diagnosis. I felt a huge emptiness at my brother-in-law's graduation; the whole family was there, except Jodie, who, despite being the oldest cousin, had to stay home with a babysitter. But I knew the hardest of all would be to let her Bat Mitzvah date pass by as if it were just any other day, without any sort of recognition or celebration.

Jodie has gone to special needs Hebrew school through a wonderful program called Matan since kindergarten. In our home, she says the hamotzi (the blessing over the bread), as well as the blessing over the candles, because she learned them in Matan. She has always loved music, so I thought maybe, just maybe, she could learn a few more songs and prayers and become a Bat Mitzvah in more or less the traditional way.

And so despite our initial failed attempts, and thanks to a well-timed, very encouraging phone call from the Sharing Shabbat coordinator, we labored on at Sharing Shabbat. Yes, we labored on Shabbat; it was not easy for either of us to get through those first few weeks. I brought her favorite Sesame Street books, and then from time to time slipped the prayer book inside and used hand over hand to point to the words. Usually she'd respond by screaming "No Book! No Book!" so loudly that everyone turned and stared. But eventually Jodie seemed to get used to the rhythm of the service. By week six, we had made it through two minutes and had sung Ma Tovu. Halleluyah! And sure enough, the next week we made it to the song Halleluyah, a full four minutes in. A few weeks later we were joining in the blessing for the Torah. And after three long months, we actual ate bagels at the oneg after services.

It was certainly not easy for Jodie, as I'm sure it was not easy for the families at Sharing Shabbat. Jodie struggles to sit still, to pay attention, to be quiet. Her behavior is unpredictable and at times loud, disruptive, and aggressive. It takes many attempts at something new before she will accept it. But somehow she came to find comfort in the music of the service and in the repetition of the prayers week after week. Her favorite part seemed to be the end of each prayer, when she would smile broadly and sing a super loud and quite off-key "Amen!" We listened to the Sharing Shabbat CD in the car and she recognized the music, saying "go to the services" and singing along with her hearty "Amen!"

Jodie works hard every day to learn things that others learn without effort and take for granted. She struggles to communicate. She doesn't know how to make friends. Her body rarely seems at peace. But she seems to have found meaning and a sense of belonging at Sharing Shabbat. On Saturday mornings, when I'd say it was time for services, she would smile. Whether she enjoyed the service or just looked forward to the bagels and donuts afterwards, I'll never really know. But she happily went to services and participated with her robust "Amen." And for this we are so grateful to the entire Sharing Shabbat community.

On June 5, 2011 Jodie became a Bat Mitzvah. Once again, she exceeded our expectations. Her thirteenth birthday didn't just pass, unmarked, like any other day. Sure, she held a baby doll while she stood on the bimah in front of the family and friends who gathered for the occasion. In her other hand she held a box of Cheez-Its (I hope they are kosher). It wasn't her best behavior at a service. And when the rabbi presented her with a copy of the Torah as a gift from the community she looked right at him and shouted "No Book! No Book!" But she said the prayers and read her line of Torah and added many joyful "Amens." Afterwards our friends and family came back to our house for lunch and several raucous rounds of the hokey pokey. We were all there to welcome Jodie into the Jewish community as an adult. A great day. And I still cry every time I hear Ma Tovu. Amen.

— Alison Singer —

39

What If It Had Been Me?

*Give freely to the world these gifts of love
and compassion. Do not concern yourself
with how much you receive in return,
just know in your heart it will be returned.*
~Steve Maraboli, Life, the Truth, and Being Free

Sitting alone in my office on a late December evening in 2013, I was too tired to do any more work, yet also too tired to face the hour-long commute home. Scrolling aimlessly through Facebook, I came across a news story about two children in Atlanta, Georgia and the one wish they had for Christmas. It wasn't a wish for the latest video game, or smart phone — it was a wish for a kidney. Not a kidney for either one of them, but for their beloved grandmother. After learning that no family or close friends were a match, and with the help of their mother, they set up a Facebook page called "A Kidney for Gran." They were asking everyone, anyone, to help.

I was struck by these kids' selfless nature, but I was also deeply moved by their decision to reach out to a world full of strangers, hoping for a miracle. What if I needed a kidney and no one I knew was a match? How hard would I pray every night that someone would not only be a match, but also agree to share a vital organ with a total stranger? How full of fear would the people closest to me be wondering how much longer we had together? What kind of person would willingly endure travel, months of testing and major surgery — to help a stranger live?

That kind of person turned out to be me. An average forty-eight-year-old divorcée from California with four kids, a full-time job in high tech and a belief that we should do unto others as we would have them do for us.

Sharing a blood type with the grandmother in need was the first sign that I should throw my hat in the ring. The next sign was simply a quiet voice inside me that said, "You know of the need and you can meet it. You'll be fine."

I picked up my cell phone and dialed the Piedmont Transplant Center in Atlanta. I left my contact information. Within a week I was contacted by a transplant coordinator, a kind woman with a warm Southern drawl. She asked questions; I answered them. After going over my answers with one of the transplant doctors it was decided that I was a viable candidate, and thus began my eight months of multiple blood tests, urine tests, travel to Stanford Hospital for a nuclear "glofil" kidney clearance test, and travel to Atlanta the next May for a full physical, mental and social evaluation.

From a treadmill stress test and a CT scan of my vascular system to a psychological exam and a review with a social worker of every personal facet of my life, no stone was left unturned.

I was not a direct match for the grandmother, who I now knew as Beverly, but I agreed to enter into the paired donation program, where another team who is not a direct match for each other would essentially "trade" kidneys with us. What this meant was that I went from volunteering to save one life to being a part of a trade that would save two lives.

During the eight months of testing I had plenty of time to think, and I received input from friends, family and strangers. Most were encouraging, some not, but only out of fear for my safety. Through it all, I never felt like I needed to turn back or rescind my offer. As simple as it sounds, it was the right thing to do. And I was never afraid. I imagined myself in Beverly's shoes. What if it had been me?

Once the testing was complete, we were entered into a database of other potential donor/recipient teams. We had an immediate match, but the recipient had too many antibodies against me. The second match came just as quickly and after a bit more testing it was confirmed: The transplant surgery would be on August 26th, 2014.

With my twenty-three-year-old in tow, I flew to Atlanta and back to the Southern hospitality of Beverly's family and the Piedmont Transplant Center on August 24th. Our families now inextricably bonded, my son waited with Beverly's family while my kidney was removed and flown to New Jersey, and a new kidney was flown to Atlanta and transplanted into Beverly. Bev's new kidney started to work immediately as did mine for the recipient in Jersey. The surgeries were a total success.

After a week of recovery I flew back to California and back to my life. Beverly is healthy and active again with her family and friends. Another person is healthy again as well, having given a new home to my kidney. I wish him or her the very best.

I came away from the experience knowing it was I who received the blessing. How often in life are we called to do the heroic, to set aside our fears and selfish natures to voluntarily help another person live? I don't feel like a hero. I feel like I paid forward a life debt and I would gladly do it all over again. During the psychological evaluation, the psychiatrist, with his measured Southern tone, asked, "What in the world would possess you to donate a kidney to a person you do not know?" My answer was simple, "What if it had been me? What if I needed one and my only hope was a stranger? I would hope someone would step up."

What if it had been me, indeed.

— Leslie Calderoni —

Chapter 5

Isn't Life Grand?

The Gift

No, I never saw an angel, but it is irrelevant whether I
saw one or not. I feel their presence around me.
~Paulo Coelho

My husband's beloved grandmother was a very nurturing person who had been raised on a farm. She was roundly plump, with white hair and kind eyes. She never had a harsh word for anyone, did not believe in spanking children, and could cook and bake like a dream. Her rhubarb and gooseberry pies were family legends. When in her presence, you knew you were loved. Babies adored her and if any of us had a colicky or fussy infant, all that Grandma had to do was cuddle the baby against her ample bosom and it immediately became content and drifted off to sleep. She was loved by all.

When she was in her nineties, her daughters placed her in a nursing home that was a distance from where we lived. My husband and I both had demanding jobs and worked long hours. But we made the effort to visit Grandma every weekend, if not more frequently.

One night, I had been at work completing a special, complex project and I was exhausted. I had been at the office about sixteen hours and it was quite late when I left. As I drove down the darkened freeway on the long commute home, I could hardly wait to get to bed. Suddenly, out of nowhere, I was startled by an overwhelming need to see Grandma. What an odd notion — I was not only tired to the core, but it would be after 11:00 p.m. by the time I would reach the nursing home, far too late to visit and certainly not appropriate visiting hours. I dismissed the feeling.

As I continued my drive, that overpowering need to see Grandma abruptly came again, this time even stronger. How foolish, I thought. Yet the feeling persisted and it became an imperative. As the off-ramp to home neared, I fully intended to turn onto it. Instead I found myself pushed forward, driving right past it. I arrived at the nursing home a little after 11:00 p.m. Feeling a bit foolish, I had to ring a bell to gain admittance.

When I got to Grandma's room, she was sitting on the side of her bed, awake, with the light on. "Land's sake, look who's here!" she declared with a bright, surprised smile. She was delightfully pleased and so was I; the anxious feeling of being pushed suddenly fell away and was replaced by an enveloping warmth.

As I hugged Grandma and sat down beside her, she asked me how my husband was. As I replied, I heard a noise in the doorway and looked up. There stood my husband! I was as surprised and shocked to see him as he was to see me. A police detective, he too had been working on a project and was on an extra shift. His project site was about an hour away from the nursing home. He had asked special permission to take three hours for a personal matter and said that he would make up the time. As he came forward and hugged me, he softly whispered that he felt like an idiot, but that he had suddenly been driven by an urgent need to see his grandmother. Despite realizing the inappropriateness of the hour, the need was so strong and so insistent that he couldn't ignore it.

We three sat close to one another, held hands and talked, reminiscing about days gone by and memories that brought smiles all around. It was a wonderfully sweet visit.

It was soon the wee hours of the night and time to leave. We promised Grandma that we would be back to visit the following day. She plaintively asked, "Can't you stay just a bit longer?" We couldn't. My husband had to make his long drive back to work and make up his time, and I had my long drive back home. We said, "I love you," and kissed Grandma a fond goodnight. Once outside, my husband and I marveled at how each of us had come to make such an unusual visit at the same time so late at night, and had both felt a strong presence compelling us to do so.

Only a short time after I arrived home, the telephone rang. It was an RN at the nursing home. The voice on the other end of the line informed me that after we left Grandma went to bed and fell asleep. When someone went into the room to check on her later, they found she had passed away. It seemed so unbelievable; I could hardly process it.

My husband and I were stunned and heartbroken. But we were also deeply grateful that we had just been with her and had one more chance to say, "I love you." We still speak of that night; how both of us, independently, had the same highly unusual guided experience.

We later learned we were fortunate that the night staff let us in to visit Grandma, as they have a strict policy against unexpected late-night visitors. It seems that even the nursing home staff felt compelled to help enable our visit.

Our experience was not one of a visitation with halo and wings. But whatever happened that night — however it came to be — it continues to leave us filled with awe and wonder.

However it happened, whatever angel insisted and compelled us to make that final visit with our beloved grandmother, we are eternally grateful for that benevolent blessing. Grandmother's name was Berta Angelia, her life reflecting the "angel" in her name. I like to think that as she left this earth our compassionate angel greeted Grandma and was gently and lovingly guided to her ultimate joyful destination.

— Johanna Richardson —

Naughty Granny

There's nothing sadder in this world than to awake
Christmas morning and not be a child.
~Erma Bombeck

Winters were extremely chilly where I grew up in Saint-Jean-sur-Richelieu, Quebec, about fifty kilometres southeast of Montreal. My siblings and I relished the cold and snow when we were youngsters, and our Christmas holidays, with a week or more off from school, were eagerly anticipated. We'd have snowball fights, make snow angels, and play ice hockey on the icy street. When the snow reached the top of our house, which it often did, we'd shovel out snow forts and play in our creations.

One holiday season in particular stands out. It was the Christmas my maternal grandmother, Granny Whiting, spent with us. Actually, it was her very first Christmas in Canada. She and my grandfather lived in Bermuda. Neither one had experienced a Canadian winter. Play forts dug into the banks of snow and snow angels were foreign to my grandparents. But after my grandfather died, my grandmother made her first visit to Canada.

Christmas Eve, my father stayed home with us children while Mom and Granny attended the midnight church service. They didn't arrive home until after 1:00 a.m., so it was late by the time they climbed into bed.

We kids always rose early on Christmas mornings and snuck down to the Christmas tree. But that year things unfolded a little differently. At three in the morning, Granny woke up my younger brother Harry and me. Perhaps, after attending church at midnight, she had never fallen asleep.

Granny Whiting was a staunch Englishwoman. Prim and proper, she did no wrong, and truth be known, she never wanted to do wrong. I'm not really sure why Granny wanted to break the rules this time, but the three of us slithered down the stairs into the living room.

"We have to be quiet," Granny whispered. "Don't want to wake the others."

One of us plugged in the tree lights and the bountiful tree glowed, creating shadows in the room. Silver icicles, hanging from the spreading branches, sparkled like a kaleidoscope as they picked up the colours of the bulbs. Below the genuine pine branches was an expanse of gaily wrapped gifts of all shapes and sizes.

"Let's look," Granny whispered with excitement. Then, gathering her nightgown she leaned into the gifts. "Cathy, do you see one for you?"

"Not yet," I said.

"I can't find one for me either," she moaned. "Harry, do you?"

Like co-conspirators, the three of us began rooting through the gifts. We were careful to whisper, for Mom and Dad's bedroom was at the top of the stairs of our split-level house. We didn't want to wake our parents, nor did we want to wake our siblings who would be too little to remain silent.

We were soon fully involved in our escapade, searching for our names on gift tags. Once we found one of our gifts we proudly showed it to the others and tried to guess its contents. Sometimes, when curiosity overtook us, we tore off a bit of wrapping paper. Granny had as much fun as we did.

Suddenly, out of nowhere, a voice bellowed, "Get back to bed!" There was a pause. "And that means you, too, Mother!" The voice belonged to my mother, and she sounded angry.

Before Harry and I had a chance to move, Granny had dropped whatever gift she held, jumped up, and bolted away, her flowing, white nightgown ethereal like a ghost floating up the dark stairs. Harry and

I remained by the tree, staring at each other, wondering what had just transpired and how Granny had disappeared so quickly.

"Get back to bed," Mom bellowed again. Like Granny before us, Harry and I scrambled up the stairs and back into our beds, giggling as we went.

The next morning there was lots of laughter when, at a more presentable hour, our entire family gathered around the tree. Granny, Harry, and I giggled as we recalled our middle-of-the-night caper.

I'll never forget that episode and how in the middle of the night our straight-laced grandmother became a child, how she instigated an adventure, how our mother had scared her, and how she got all three of us into trouble. For Mom blamed her, of course. Granny was certainly old enough to know better!

— Catherine A. MacKenzie —

Reserved for Seniors

*My goal is to say or do at least
one outrageous thing every week.*
~Maggie Kuhn

I was taking my fourteen-year-old granddaughter to soccer practice and I was running behind. As we backed down the driveway, she drummed her fingers on the armrest.

"What's wrong?" I asked.

"Coach's rule is we have to run a lap for every minute we're late."

"That seems harsh," I said. "But don't worry, sweetie. We'll get there on time."

I eyed the dashboard clock. The practice field reserved that day was located at the farthest end of a local high school, just beyond their outdoor stadium. That added several minutes to our drive.

My granddaughter jiggled her foot while we waited at a red light.

"So, what other rules does your new coach have?" I asked, trying to divert her attention.

"No earrings. Our shin guards have to be in place, our soccer shoes tied tight, and he doesn't like us to wear our cleats off the field." She turned to me. "And we have to be picked up on time."

When the light finally turned green, she twisted her long blond hair into a ponytail. "Can you drive faster?"

I patted her knee. "Almost there."

Then we ran into a traffic jam. She took off her sneakers and put on her shin guards as we pulled into the parking lot.

Rows of out-of-town buses lined the perimeter. A sign on the marquee announced the school was hosting a regional sports tournament. I drove down row after row searching for an empty space.

With few minutes to spare, my granddaughter pulled on her thick athletic socks and laced up her soccer shoes.

"I thought you weren't supposed to wear your cleats off the field," I said.

"I'm not, but I don't have time to change on the bench. Just stop and drop me off here."

I kept driving. "Hold on. I'm sure we'll find something closer."

As if in answer to my wish, several slots were open near the entrance to the stadium. A sign printed in bold letters read: "RESERVED FOR SENIORS."

"Whew!" I pulled into the closest space.

"You can't park here, Grandma."

"Sure I can." I pointed to the sign. "I'm a senior."

She grabbed her gear and opened the door. "Um, Grandma, these parking places are reserved for HIGH SCHOOL seniors, not senior citizens. You'll get a ticket if you don't move."

I shrugged and smiled. "Don't worry about me, sweetie. See you in an hour."

I rolled down my window and inhaled the scent of freshly cut grass as I watched her trot to her practice field just in time. A wave of nostalgia washed over me as I recalled how fearful I was of getting into trouble when I was her age. My parents were strict, and the nuns at the all-girls' high school I attended were the same. Disobeying rules or questioning authority weren't tolerated.

But I've grown older — and bolder — since then.

If I was asked to move, I'd argue that since the sign didn't specify which type of seniors the parking spaces were reserved for, I wasn't breaking any rules. Feeling sassy, I tuned the radio to a station that played music from my high-school days.

When "Wild Thing" by The Troggs came on, I sang along and danced in my seat, enjoying my rebellious senior moment.

— Donna Volkenannt —

Isn't Life Grand? |

Grandma Lillie's Red Cadillac

When in doubt, wear red.
~Bill Blass

Grandma Lillie always drove a red Cadillac. I'm not really sure why except that red was her favorite color. Not just any red, of course, but a gleaming candy-apple red with a hint of metallic that glistened in the sun. Grandma always told me that men "always look twice at a pretty woman in a red car." She did seem to get plenty of glances when she was behind the wheel of her Caddy, but I wasn't sure if they were directed at her in admiration or in anger over her limited driving abilities.

I used to stay with Grandma during the summers, and washing her car once a week was one of my chores. I never dared miss a spot, either inside or out, or I would have to redo the whole task. Grandma was of the school that a job worth doing was worth doing perfectly, so I tried to do it the way she wanted, as best as I could. She would come out and survey my work when I was done, bringing me a glass of ice-cold lemonade or a Coke in a bottle, and if I had done well, a homemade cookie. She would inspect her car and then remark, "Pretty doggone good for an eight-year-old," which made me feel like a queen.

After the car was cleaned up, Grandma and I would ride over to the Navy base to get her hair done and a "man-cure" on her nails. Grandma had long, thick acrylic nails, painted, of course, the same deep red as her car. She vowed you could always tell a real lady by the condition of her hands, and long red nails were another "man magnet."

Paw-Paw was in the Navy, so the base was where Grandma and I did all our shopping. Grandma would get her nails filled in by a nice lady from Barbados, and I would listen to their conversations, enthralled by the topics they discussed — everything from witchcraft to voodoo. Most of it was far above my eight-year-old head, but intoxicating nonetheless. Although Grandma was a devout Catholic, she and Paw-Paw had lived in Barbados for many years, and she had embraced many of the customs of the local people she befriended there. I loved looking at the photos she brought back of the ebony-skinned people and the palm trees waving in the tropical winds, and imagined the most magical place on Earth. Grandma told me that any time a good-looking man was married to an ugly woman, the woman must have "put the voodoo on him." I had no idea what she was talking about, but figured it must be true because Grandma said it was.

Of course, these ideas of Grandma's, along with her salty tongue, were of great concern to my parents. After one of my visits with Grandma, Mama and I were walking through JCPenney when I witnessed a nice-looking man strolling with a most unfortunate-looking lady. Upon seeing them, I commented loudly to Mama, "Look at that man with that dog-faced woman! She must have put the voodoo on him!" Then, after a pause for dramatic effect, I stated, "Either that or poontang." Of course, I had no idea what "poontang" was since Grandma had never explained it to me. I tried to tell Mama that, but she still gave me a butt-whipping all the way back to the car.

Later, I learned that was a slang term Grandma used for lovemaking. She never used the right words for any body part that was "down there," but had her own vocabulary for the "privates," as she called them. The girl part was either a "hoochie mama" or "pocketbook," and the boy part was a "weenie" or a "pecker." Grandma always told me and my cousin Scarlet to keep our pocketbooks closed until we got married. We never really did get why it was bad to open up your purse prior to marriage, but again, if Grandma said it, we thought it was the gospel.

After Grandma would get her nails done, she would usually get her hair dyed jet black and teased up till it looked like cotton candy. I thought it was so pretty and wished I could get my hair dyed or teased. To me, Grandma looked like an older, racier version of Priscilla when she married Elvis. Of course, everyone in the South knew that Mrs. Presley was the most beautiful woman on the planet. Otherwise, Elvis would have never married her.

Grandma usually took me shopping after her hair/nail appointment. She had to show off her freshly done "do," and the first place we always went was the lingerie department at the Navy Exchange. Grandma loved lingerie and bought it in her favorite color as well. She thought black lingerie was only worn by "open-bottom hos," and white was only for your wedding night—if you kept your pocketbook closed and deserved to wear white, that is. She said red lingerie meant a woman was ready to "get down to business." I didn't know what "business" meant either, but I noticed Paw-Paw always seemed real happy the next day after Grandma got her new lingerie. He would wake up smiling, "whisker" us grandkids with his unshaven face, and walk around the kitchen singing, "She's got dimples on her butt, she's perty, she's Lillie Helen Miller, and she's perty!" at the top of his lungs while Grandma fixed his breakfast.

Grandma was a real good "cooker," and I never tired of helping her in the kitchen. Rolling out her yeast rolls and feeling the sticky dough between my fingers, or rolling out homemade noodles for her vegetable soup, began my lifelong love affair with cooking. The smell of the yeast and the fresh-baked bread was the first thing to greet anyone who came to Grandma's house on a Sunday or holiday. Paw-Paw would help out by grilling steaks on an old charcoal grill out back of the house, marinated in a "secret sauce" that only he knew the recipe to, but which made the steaks fork-tender and scrumptious. Grandma would cook us a baked potato to go with our dinner, topped with mounds of freshly made butter and sour cream. "Low-fat" wasn't a word heard in Grandma's kitchen, and all of us grandkids would come home from a visit a little "healthier"—i.e., with about ten extra pounds.

I continued to visit Grandma throughout her life, even after I married and had children of my own. After Paw-Paw passed on, Grandma lived at home for a while, making one of the bedrooms a shrine to him with all his military medals and photos on display. After a while, she had to be put into a nursing home, but continued to be feisty in spirit. Her worn-out body still housed a little fireball. The workers at the home called her "Ms. Froufrou" because of the many demands she placed on them. Even in the home, she wanted to keep up her appearance and gave the staff of the nursing home fits. Still, they loved her and tried to keep her looking pretty whenever anyone would come to visit. However, she was saddened by the fact that she was no longer at home and continually asked about her precious red Cadillac. She was sure she would go back home some day and drive it again.

Grandma died just shy of her ninetieth birthday. When my brother called to tell me she had passed away, I was saddened, but glad that she did not have to live in the nursing home any longer. In my haste to get down to Florida for her funeral, I didn't have time to get a manicure, and I was glad Grandma wouldn't see my ratty-looking hands and un-"mancured" nails.

Her funeral was beautiful and meaningful, and brought back a flood of memories. My cousin Scarlet had written the eulogy, which made all of us laugh and cry. All the things that had made Grandma a unique Southern lady came back to us all that day.

I got up to see Grandma's body and tell her goodbye before the casket was closed. As I looked at her frail little hands, I noticed something that would have made her real happy. Her nails had been painted red — not just any red, but a candy-apple red with a little sparkle that matched the paint on her Cadillac. I smiled, taking comfort in the knowledge that Grandma was finally home, driving her red Cadillac around heaven and scaring the heck out of any angels who might get in her way.

— Melanie Adams Hardy —

Just Press Play

*Memory is a glorious grab bag of the past from which
one can at leisure pluck bittersweet experiences of
times gone by and relive them.*

~Hal Boyle

I awoke at 5:00 a.m. and instinctively turned on my phone to see the scroll of missed calls, messages, and texts. Sadly, I saw that my beloved ninety-two-year-old grandmother, Margaret Amelia Sullivan, had passed away. In her sleep, at home, in the still of the night, she had floated peacefully to heaven — the way we all wish to slip from this world into the next.

While my family and I were hunkered down in a puppy pile of tears, hugs, "I love yous," and our favorite stories about Granny, my husband received a phone call from the owner of the recording/production studio we'd been renting for the past five years saying that the studio had been sold. We had two days to move out. We had known we would soon be moving, but we thought we had months to do it gracefully and gradually. But now, the clock was ticking, and we had forty-eight hours to move our belongings.

The last place on earth I wanted to be was at our 24,000-square-foot studio on the other side of town, away from my family. My heart was so heavy with emotion that I was not in the mindset to sort out our mountains of business files and boxes.

With tears, sniffs, and a lot of pouting, I dutifully accompanied my husband to our studio.

As we were sorting, sandwiched between my teary thoughts of missing my grandma, I vaguely remembered dragging my husband, Dana, with me years before to visit my grandma to film her telling some of her stories. It was just after she'd suffered a broken hip, and I knew that her time on this earth with us was limited.

My husband turned on the camera, and Granny lit up like a Christmas tree, eyes sparkling and smile radiant. With her gray hair done in her classic style and wearing a lavender sweatshirt, she animatedly shared stories about sneaking out her bedroom window as a teenager to hop on a train to meet the man who would be my grandpa. She reminisced about raising five children alone while my grandpa was at war in the Navy, surviving fire, floods, storms, and keeping her highly energetic kids safe while having as much fun as possible.

I didn't dare ask Dana where those tapes might be. I knew it would be met with a sigh and an eye roll at the impossibility of finding them. My husband is an incredibly talented music producer, videographer, and editor, among many other gifts. But one of his talents is *not* in the domain of organization. There were hundreds of boxes of MiniDV tapes he had filmed over the past seventeen years since we'd been together… all of which needed to be moved.

And because all my heart wanted to do was get back to my family, I was in the spirit of "let's get rid of everything!"

Dana was contemplating agreeing with me about just torching the whole mess when, out of the blue, he stuck his hand into a random box. Like a grab bag, he pulled out two random tapes, and then he yelled across the cavernous studio, "Kelly, you'll never guess the names of the two tapes I just found!"

I responded with a despondent blank stare and shrugged shoulders. "Granny 1 and Granny 2!"

Those were the only two tapes he'd pulled out of boxes of hundreds!

New tears streamed from my eyes… tears of gratitude… tears of awe… tears that only take place when something truly miraculous and unexplainable happens.

If we didn't have to move that weekend—the day after my grandma passed away—we never would have been at the studio sorting through boxes.

Of all the boxes of tapes, how was it possible that Dana was led to the exact box that contained those exact tapes?

Did my granny orchestrate this? Was it God? An angel?

Whoever or whatever it was, it felt like the reassurance that my family and I needed that Granny was well situated in heaven, and soon we would be at peace, too.

To add the icing on top of this unexplainable miracle, I found someone who had the rare technology to transfer nine-year-old tapes to a digital format just in time to share the video of my sparkling-eyed grandma at the reception after her funeral for my whole family to enjoy.

These tapes are treasures, soul gold that we are all so grateful to have… and all my family and extended family will always treasure.

Now, when I miss Granny and just want to see her again, to hear her voice and laughter, all I have to do is press Play.

— Kelly Sullivan Walden —

45

Mammie's Meatloaf

If God had intended us to follow recipes,
He wouldn't have given us grandmothers.
~Linda Henley

My grandmother, Mammie, has lived alone for more than twenty-five years. But you wouldn't know it to look inside her fridge. On any given day, you might find several types of meat, two heads of cabbage, potatoes, carrots, and a few bricks of cheese. Usually, she has a specific meal in mind when she purchases these items.

"Why don't you and Craig come over for dinner?" she'll ask. "I've been making cabbage and a roast."

That's a hard meal to pass up. So if we aren't busy, we indulge.

"What did you do today, Mammie?" I'll call and ask her.

"Well, I washed a few loads of laundry and did some dishes. Oh, and I put on a pot of homemade vegetable soup. You want Craig to come by and pick some up for dinner?"

"Of course, that sounds great!" I say. And then I call Craig and ask him to stop at Mammie's. Sometimes he has already passed her town but there is no such thing as "driving out of the way" when it comes to her cooking.

Mammie cooks for all of us: her sisters, her four children and their spouses, her nine grandchildren and their spouses, and her three great-grandchildren. And though we sometimes joke that her house contains more food than a nuclear fallout shelter, we don't know what we would do without Mammie's meals. In fact, we all have our personal favorites.

Aunt Connie loves Mammie's sweet potatoes. They're peeled, sliced and fried in bacon grease and then topped with butter and sugar. Susie likes Mammie's homemade chicken rice soup. My uncle prefers Mammie's beef roast, seasoned to perfection and tender enough to cut with a fork. My cousins like Mammie's fried chicken and stewed potatoes. And my mom is a big fan of her cabbage and potatoes.

Each of us has a favorite "Mammie" food. And several times a year, she fixes our favorites and invites us over individually. I'm not quite sure how my favorite came to be. I don't remember the first time I ate it but I was probably very young. It's not something that I eat anywhere else; I certainly don't order it at restaurants. As a rule, I don't even eat that much meat.

Mammie's meatloaf is the exception to the rule. It is the most delicious food that has ever entered my mouth. Mammie starts with high-quality ground beef and adds in a mixture of breadcrumbs, onions, and tomato sauce. After it has cooked, she carefully tops it with homemade French fries. Then (this is the best part) she drizzles the fries with a gooey ketchup garnish.

Her meatloaf puts any gourmet meal to shame. Best served when fresh from the oven, the first bite is always soft and tender. The edges, a bit browner than the rest, have a hint of candied sugar. And the French fries, meant to accompany each bite, are just as good when eaten by themselves.

Mammie's meatloaf is consistently delicious — the same cannot always be said about foods from popular restaurant chains and grocery stores. Last July, Mammie called to ask me what I wanted for my birthday. That was an easy enough question to answer.

"I would like a meatloaf! Can I have one?" I begged like a little child.

"I think I can do that," Mammie said.

For my twenty-ninth birthday, my husband, my parents and I gathered around Mammie's table. We ate slice after slice of meatloaf and heaping helpings of cabbage and potatoes. Then, she gave me my own meatloaf to take home. I didn't want to share it with my husband, but I did. It was a fabulous birthday.

This year was the big one. I turned thirty.

"Let's go out for a nice dinner in Virginia Beach," my husband suggested.

"Yeah. This is a big birthday, honey. Don't you want something special?" my mom asked.

I did. I wanted Mammie's meatloaf. That would make it special.

Mammie went shopping for ground beef, potatoes, and a couple of heads of cabbage. And on the night of my birthday, we gathered at my parents' house for our meal. It was a scrumptious dinner.

Maybe if I had her recipe, I could explain it more precisely and its delectableness would be easier to share. But right now I don't have it. And I don't need it. That's because Mammie's meatloaf cannot be replicated. It wouldn't be nearly as good if it were made by anyone else.

I guess that's how most people feel about their favorite foods. The cooks, more so than the ingredients, make the dish special. Mammie's signature meatloaf is the most succulent food in the world. And as long as she feels like fixing it, that's what I want for my birthday.

— Melissa Face —

46

My Two Grandmas

Grandmothers always have time to talk
and make you feel special.
~Catherine Pulsifer

I'd known these two women for my whole life, but I'd never seen them in the same room. Both were my grandmothers, one by blood and one by marriage. They'd married the same man — my grandfather. He'd divorced one of them and then married the other. He'd passed away four years earlier.

My two grandmothers hated one another. Even though the man they'd fought over was gone, they still despised each other. For my entire life, we'd celebrated holidays with them separately because they'd insisted on it. Even after my grandfather had died, they still refused to be in one another's presence.

Until today.

Today, the three of us were meeting for lunch to discuss the one thing we all shared: divorce.

I was going through one, and it was positively excruciating. When Grandma-by-blood heard that my husband had left me, she'd called Grandma-by-marriage for the first time ever.

"We have to help Sarah," she said. "She's my granddaughter, and she's your, well, I guess when you married my husband, she became your step-granddaughter."

Grandma-by-marriage said, "I married her grandfather — your ex-husband — before she was even born. She's my granddaughter, too."

"Well, that's all semantics," Grandma-by-blood said. "Anyway, I've been through a divorce, and my husband was your second husband because you were divorced from your first husband, so we both know what she's going through."

"Yes, I married your ex-husband eight years after you and he split up," Grandma-by-marriage reminded her. "Your divorce had nothing to do with me."

"Yes, and you were married to him longer than I was anyway, but he never had any kids with you," Grandma-by-blood said. "A real marriage produces children."

"But he didn't divorce me," Grandma-by-marriage said. "We were married until the day he died. He never left me."

"Which brings me back to the reason why I called you for the first time ever in my life," Grandma-by-blood said. "My granddaughter needs us. Both of us."

So we went to lunch. It was strange to see these two septuagenarians in the same room after all those years. It felt strange, especially when I remembered that they only did it because they wanted to help me.

"How are you doing, honey?" Grandma-by-blood asked, reaching for my hand.

Before I could answer, Grandma-by-marriage grabbed my other hand. "Yeah, sweetie, tell us how you're doing," she said.

"I'm all right, I guess," I said. "It's hard. Divorce sucks."

"Oh, you're right about that," Grandma-by-blood said. "When your grandfather and I split up — you know, so he could marry her," she nodded at Grandma-by-marriage and continued, "I felt like my heart was ripping out of my chest."

"He did not divorce you to marry me," Grandma-by-marriage snapped. "I didn't even know him then." She shook her head, suddenly seeming to remember that she was supposed to be helping me. She patted my hand. "So does it feel like your heart is ripping out of your chest?"

I shrugged. "Yeah, kind of. I have good days and bad days."

"What kind of day is today?" Grandma-by-blood asked. Before I could answer, she said, "I'd say it's an historic one. You know, because me and her," she nodded at Grandma-by-marriage again, "are here together in one place just for you because we love you, and you need us."

"I sure appreciate that," I said. "It means a lot to me."

"I would think so," Grandma-by-blood said. "Because me and her," another nod, "haven't always gotten along that well."

"Yes, I think my mom might have mentioned that once or twice," I said.

"Well, you know, it's on account of your grandfather," Grandma-by-blood said. "He caused a rift in the family when he divorced me to marry her." Again, she nodded at Grandma-by-marriage.

Before Grandma-by-marriage could jump in, I jumped up, thankful that the restaurant had a buffet. "I'm going to get some food now," I said.

As I ate, my two grandmas continued to pretend to talk about me, all while taking jabs at each other. Grandma-by-blood nodded at Grandma-by-marriage about fifty more times, I think to avoid saying Grandma-by-marriage's actual name. Grandma-by-marriage defended herself and her relationship with my grandfather in the calmest possible way, gritting her dentures until I feared they would grind into dust.

When Grandma-by-blood asked me if I thought my husband was seeing another woman — while nodding like a bobblehead at Grandma-by-marriage — I knew I'd had all I could take of their wise counsel.

I grabbed their hands and said, "This has been lovely. I appreciate you putting aside your differences on my behalf."

Grandma-by-blood squeezed my hand. "It wasn't so hard. I'm not sure why we waited so long." She looked at Grandma-by-marriage and smiled tentatively. "Do you want to do Christmas together this year?"

Grandma-by-marriage nodded. "I think that would be wonderful for the kids."

"Well, they're my kids," Grandma-by-blood said. "They're only your step-kids."

I sighed. "Grandma, I speak for my mother, her siblings, and all of your grandchildren when I say that we belong to both of you. And Christmas as a family sounds terrific."

And, oddly enough, it was terrific. As the years went on, my two grandmas actually became friends, and their problems in the past were finally forgotten.

Most of the time, when a couple gets divorced, it tears apart a family. But my divorce brought together two of the most amazing women I've ever known.

— Sarah Foster —

47

The Barbie Christmas

Children make you want to start life over.
~Muhammad Ali

My five-year-old granddaughter, Anna Grace, was sitting on a child's wooden bench in my living room and staring at the decorated Christmas tree. It was most unusual for her to be silent. She hadn't said a word in an hour and I was wondering if she was okay. Her big blue eyes were larger than ever.

Finally, she turned to me and said, "GG, why didn't you tell me?"

"Because I wanted to surprise you."

"Where did you get all the Barbies?" she asks. "And all the pretty dresses?"

"I was shopping at Goodwill. Someone dropped off fourteen Barbies in pretty dresses. I thought they would be beautiful on a Christmas tree and you would love it. I decided to search for more after that."

After discovering the first fourteen dolls, I kept looking for secondhand Barbies in party dresses for the Christmas tree. At Salvation Army and Southern Thrift, I found more dolls and plastic bags filled with sparkling clothes to dress the Barbies we already had. My plan fell into place. I had a variety of forty Barbies ready for the tree — all dressed beautifully.

Anna Grace enjoyed the tree throughout the Christmas season. At year's end she was delighted to take it down. She placed the Barbies in a line on the floor, counting each one. It was time to play with the best Christmas decorations ever.

Anna Grace played with the Barbies for hours. We dressed and undressed them, cut and styled their hair, named them, and went on imaginary adventures with them. They were swimmers, gymnasts, shoppers, and explorers. They had Ken dolls to escort them to fancy parties or the beach. I don't know which one of us had more fun playing with our collection of thrift store Barbies.

Months later, Anna Grace said, "GG, I have beautiful Barbies somewhere at my house, but these thrift store Barbies are the ones we played with the most."

It's been eleven years since the Barbie Tree Christmas. Our family and friends still talk about it. Now, the Barbies wait in their pretty dresses, tucked away in tissue-lined boxes. A few will be selected for a small Christmas tree. It's a grandmother's tradition and a story I've told over and over and over.

— Gloria Hudson Fortner —

Chapter
6

Mom Knows Best

48

Christmas with a New Family

I don't remember who said this, but there really
are places in the heart you don't even know
exist until you love a child.
~Anne Lamott

When I married my husband, we blended our families and I got a new twelve-year-old daughter. She came to live with us and my eight-year-old daughter. When Christmastime came, I started hearing a certain phrase: "We used to…"

"We used to make sugar cookies for Christmas and decorate them," my husband said to me. So, I made sugar-cookie dough — the kind you stick in the fridge for hours and then come back to roll out and shape. I botched it. It got warm beneath my rolling pin and stuck to everything. My husband tried to comfort me by saying, "I remember when we tried to make them for the first time. We screwed it up, too." I started to feel jealous.

"We used to make breakfast pizza and cheesy potatoes for Christmas morning," he said to me on a walk through the grocery store. My throat tightened. I felt like a replacement — a stand-in for some once-upon-a-time that I had nothing to do with.

At home, I put the groceries in the fridge and heard the intro of yet another anecdote beginning with, "We used to…" He started to say it, but I didn't let him finish.

"If you're trying to recreate something you had with someone else, then why am I here?" I asked. I wanted to create new, different memories with the man I loved and our blended family. The last thing I wanted to bring into our home were traditions of some other marriage that ended badly.

He stopped unpacking a grocery sack and looked at me. "I hope you understand that all of this isn't for me."

The knot inside me unclenched. In his face, I saw the worry that only a father could carry. This wasn't about what he needed for his holiday. How could I have missed that?

Later, I retrieved the Christmas decorations from the basement. "I love ornaments," the twelve-year-old said to me.

Smiling, she reached into the plastic tub, looked over the decorations and pulled them out one at a time. There were crocheted ornaments and wall hangings that my mother had made when I was a child. I even had the crocheted stocking that Mom had made. Ornaments I had made in school were in there as well as my eight-year-old's baby ornaments and more decorations from her craft days at school.

I watched my twelve-year-old grow quiet and her excitement vanish. In this tub of decorations, she didn't exist. Her childhood ornaments and holiday memories were someplace else. I didn't have to say the words. Every item in the box screamed, "We used to… without you."

"Great," she said. "So, everyone's going to have stuff to put up except me."

She started to walk away.

"Wait a minute," I said. Then I shouted to my husband, who was in the other room, "We're going to the store!" We got in the car and I wanted to say something. My face was pinched, and I was mad. What was I doing? I had no idea. All I could see was my husband's worried face and hear his repeated attempts to save the pleasant scraps from his past for his little girl — *our* little girl — the now silent, angry girl in my passenger seat. We arrived at the supermarket. I turned off the engine.

"Listen," I said with a heavy sigh. "I can't bring back the past or duplicate your traditions. I can't go get your ornaments. I wish that I could, but I can't."

She looked out the windshield and didn't blink. It wasn't like I was telling her something she didn't already know.

"Here's what I can do," I said. "I can promise you that we'll create new traditions together." She looked at me doubtfully. "Let's go," I said.

We got out of the car, and I took her to the seasonal department of the supermarket. "Pick out some ornaments, whichever ones you want," I said. She looked at me, and I knew it wasn't the same, but we had to start somewhere. She went up and down the aisle and settled on a multi-pack of blue and silver ornaments of varying shapes and sizes.

At home, I opened my sewing machine. I sewed everyone a stocking to hang over the fireplace. The twelve-year-old's stocking had penguins on it, the eight-year-old's stocking was adorned with cookies, and my husband's stocking featured bears.

While my mom was visiting, we made salt-dough ornaments, which are made like cookies. Once they were baked and painted, they would keep forever thanks to the salt. Well, the ones the dog didn't eat off the tree would keep forever....

Then, the twelve-year-old and I went to a local paint-and-bake ceramic studio. We painted Christmas ornaments for a family gift.

Each year since then, I've made the girls a Christmas ornament with their name and year on it. Some are cross-stitched, and some are painted.

"For how long will I get these ornaments?" the older one once asked.

"Until you have babies," I told her. "Then I'll make the ornaments for my grandchildren."

"I might never have kids then," she said, and I laughed.

Last year, I cross-stitched an extra ornament for my now eighteen-year-old. It had the year of her birth on it along with her name. I gave it to her privately on Christmas Eve. "Every baby deserves a first Christmas ornament," I told her. If I could've turned back time and made her mine from day one, I would have.

I've also mastered the sugar cookies in my own way. A friend gave me a recipe that doesn't require the dough to be refrigerated. This works for me. I make cookies with the girls every year. I also make cheesy potatoes. Turns out, they're really good.

—Bonnie Jean Feldkamp—

49

Rich Is Better

Concentrate on counting your blessings, and you'll
have little time to count anything else.
~Woodrow Kroll

The winter wind bit through my coat but didn't dampen my cheerfulness as I carried my four jars of home-canned tomatoes into the church basement. Excited to participate in feeding the less fortunate in our community at Christmas, I joined my Sunday school classmates as we boxed the goods for delivery.

That year, we went to Bobby's house. He was one grade ahead of me in school, but I never knew he was poor. When we took the box inside the small house, I saw bedrooms had been created by hanging sheets over ropes. Bobby came home while we were there, blushed, and disappeared behind a divider.

My heart ached for him. Even as a seven-year-old, I understood embarrassment. After we returned to the church, my teacher pulled me aside. I thought she was going to discuss Bobby's situation, but she didn't.

"Linda, we collected a lot of food this year. You have a large family. Why don't you take this extra box home with you?" She picked up the cardboard container, expecting me to accept the food.

"No. That's for poor people."

"All people need help at times," she said.

"Well, we don't." I pushed open the door and walked the three blocks to my house.

Were we poor? I began to look at our family with what I considered impartial, grown-up eyes and concluded that we were definitely poor.

My mother never suffered fools, and she didn't tolerate whining. After two days, she demanded to know why I'd been moping.

"We're poor."

"Who said that?" she demanded.

"Nobody said it. I figured it out." I couldn't look her in the eye. She'd been hiding this important truth from us.

"Why do you think we're poor?"

I listed reasons, becoming bolder as I elaborated on my realizations. "The church wanted to give us food. We don't have a car, only a pick-up, and we have to ride in the back when we go places. The women's missionary group offered to buy us shoes for this school year. And most of the clothes in my closet are hand-me-downs from a girl in my class. I never thought about it, but what if people are laughing about me wearing her clothes?"

"Are you done?"

I wracked my brain for other examples but came up with none.

My mother poured a cup of coffee and sat at the kitchen table, a rarity as she worked constantly. Maybe she hadn't known what people thought about us.

She stirred in a spoonful of sugar and sipped. "We are not poor. We are exceedingly rich."

This statement got my attention, and I grabbed a chair. "We are?"

"Do you have a healthy body? Can you run and play without any problem?"

I nodded. I was the fastest girl in our class.

"Do you have a good mind? Are you a good reader? Is there a library where you can learn about anything that interests you?"

I nodded again. My mother often reminded us that she only had an eighth-grade education, but she expected every one of her seven children to earn college degrees. I now felt embarrassed about bringing up the subject.

"Do you ever go to bed hungry?" She put down her cup. "I know you don't. We have a wonderful garden, and you eat well year-round. Canned food doesn't taste as good as home-grown. I should buy some tins just to prove it."

"But the rich people buy their food in cans," I protested.

"Because they don't have gardens. People in China don't get enough to eat. You do. And people in Africa don't have many clothes, hand-me-downs or not. Clothes aren't important. Consider the lilies of the field." She used that Bible reference when any of us complained about the clothes we wore.

"But people think we're poor."

"Well, they're wrong. You get to go to school and play, while some children in this world have to work. You live in America. You're free. You can go where you want to go, worship in any church you choose, and pursue any dream you can imagine. You are not poor! You're rich! I expect you to remember that every day of your life."

I never brought up the subject again.

Now that I'm older, I marvel at the riches we enjoyed, even on Christmases when there weren't many presents under the tree.

I've often heard the saying, "I've been rich, and I've been poor. Rich is better."

I know rich is better, for I'm an exceedingly wealthy woman.

— Linda Baten Johnson —

50

A Mother Knows

A mother's love for her child is like nothing else in the
world. It knows no law, no pity. It dares all things and
crushes down remorselessly all that stands in its path.
~Agatha Christie

I stared at the pregnancy test, willing the lines to appear. Then I saw the faint pink squiggles morph into two deeper pink lines. "Oh, my goodness! I'm pregnant!" I screeched to my husband who was waiting outside the bathroom.

We hugged each other while crying happy tears. Our eighteen-month-old daughter, Abby, was going to be a big sister!

Imagining another picture-perfect pregnancy, I started a baby registry and scanned the Internet every evening until I had my top three choices for boy and girl names. Then, at the seven-week mark, I began experiencing painful cramps, strong pelvic pressure and heavy bleeding. After rushing over to my OB's office, I lay on the exam table with an ultrasound wand over my stomach. The exam room was silent as my doctor stared at the pulsating screen.

"Look at this, Crystal — there are two heartbeats. You're having twins!"

"I can't believe there are two little humans in here," I said, smiling as I rubbed my stomach.

The ultrasound also revealed a blood clot, which was the cause of the cramping and bleeding. The doctor placed me on bed rest for a month, hoping that the blood clot would re-absorb into my body.

I sucked on ginger-flavored lollipops to help soothe my nausea and snacked on Saltine crackers while binge-watching episodes of *Game of Thrones*. Now I could relax and enjoy the rest of the pregnancy — or so I thought.

But at twenty-two weeks, my doctor made a shocking discovery during a routine ultrasound.

"There's an abnormal amount of amniotic fluid surrounding the babies. You have a disease called twin-to-twin transfusion syndrome. It's a serious condition."

He explained that our twin girls shared a placenta, which meant that one baby was pumping blood disproportionately to the other baby. While one baby was receiving too many nutrients, the other was being starved.

An army of maternal fetal specialists advised us that our only hope for both babies' survival was for me to undergo a risky laser ablation surgery. The procedure required inserting a laser into my uterus to sever all the connecting blood vessels so the placenta would be separated. Since the disease had weakened them, we didn't know if both babies would survive the surgery. I swallowed my doubts, opened my heart, said a prayer and poured my faith into advanced medical technology and the incredible team of nurses and surgeons.

It worked. The surgery was a success, and both babies survived. Yet I couldn't shake a premonition that there was another roadblock coming on my pregnancy path. I tried to ignore that feeling and envisioned myself sitting at home in my rocking chair with my babies.

A week later, we learned that the procedure had created a small hole in the inter-twin membrane. One of the babies tore the hole, joining her sister in the same amniotic sac, which was dangerous because they wouldn't have enough room to grow without entangling themselves.

Each night, I knelt underneath the nursery window, clutching a pink baby blanket, and begged for my solemn request to be fulfilled. "Lord, you have been by our side this whole time. Please continue to guide us through this time of uncertainty. Help my precious babies," I pleaded.

My doctor admitted me to the hospital for bed rest and

Mom Knows Best | 159

around-the-clock monitoring until my due date. Five uneventful weeks passed, and I was beginning to doubt my premonition. We had already battled major medical mishaps. What else could possibly happen? Then I woke up one morning with my sheets drenched in sweat, a clawing in the pit of my stomach, and the overpowering feeling that something was wrong. I was certain that my babies were in mortal danger.

I banged repeatedly on the red call button until my nurse flew into the room.

"There's something wrong with my babies!"

"How do you know?" she asked, looking confused.

"I'm the mother. I just know! Please listen to me," I pleaded.

Soon, I was entangled in wires and cords attached to monitors. I was having full-blown contractions although I was only thirty weeks along. I welcomed the pain, convinced that I needed to get the babies out of my body that moment.

"What is taking the doctor so long to get here?" I demanded. The nurse scurried to find the doctor. When he finally arrived, he put me on magnesium to try and stop the labor. Sensing there was still a problem, I fought him with every fiber of my being.

"No, we need to deliver the babies today," I cried. "Something doesn't feel right."

"But the babies are only thirty weeks, and everything looks fine according to the monitor," my doctor said, patting my shoulder reassuringly.

"I don't care what that machine says. I'm telling you something is wrong!" I yelled. By now, the nurses walking by in the hallway had gathered around me, consternation on their faces.

"I know the babies will have a longer NICU time, but I need to see them and know that they are okay…. That's what I want. That's what you have to do."

He stared at the sheet of white paper with zigzag lines coming out of the monitor.

"Okay," he nodded. "You win, Duffy."

I prayed fervently for my unborn babies as I was wheeled through the corridors to the operating room. Once there, the bright lights, scrubbed and masked doctors and nurses calmed me. I didn't know what the outcome would be, but my prayers and my feeling that I was dealing with a greater power gave me faith that my instincts were correct.

As soon as the C-section began, the doctors saw that my placenta had abrupted. I was bleeding heavily internally. The premonition that kept gnawing at me was a warning that my babies and I were in grave danger.

It took a team of talented surgeons and nurses to save my baby girls and me.

If I hadn't trusted my intuition, there would have been a very different outcome.

Katherine Maria and Lauren Elizabeth weighed three pounds when they were born and spent thirty-eight days in the NICU. Today, at five years old, they are happy, healthy, and energetic girls who love building sandcastles on the beach, taking their dog on walks to the park, and playing dress-up with their older sister.

Does maternal instinct trump medical science? Does the power of prayer work? The mystery in life is great. All I know is that I asked for a miracle in my time of need, and I received one.

— Crystal Duffy —

51

Is Everybody Smiling?

Family quarrels are bitter things. They don't go by any rules.
They're not like aches or wounds; they're more like splits
in the skin that won't heal because
there's not enough material.
~F. Scott Fitzgerald

I
n my family, no gathering is complete without a camera. It's genetic, inherited from my father. Dad would have liked pictures taken at his funeral, too, but none of his five children were speaking to each other at the time. Requesting a sibling to "smile for the camera" would have been considered speaking first. It's a well-known rule that if you speak first, you lose. We're a family of winners.

It is amazing that in this clan of chronic chroniclers, we had been missing the picture that became so important to my mother that it forced all of us to spend our first Christmas together in six years.

The hole in the family album was pointed out to me one December morning when my mother and I passed the piano in my living room at the same time. Mom cast a longing look at a picture of my late father taken at his wedding to my stepmother. He was surrounded by his five loving children.

"What's wrong, Mom?" I asked as I watched her pick up the picture.

"Oh, honey, I'd love to have a picture of myself with all of you kids like this one. That's all." Sniff, sniff.

"Sure, that would be good," I said as I removed the picture from her grasp and put it back on the piano top. "Don't you have the one from when you and Larry were married? I can have mine copied for you." I handed her that picture.

"This was taken nineteen years ago."

"But we all looked good. Everyone was smiling." My hair had looked spectacular.

Does the expression "if looks could kill" mean anything to you? "I was thinking of next Christmas, dear," she said as her jaw set and her mouth tightened into a straight line.

"Oh," was the only thing I could say that wouldn't be the subject of a prayerful letter to Sister-Mary-What's-Her-Name at the monastery. Plus, this was December twenty-sixth, and she might forget by next year. Let one of her other children question the sanity of this. Not me. I knew I was not the only one who had no interest in celebrating anything together, but I was still trying to redeem myself for my behavior during my teenage years, when the letters to Sister Mary began.

My family hadn't always been like this. My three sisters, my brother and I, dubbed the "Taylor Tots" by my dad when we were younger and forced to dress alike, had been very close. We spent a lot of time together, especially after Mom gave up on the matching outfits. Sundays meant Lake Harriet. The children swam, the men read the newspapers, and the women gathered in lawn chairs at the water's edge, adding a fresh coat of burn to the previous Sunday's tan. Ours was a family that couldn't imagine celebrating anything without each other. I have the pictures to prove it.

Times change and so do families. We all got busy. The three younger siblings married and began having children at the same time the two older divorced and remarried. Still, no one would have thought to stop celebrating Christmas together. We gathered at Dad's condo: Mom and her husband, Dad and his wife, the five children and their spouses, fourteen grandchildren, a grandchild's spouse, two grandchildren's intendeds and a great-grandchild. That's a lot of flashbulbs.

Then Dad passed away. Grief turned to anger. Even the pictures stopped. Christmas wasn't a consideration with no one speaking to everyone. Oh, this one spoke to that one but not to this other; if you spoke to her, you'd better not mention him. It required a scorecard, and we were allowed no errors. Why? The usual after-a-parent-dies stuff: misunderstandings, hurt feelings, words said that shouldn't have been.

That's how we got to the day after Christmas and my mother's incredible wish. Praying that she'd forget was useless because Sister Mary and You-Know-Who were on her side. In fact, Mom's memory improved now that she had a mission. When she brought up the subject in March, I told her about my brainstorm.

"This is perfect, Mom. We set up appointments at a studio, and each of us can go in for a separate picture. We never have to speak to each other. They can take a picture of you, put it in the middle and have our pictures circled around yours."

"Oh, you're so full of good ideas, aren't you?" I said goodbye to redemption.

The year passed faster than any I remembered, and the picture was a certainty as far as my mother was concerned. Unfortunately, I was the only one who knew about it, and the responsibility of being the oldest and doing the right thing was a burden. My youngest sister called from Florida; she and her family were coming for Christmas. I became suspicious.

By the end of summer, the picture was taking over my life. Why was this so important to her? Whenever we spoke, there was a sniffling sound and some mention of the picture. Why did she want to force us to pose for a family picture when we weren't feeling familial? Who was going to host this celebration? Not me. I wanted to be able to make a quick exit when the yelling started.

Saved! My otolaryngologist, Dr. Super Hero, recommended I have sinus surgery. He assured me there would be swelling and heavy-duty bruising. He mentioned black and blue. I scheduled the operation for the week before Christmas and then rushed to the phone to share the sad news with my mother. And garner some sympathy.

"You'll be all right in time for THE PICTURE, won't you? Your sister's going to have Christmas." Yikes! Which one? It didn't matter; Mom had been working on this behind my back. I canceled the surgery.

Christmas arrived. I was fat. My hair was too short, and I was overdressed. Why hadn't I gotten cucumbers for the vegetable tray? I should have made dill dip, not spinach. I was sweating. The flu. I prayed it was fatal.

"You look great, honey, even better than the vegetable tray, which is a work of art," sang my husband, Mr. Wonderful. Couldn't he see I was dying?

Flu or no flu, I found myself standing at my sister's door, wondering if I should knock or walk in like "the old days." Four children answered the question for me as they came barreling out the door, carrying sleds.

My husband joined the brothers-in-law in front of the television. The teenaged nephews had assumed their now-rightful places among the men in the family. Who was trouncing who on the football field was all that mattered to them.

I put the vegetables on the dining room table and made my way slowly toward the kitchen, stopping in the bathroom first to check my oh-so-short hair. What had I been thinking? I was bald.

There they were—mashing potatoes, stirring gravy, talking. Talking? I took a step. They turned toward me.

"Cute hair!"

"Get her some champagne."

"Someone take a picture of that cute haircut."

I finally got it: my family doesn't say "I'm sorry," or "I love you." We say it in other ways like "Cute hair." Could "Take a picture" mean "I don't want to forget you"?

A year and a half later, four daughters and one son walk down the church aisle to place a gold-framed copy of the picture next to their mother and to say goodbye. We realize that Mom hadn't needed the picture for herself. She wanted it for us, for this day—for the mantle, a table or the top of a piano. Mom knew if she could get us all together that Christmas everything would be as it had been—a family not perfect, but connected in spite of its imperfections. We turn to take our places in the front row—together, the way our mother wanted us.

— Andrea Langworthy —

52

Dream Date

Love makes your soul crawl out from its hiding place.
~Zora Neale Hurston

The wedding ceremony took place on a sunny August day, charming everyone in attendance. Blossoms filled each corner of the garden at the historic inn and a soft breeze rustled the leaves as we all waited for the bride to appear.

And then, she was there, moving with grace down the length of the aisle, a picture of simple beauty and style. Her dress and the estate grounds reflected a modest elegance in a silent nod to this, her second marriage.

I wiped away a stray tear. This wasn't her first time to recite the vows, but I was certain it would be her last.

She reached the podium and turned to gaze at her groom, his face beaming with an infectious joy.

I smiled as I watched this young man, once such a mystery, now as familiar as if he were my own God-chosen son. And in a way, he was.

***

It all started around a year earlier in the middle of the night. Was it too much pizza, or had I watched one too many romantic comedies? Or was it something more that caused my subconscious visitation?

The dream had felt so real.

I stared at the man, his tall, stocky frame filling the crowded kitchen's threshold. He looked about five or ten years younger than I, with curly salt and pepper hair topping a sensitive, intelligent face. Brown eyes shone behind wire-rimmed glasses, his grin exuding confidence.

Watching him from across the room, I felt an impulse to speak with the stranger. Somehow I sensed his kindness and knew he'd protect those he loved. In an instant, my thoughts flew to my twenty-something daughter. My single daughter.

I glanced away to scan the space, hoping to spot her long blond hair or hear her laughter nearby. I couldn't see her anywhere. A moment later the people overflowing the area vanished. When my gaze returned to the doorway where the figure had stood waiting, it was empty.

I jolted awake, the glow of the bedside clock my only witness in the midnight quiet. Darkness shrouded the bedroom, and the street lamp outside my window sent a solitary ribbon of light across my comforter.

What was that all about? The gentleman's visage burned into my mind like a brand, forever committed to memory, whether welcome or not. But why? What was so special about this dream figure? Questions riddled my rest until morning.

As sunlight brightened the sky, I headed downstairs to set some coffee to brewing. Sounds coming from my daughter's room alerted me she was awake. The door squeaked open and she joined me in the kitchen.

"Morning."

"Hi, honey. Did you sleep well?"

"Yes, fine." She poured some of the brew into our cups and passed one to me. I had waited a long time for "fine" to become the norm for her.

Our daughter had left an abusive marriage and accompanied my husband and me in a cross-state move. Three years had passed and for the most part the scars had healed. There were no more nightmares or flat, unemotional responses. No crippling self-esteem issues. Even her pets seemed secure sharing their lives in our home.

I sipped the coffee and gazed at my child, her blond hair flowing down her back in a silky stream, her dark brown eyes reflecting warmth from within. My heartstrings tugged a notch tighter. "Do you work tonight?"

"No. I'm getting together with one of my friends."

I glanced out the window. A blue jay perched in our old walnut tree, preening, its azure feathers catching the light like a blue flame. A few fleeting moments later it took flight and was gone. My throat tightened.

I refused to ask whether or not she had a date — I knew the answer. The men she'd met since her divorce had left her hurt and wary and she'd all but stopped pursuing romantic relationships. A couple of months earlier, she'd joined the online dating community, choosing a service that focused on our faith and offered a free trial period. Nothing lasting had developed from that venture. Over time, both her interest and participation waned.

I was worried. Would she never experience the blessings I'd found in marriage — laughter and tears born of time-tested love?

"Let's go upstairs and check out the dating site together."

"Mom." She rolled her eyes as well as any teenager.

"Come on. It'll be fun." Crossing the dining room, I turned my head to see if she would follow.

"Oh, all right."

Minutes later, we snuggled together in our pajamas in front of the computer. She scanned a few profiles, not settling on any one.

She opened another and there he was, the man from my dream! His smiling face seemed much younger and his hair darker than the fellow in my vision, but he was unmistakably, undeniably the individual who'd stood in my kitchen's entry, as if waiting for something... or someone.

I gasped. "That's him."

"Who?"

"That's the man I dreamt about." My heart skipped a beat. "I think he's the one."

"The one what? What are you talking about?" Her gaze remained on his photo.

And I knew. "The one you're going to marry."

Disbelief shadowed my daughter's expression, but she listened as

I relayed my nighttime vision to her. "So you think I should meet this guy?" I could hear the excitement in her voice as her focus returned to the picture.

"I'm sure of it." I stretched an arm around her for a hug. "He's been waiting."

Her head rested on my shoulder for a moment and she sighed, long and slow, like a runner finally crossing the finish line.

As her gaze met mine, I smiled. "And so have we."

***

A blue jay zipped past, returning my thoughts to the present as the pastor spoke. "Will you promise to love, honor, cherish and protect her, forsaking all others and holding only to her forevermore?"

My dream son-in-law leaned a few inches closer to my child to answer, his voice lowered. "I will."

I believed it then and I believe it still. The wait is over. And this dream came true.

— Heidi Gaul —

53

ThanksChristGivingMas

I don't think quantity time is as special
as quality time with your family.
~Reba McEntire

Ted and I watched our daughter Elizabeth get married in Ogunquit, Maine over Memorial Day weekend, and then we flew back to Ohio while the young marrieds went home to New York City. When the winter holidays rolled around that year, Vince and Elizabeth decided to spend Thanksgiving with Vince's family in Massachusetts and Christmas at our home in Ohio. It was a beautiful Christmas, and we had quite a bit of fun. Vince got to experience our family traditions, including playing board games on Christmas Eve attired in new Christmas pajamas.

We laughed, baked, ate and ate some more. We also bundled up to take a walk through the neighborhood and look at the Christmas lights. Christmas morning brought an array of gifts under the tree while an egg casserole cooked in the Crock-Pot over the wee hours, leaving a wonderful aroma throughout the house. When I talked to Elizabeth after they returned to New York, she told me how thankful Vince was for being with us. Ours had been the first Christmas spent away from his family, and he so much appreciated the warmth and traditions that were shared. After all, Vince is now part of both families, as is Elizabeth.

The next year, the tables were flipped, and Vince and Elizabeth were going to spend Christmas in Massachusetts and Thanksgiving in

Ohio. In October, I was chatting with Elizabeth on our usual weekend call. Elizabeth said, "Wouldn't it be fun to celebrate both Thanksgiving and Christmas while we are home?" I'm not sure if she actually heard the thoughts flying around in my head… *I have less than a month to plan, bake, cook, decorate, shop, wrap and clean!* I wasn't quite sure how we were going to do both holidays in one chaotic week, but my reply was, "Sure! Why not?" The newly dubbed ThanksChristGivingMas holiday was born.

Immediately, I began online shopping from wish lists that I asked Elizabeth and Vince to prepare. Packages were arriving nearly daily, and I tried to wrap the gifts as they came in so as not to get behind. I wrote a grocery list for the feast, and we picked up any nonperishable items with our typical grocery shopping. Ted did much of the cleaning while I was at work. After a couple of weeks, I found I was enjoying the preparations for the ThanksChristGivingMas season!

Vince and Elizabeth were scheduled to arrive the Sunday before Thanksgiving. Ted and I put up the Christmas tree in the living room with lights and beads as usual, but this year the angel on top was replaced with a large and incredibly ugly papier-mâché turkey. Ted had purchased the decoration years prior, and it had become a Thanksgiving tradition. Small pilgrim decorations were also hung on the tree. We had our typical Thanksgiving dinner on — well, Thanksgiving.

On Friday, the next day of ThanksChristGivingMas, we did the rest of the decorating. I gave Vince a Disney Christmas tree hat, Elizabeth wore a Santa hat, Ted wore a Grinch hat, and I wore a reindeer mask made by Elizabeth when she was quite young. The Christmas Village went up in the family room, and the actual ornaments and angel replaced the turkey and pilgrims on the tree. Vince and Elizabeth arranged our nativity and our decorative scene of the entire cast of Rudolph the Red-Nosed Reindeer characters. As we decorated outdoors, we said "Merry Christmas" to our neighbors!

That evening became Christmas Eve, and outfitted in new Christmas pajamas, we played *Life*. I could not believe that Vince had never experienced this game, and we laughed continuously. Vince ended up being the big winner to boot!

Saturday morning, the house was filled with the breakfast casserole aroma as we woke to see what Santa had brought. It was so nice that he delivered early for our special ThanksChristGivingMas holiday! The gifts were opened and hugs given all around. Vince, Elizabeth and I all have December birthdays, so we went ahead and threw in those as part of the celebration.

I must admit, I wasn't sure how we would possibly pull off our combination holiday, but it could not have gone better. Everyone had so much fun, and we were immediately filled with the warmth and spirit of the season. Now I look forward to celebrating our new combination holiday in November — every other year.

— Lil Blosfield —

54

The Christmas
of My Dreams

Christmas now surrounds us, happiness is everywhere.
Our hands are busy with many tasks
as carols fill the air.
~Shirley Sallay

I have a recurring stress dream about Christmas. It always starts the same way. *Suddenly, I realize that it's Christmas Eve, and nothing is done. There are no trees, gifts, or groceries ready to be cooked into a holiday feast. The halls are decidedly un-decked. I panic and rush to the store, but the shelves are bare. There's no food left. All the presents, decorations, and rolls of wrapping paper are sold out. There aren't even any Christmas trees. Christmas is ruined, and somehow it's all my fault.* Then I wake up in a cold sweat.

I know exactly where this dream comes from. My family never did Christmas "right." We were those slackers who finally got around to getting a tree on December twenty-third. I have no memories of my mom ever hanging a wreath, and we had zero lights around our windows. Sure, we had a nice dinner. My mom was a great cook, but the turkey and candied sweet potatoes were served on paper plates because she liked everything casual. No fuss. That was why she never wrapped our gifts. My sister and I would get our gifts — tags still dangling — in the bags they came in. And since Mom hated surprises, she could never wait until Christmas morning to give them to us. It drove me insane.

As a kid, all I wanted was to be in charge so I could "fix" Christmas and make ours like the ones I saw on TV.

I vowed that when I grew up, I'd never put together such shoddy holidays. I'd watched a Martha Stewart Christmas special when I was about twelve, and the elegant tables, handcrafted ornaments, families in matching plaid, candles glimmering in real crystal holders, holly sprigs, and homemade eggnog enchanted me. That was a real Christmas, I thought, and that's what I wanted.

Motherhood finally gave me the chance I'd been waiting for. It had been two and a half decades since I'd first seen Martha artfully arrange those poinsettias, but the image had been burned into my memory forever, and I recalled every detail. My daughter was four now, and she'd be able to remember this year. I felt like I owed her the picturesque Christmases I never had, so as soon as Black Friday was over, I embarked on what can only be described as a Christmas blitzkrieg. I was going to do everything, and it was going to be perfect. My little one was going to be so happy.

Except… things didn't go exactly as planned. What was supposed to be a magical morning spent decorating the tree while sipping hot chocolate (homemade, with organic artisan cocoa powder), and listening to classic carols ended up with my daughter in tears in a heap on the living-room floor, while a blackened pan of snickerdoodles smoked in the oven. This wasn't exactly what I'd imagined.

I don't know what music was playing at the time, but it wasn't the Mormon Tabernacle Choir version of "O Come, All Ye Faithful." I'm pretty sure it was heavy metal. My daughter thought the holiday choir music was "scary" and wanted to play her favorite movie soundtrack (which was highly annoying). Then she seemed uninterested in trimming the tree and wanted to make cookies. When they were done, she tossed sprinkles all over them, completely destroying the tasteful, minimalist Scandinavian look I was going for, which I'd seen in an issue of *Martha Stewart Living*.

When she finally wanted to decorate the tree, it seemed we had very different ideas about what that entailed. She liked a low grouping of ornaments clustered within a single, ten-inch radius while leaving the rest of the tree stark naked. This fir was nowhere near magazine-worthy. To tell the truth, I was embarrassed to even post it on Instagram. We weren't wearing our matching plaid jumpers anyway, and that's because we didn't have matching plaid jumpers. We were still wearing our pajamas.

It got worse when I tried to make a gingerbread house. Apparently, to really do it right, one needs an advanced degree in cookie architecture. My house collapsed. Its roof slid, and the chimney was crooked. Once I finally got the thing to stand up, my daughter attacked it with a zeal and fervor that was frankly alarming. It looked like a Jackson Pollock painting when she was done. I kept trying to tell her where to place the Skittles and marshmallows, but the kid was having none of it.

"Mommy, it's beautiful," she sighed, with a clump of dried frosting stuck in her left eyebrow.

It was not beautiful. It was the stuff of nightmares — my recurring nightmares, to be exact. Maybe I was psychic, and now my dreams were coming true. The holidays were going to be ruined because I couldn't get my act together. I felt like the tragic heroine of every made-for-TV holiday film — it was up to me to save Christmas, and I was failing.

"Honey, the gingerbread house looks a mess. Let's try to make it look like this one I saw on Pinterest," I suggested.

My daughter looked crestfallen.

"Why, Mommy? I like my gingerbread house. I think it's pretty like this. You don't like what I did?" she asked.

I didn't know what to say.

"You thought the tree was ugly, too, and I was trying to help you make it nice," she said.

She got up from the kitchen table, wiped her hands, and went into her bedroom to watch her iPad while I cleaned up.

That's when I remembered a story my mom had once told me about her own childhood.

"My mom always had to have everything perfect," she said. "We weren't even allowed to go into our living room when we were kids, and on Christmas we'd be in hot water if we got anywhere close to the tree. My mom wouldn't let anyone touch it."

My mother told me that their Christmas tree was a showpiece that stood proudly in their picture window so all the neighbors could see it. There'd been no festive tree-trimming parties because my grandmother had meticulously decorated every branch herself, usually when the kids were at school.

"She knew we'd mess it up. The ornaments wouldn't be spaced evenly. We'd put too much tinsel in one spot, not enough in another, and probably break a piece she loved. She wanted it to look just so, and you know how children are. Little kids can't make it look perfect," Mom told me.

"That's so sad," I said.

"As kids, we never cared about that stuff anyway. It didn't matter to us what the tree looked like. You know what we cared about?" Mom asked.

"Toys?" I guessed.

Mom smiled and shook her head.

"We were poor, so we didn't get a lot of toys. A doll and a new dress maybe."

"What was it then?" I asked.

"We cared about people. My brothers and sister and I loved visiting my grandparents. We loved having a big dinner with our family. My grandmother made every kind of pie you can imagine, and everyone was happy and talking and hugging. I'll never forget how special it felt. That's why when you were growing up, I never stressed out about the garlands and bows. I focused on being with you kids, having fun, and being relaxed."

Mom was telling the truth, and because I was too busy complaining that our family holidays didn't look like a scene from Currier & Ives, I'd overlooked what had mattered most — the fun we'd had, the memories we made, and the laughter we shared. Our Christmases were a blast. Sure, Mom may have slacked on the decorations, but she gave her all when it came to love and generosity.

Our family had never missed out on togetherness, and neither would my daughter. I knew now how ridiculous I'd been. It was time to relax and prioritize my *presence* with my daughter instead of perfectly wrapped *presents* for her. Kids don't want a tree that's a museum piece. They just like the process of decorating it with people they love.

I owed my little girl an apology for being such a perfectionist, which she happily accepted with a hug. This yuletide wasn't a nightmare after all. It was the real Christmas of my dreams.

That year, our tree may have been a little wonky, and our ginger-bread house a bit slipshod. The snickerdoodles went in the trash. In the end, when I finally let go of my ridiculous expectations and really started having fun, I realized what truly matters during the holiday season: spending time with the people we love most.

— Victoria Fedden —

55

The Bird

*Good manners are just a way of showing other people
that we have respect for them.*
~Bill Kelly

irst there was a knock on my bedroom door. Then my mother's voice called out: "Jean, there's a bird in my bathroom." Before my husband, Doyle, or I had time to respond, Mom appeared like an apparition at the foot of our bed. "Come quickly," she said. "You've got to get it out."

Doyle pretended to be asleep. I peered over the top of the covers that were pulled to my chin. In the semi-darkness I could see my eighty-four-year-old mother's eyes ablaze with conviction. Her short white hair stood on end, spiking off at irregular angles. She wore a light summer nightgown, inside out, backward and slightly askew. I wanted to cry.

Mom lived with us because she had early-stage Alzheimer's disease. We had grown accustomed to her quirks: the searing hot Florida days when she applied layer upon layer of clothing to her frail body, the storing of canned goods and buttered garlic bread under her pillow, the repetitive questions. But a hallucination caught me by surprise. That was enough to send me under the pillow, at once trembling in fear and denial.

"Mom," I said, "birds can't get in the house." This was an eighty-eight-degree September day. We never opened the windows. Our air conditioning hummed twenty-four hours a day.

"Je-e-an." Her hands went to her hips; her chest rose and expanded.

I cleared my throat, hoping that would clear my head. "He won't hurt anything," I said. "We'll get him out in the morning."

"Je-e-an." She was accustomed to being in charge, like the fourth grade teacher she had been for thirty years.

Arguing seemed pointless. A bird was in her bathroom — a windowless, second-floor room with a skylight that did not open, a room entered only through her bedroom — and she wanted that bird out *now*. Her face wore a look that, even with her teeth out, said she was not leaving my room until I followed her out.

I slid out of bed and down the worn oak floors in the hallway, into her darkened bedroom. "There's no bird here," I said.

"In the bathroom." She pointed to the door. "Go look."

I stepped into the bathroom. My eyes struggled to adjust to the bright lights that only illuminated the dreadful floral wallpaper I had regretted choosing the moment the paste dried.

No bird. I checked the shower, behind the toilet, under the sink. "Maybe you had a dream, Mom."

"I know what I saw." She pointed to the skylight. "Right there. A bird was flapping around, trying to get out."

"Well, I guess he made it." I clapped. "Good for him. Can we go to bed now?"

Mom hung her head and wrung her hands. "I know you think I'm crazy," she said. The smartest woman I'd ever known looked bewildered and close to tears.

Guilt over being too flippant weighed on my conscience and pulled my shoulders into a slump. I turned my weary self back into her bedroom and looked up to the heavens for guidance.

From the top of the armoire across her room, a huge black bird looked back. "Whoa!" I screamed.

To my stunned eyes, the bird appeared the size of a giant condor. I threw my arms around Mom, although she showed no sign of needing my protection. She drew in a breath that raised her shoulders all the way to her ears, then sighed relief, like a witch whose burning had been called off when her visions proved to be true.

The grackle, in reality about a foot high, took wing. Black, iridescent plumage glistened in the low light as the bird zigged, then zagged over our heads. Panic glued my feet to the floor, my hands to my mother.

The sounds and smells of fear must have jolted our cat, Ray, from his nap on the first-floor sofa. Little padded feet pounded up the wooden steps, then galloped full speed down the hall and into Mom's room.

Swoop! The bird found the door. Screech! Ray ground to a stop, jumped in the air and reversed course. The bird, the cat, and the panicked daughter flew, raced and bumbled our way out of the room, along the hall and down the stairs. At the bottom, I turned to see Mom gliding behind, head held high.

The terrified bird careened around the kitchen, seeking an escape. I sped to open the back door where I stood like a flight attendant, pointing to the exit, wishing I could whistle to get the bird's attention, failing to see the imminent danger posed by Ray. After all, cats can't fly, I reasoned, as Ray jumped onto the kitchen counter and soared into space. Snap! He caught the bird in his jaws mid-air. Plop! Ray landed. The bird hung in limp clumps of black out of either side of his mouth. Out the door they went.

Doyle arrived in the kitchen. "What is going on?"

"You'll think I'm crazy," I said. Mom and I laughed.

"What's so funny?"

"A bird was in the house," I said.

Doyle rubbed his chin and regarded me with suspicion.

And for one enlightening moment, I imagined how desperate I would feel if my husband didn't believe me, if he second-guessed everything I said or did.

When my children and friends called in the morning, I spun elaborate versions of Mom's triumph. She pressed against me, soaking in every word as I told of her patient effort to make me see. Mom knew she was losing control over her life, giving up her freedom and her home, but she seemed to find comfort in believing that we still listened to her and trusted her judgment.

Rather than a harbinger of death, our black-plumed visitor served to remind me that my primary mission in caring for Mom was not to prevent her dying, but to preserve the dignity of her life.

—Jean Salisbury Campbell—

Life Is for the Living

Mother, the ribbons of your love
are woven around my heart.
~Author Unknown

The first hitch in our travel plans occurred when our luggage did not arrive in Atlanta. My normally calm husband, Ken, shouted at innocent airport personnel. We finally filled out forms and were told we'd be contacted when the luggage arrived. We were scheduled to fly on to Johannesburg, South Africa, the next morning for a long-planned three-week visit with dear friends, and this was no way to begin.

We returned to the hotel after dinner and were dismayed to find no message or luggage. "What are we going to do?" I asked my husband. "We've spent months planning this trip. How in the world can we cancel now?"

Ken put his arm around my shoulders. "We'll be on that plane tomorrow morning. What you're wearing now will work out fine for the next three weeks." Then he laughed.

I used the toiletries the airline had supplied and went to bed imagining two different scenarios: wearing the same clothes for three weeks straight, or going on a big shopping spree upon arrival.

I'd finally drifted off to sleep when the phone woke me. "Mom, it's Kirk. Uncle Paul called a few minutes ago." He hesitated before saying, "Grandma died tonight."

I clenched the phone. My eighty-seven-year-old mother had been in a nursing home for well over a year, body and mind deteriorating rapidly. Dying was a blessed release. I understood that, but why now?

"Did Uncle Paul say what the plans are?" I felt Ken's hand on my shoulder, rubbing gently but sending a clear message of comfort.

"No, nothing's been set. Didn't you talk to him and your other two brothers about this before you left?"

"I did, Kirk. I told them that if we were still in South Africa when it happened, we'd probably not return for the funeral. I said my goodbye last fall when I visited Grandma. At least then, she was aware and knew me, but I realized it was our final visit. But now—I'm just not sure what to do." My hand kept smoothing the comforter on the bed until I broke the silence. "The doctors said three months ago she had only days left."

My son did his best to give me a guilt-free way out. "If there's a funeral right away, I'll go for you. You and Dad should continue with your trip."

"I'll call in the morning with our decision. You phone your sister and tell her." I choked on the final words.

Ken put his arms around me. "We'll do whatever you want."

Suddenly, the man who proclaimed we'd go on with or without our luggage had changed completely. His concern for me took precedence over everything else.

The big question was: What did I want? I wanted to go on this long-planned trip. I wanted to honor my mother at a service for her. I wanted to talk to her. I could barely swallow around the lump in my throat.

I lay down and reviewed a conversation I'd had with Paul only days earlier. I suggested that, if the worst happened, they have a burial immediately and then a memorial service later when we could all be there. My brother hadn't readily agreed, but he didn't veto my idea either. It sounded reasonable to me then, but it suddenly seemed selfish.

But was it? We'd spent a lot of money on airfare, our friends had reservations at places we'd travel to, and they'd arranged visits and activities with others. They'd worked hard on plans. Even so, I wrestled with my conscience in the darkness. Ken's even breathing let me know he was asleep. I lay there for what seemed like hours.

Suddenly, I heard my mother's voice. "Go. Life is for the living." Did I imagine it, or was it real? As if in answer, she repeated it. "Go. Life is for the living." I could not see her in the darkened hotel room, but I felt a warm presence close to the bed. Had she come on the wings of an angel?

The voice and message were clear and strong. This was the mother I'd known for so long, not the very ill woman I'd visited in the nursing home months earlier. I reached out from the side of the bed, but felt nothing. I had only the memory of the few words she'd spoken.

My heart beat faster. I shivered and moved closer to my sleeping husband. I spent the remainder of the night thinking about the vibrant person my mother had been up until the past year. I had no doubt that it was my mother speaking to me and advising me as she had always done when I needed her most.

The sun hadn't made an appearance yet when Ken rolled over and put his arms around me. "What have you decided?"

Before I could answer, the phone rang again. Our luggage had arrived.

I related my nighttime message from Mom, wondering if Ken would think I'd gone around the bend. He never questioned what I told him and agreed with my decision to go on with our trip. Quietly and quickly, we got ready for our overseas flight after he retrieved our luggage.

Before leaving for the airport, I called my brother to tell him my decision. "Do what you have to do," he said. He hadn't censured me, but I knew my mother approved, and that was all I needed.

I called both our children to tell them what we'd decided. Each said they'd hoped that is what we'd do. Karen laughed when I told her about the message. "That sounds just like Grandma," she said.

I boarded the plane with a heavy heart, but I had Ken's love and support plus a wonderful message from Mom to sustain me. Her words gave me the strength I needed during the visit with our friends and their family, all of whom were so kind to me. Whenever I felt sad, I remembered my mother's sage advice: Life is for the living.

Later that spring, I prepared a photo board of Mom's long and full life for her memorial service. Our guests studied the pictures, many commenting on how full of life she'd always been. They listened as I read a tribute I'd written, many nodding their heads at one thing or another. She lived her life to the fullest, and so would I, thanks to her advice.

—Nancy Julien Kopp—

57

Third Time's the Charm

Try, try, and try again. Never stop trying.
~Lailah Gifty Akita

"I can't like it." My toddler made a face and spit her spinach back onto her plate. "I want nuggets."

Exasperated, but bound and determined not to be one of those moms who gave in to her child's picky eating habits, I gathered myself and tried a different approach. I firmly believed that junk food should be for special occasions, not a daily habit.

"Mommy worked hard to make you a nutritious and delicious meal. Please eat it," I begged, almost at my wits' end. This was the fourth time that week I had made dinner, only to have her refuse it.

"No!" she yelled. "I WANT NUGGETS! All my fwiends at school get whatever they want for dinner. I hate you!" She was screaming while tossing her food on the floor. I bowed my head in shame, feeling as if I was failing as a parent.

I took a deep breath and tried to keep my cool. I gave her a stern "don't-mess-with-me" look and said, "Come on, you know the rule."

"Yes, I should try evwething tree times," she replied with a roll of her eyes.

"That's right," I said in my sweetest mom voice. "So two more bites."

When I was a child, my mother refused to make me eat everything on my plate. Her mom had insisted that food never be wasted, and she was convinced that this training was the reason for her being overweight.

My mother had a different approach. She said I had to try every food three times. Her reasoning was this: one time to try it, the second time to get over the fact that you had just tried it, and the third to make sure that you don't like it. After those three attempts, if I still hated the taste, she would never make me eat it again. Her rational and supportive approach worked almost every time — except with liver and bananas (which I still won't eat to this day).

I was raising my daughter with this same — reasonable — rule. A small smile crept onto my face now as I saw her swallow her second bite of spinach and then open her mouth for the third. She slowly chewed her final forced bite, and my thoughts returned to how the "three things rule" had affected my life.

As I grew older, I brought that three-times philosophy into my daily life. I had been terrified of the diving board at the pool, but I had managed to make that first terrifying jump off the board. When I breathed in water, my mother, who was carefully watching me, jumped in to help me. Before she could even reach me, I was up and out of the pool, heading back to that diving board. I barely paused before I jumped off with a flourish the second time. More coughing ensued, but I was steadfast in beating this fear. When I got out of the pool the second time, my mom tried to cover me with a towel and escort me home. Instead, I threw off the towel and finished my mission.

The third time there was no fear and no water in my nose. In fact there were cheers from the others at the pool. At that point, I was hooked. For the next few summers, you couldn't pull me out of the water unless it was to dive into it. I have still never met a pool I didn't want to jump right in.

Every time I am faced with something that is outside my comfort zone, I repeat to myself that I must try everything three times, and it gives me the strength to forge ahead. From public speaking to job interviews, how am I going to know the outcome unless I go for it? Roller coasters, flying, changing careers, dating… all my major fears have somehow been faced by one simple idea that my mom came up with to get me to eat my vegetables. Sure, he may have not been great on the first date, but perhaps the second or third would be better.... This thought process even led to my marriage! My life has been full because my brain repeats this one simple rule: Try everything three times.

"Mommy?" My daughter's voice pulled me out of my memories. "I can like it now," she said as she finished all the spinach on her plate.

We are all afraid of the unknown. But how can we be sure that something won't be enjoyable unless we give it a shot? After all, if I hadn't tried everything three times, you would not be reading this. Instead, I would be stuck at a job that made me miserable, only dreaming of things that I could accomplish. In my mid-thirties, I left a successful job that did not fulfill me in order to pursue my dream of being a writer. After two rejections, I took a deep breath and tried for a third time, all while picturing that diving board. I have been happily living the life of a writer ever since.

And my daughter the picky eater? She's now a sixteen-year-old vegetarian. Spinach is one of her favorites, although she also still likes nuggets if they are soy — but only on special occasions.

—Jodi Renee Thomas—

58

The Question

If you are really thankful, what do you do? You share.
~W. Clement Stone

I stood in my tiny apartment kitchen, drinking my coffee and staring at the words I had written on a chalkboard: "My beautiful loving thoughts create my beautiful loving world."

I did this each morning, hoping this quote would help me find my own happiness. My life was stagnant. I was twenty-five and living alone with two cats. I had been mostly single for six years and was working as an underpaid reporter for a local newspaper.

I wondered if I was miserable because I was single. I had watched all three of my sisters and many friends from high school get married, have children, and buy their first homes. I wanted to find a man to marry, so I could "start" my life, too.

I had created a bitter, lonely world for myself — the opposite of the chalkboard quote. One day, I was complaining to my mom about all the things wrong in my life. She was wiping down the kitchen counters when she stopped and looked at me.

"What if you only had today what you thanked God for yesterday?" she asked.

I blinked back the tears her simple question immediately caused. I couldn't reply. I realized that even though I wasn't happy with some aspects of my life, there were many things I wouldn't want to give up. I hadn't taken the time to be grateful for them.

In John Eldredge's book, *Walking with God*, he wrote about keeping a prayer journal as a way to talk with God and organize his prayers. I decided this would be a good way to organize what I was grateful for, so I bought an eighty-nine cent journal on the way home that day.

I began each day by writing down five things I was grateful for in my life. It started out as simple things: my morning cup of coffee, sleeping in on the weekends, and having holidays off from work. After a couple of weeks it became more specific: the first signs of autumn, homegrown pattypan squash, and hearing the birds sing in the morning.

After a month I started being grateful for everything, including: the people in my life, playing games after dinner with my grandparents, my coworker Karen giving me a souvenir from her vacation, and my teenage niece Madison going to a movie with me on a school night. If I ever struggled with something to be grateful for, I would ask myself my mom's question.

I started feeling joy again, despite my life situation still being the same. Small things I didn't normally notice caught my attention. The air was light, the breeze was refreshing, and my coworkers' jokes were funny.

Feeling joy caused me to pursue my passions again. I started reading and writing for pleasure as opposed to writing for the newspaper. I joined a writers' group and met once a month with other writers and published authors to exchange ideas, receive tips, read each other's work, and offer advice on techniques and style.

I started walking every night after dinner instead of watching TV, and I also joined a Zumba class. I lost weight and now I'm becoming more confident about my physical appearance.

I experienced the most change when I got involved with a fundraising and community involvement program. I would never have done this before. I named the program Smart Cents, after my last name, and used it to raise money for local ministries and to volunteer for community projects. My first fundraiser was for a nonprofit café that fed people who could not afford a meal. My goal was to raise $1,000 in one month, which a few naysayers called too ambitious. In one month, I raised $2,525. Delivering the money to the café and having photos taken of them holding their big check was the most rewarding day of my life. I finally believed I had real purpose and was not put on earth to serve only myself.

My long time friend Aarika called me after reading an article about Smart Cents. "You're such an inspiration. The world needs more Haylie Smarts." Her words touched me deeply. I finally believed I had started my adult life.

With my newfound purpose, I decided to become a teacher in Oklahoma. Teaching had been my first major in college, but I had given it up when I couldn't pass college algebra. I heard about an alternative pathway to certification and worked through the process to become an English teacher.

I can't wait to teach my students the power of gratitude through the same exercise I still use on myself. I want to inspire my students the way I was inspired.

It's amazing how much my life has changed since I started being grateful for all the things I never want to live without. It didn't take a husband, a new house, or a new job to start my life. It took an eighty-nine cent notebook and the question, "What if you only had today what you thanked God for yesterday?"

— Haylie Smart —

59

Listen to Your Mother

The person who is waiting for something to turn up
might start with their shirt sleeves.
~Garth Henrichs

My grandmother always said, "Can't never could until he tried." My mother took up the mantra and recited it to me many times during my childhood. She normally used it to try and coerce me into doing something I didn't want to do. It was like waving a red flag in front of a bull. Irritating as it was, it took root.

Many years ago, my husband was downsized out of his job, leaving us with a single income — mine. We were a two-income family with two-income bills and two children to support. He had been given a generous severance, but that money would only last so long. Just when it looked like things couldn't get any worse, they did. I lost my job too.

While my husband was out pounding the pavement, knocking on doors, making calls, and scanning the papers for another job, I stayed home and did my best to figure out how to make the most of every cent. It was often difficult to maintain a hopeful, positive attitude, but we did our best.

One day I took some milk from the refrigerator and noticed that it was lukewarm. We could not afford to call a repairman, so we just turned the refrigerator up as high as it would go and prayed for the best.

Anxious about our situation, I tried to think of something that I could do to earn some money. Even a little would help. Maybe we could at least get the refrigerator repaired. But what could I do? I, too, began searching the want ads, applying for anything for which I was even remotely qualified.

One day I had lunch with a former coworker who insisted that I would be great at teaching computer classes. I had used word processing software extensively at my former job and was definitely an expert, but could I sell that skill? Was it possible that people would actually pay me to teach them? The only teaching I had ever done was in Sunday School. I remembered my mother's mantra — "Can't never could until he tried."

I wasn't sure where to start. Finally formulating a plan, the first thing I did was check on the availability and the cost of a meeting room. After securing a room, I went down to the Chamber of Commerce and got a list of local business addresses. I typed the addresses into my home computer and printed them on labels. I then designed a brochure that could be mailed, advertising my class. I sat on the den floor, folded my brochures and stuck address labels and stamps on them. The next day I sat in my car and prayed outside the post office, then went in and mailed the brochures. We could not really afford to spend the money that all this had cost.

I was filled with self-doubt as I waited for responses. I had absolutely no experience in running a business, even a small endeavor like this one. I had no training experience. I just had a need and I remembered my mother's words, "Can't never could until he tried." Well, "Can't" was trying.

Every day, I waited eagerly for the mail. On the third day, I got my first response. I ran inside to show my husband. "Why haven't you opened it?" he asked. I carefully opened the envelope to find a check and two registrations. I couldn't believe it! I needed ten people to break even on my expenses. Over the next two weeks I got more checks and registrations in the mail. On the day of my first class, I had seventeen students.

I had rented computers, but could not afford for them to be delivered and set up. "Don't worry, honey," my husband said, hugging me. "You've got me. I'll help you out. We can do it." On the day of my class, he and I left early and picked up the computers. It took two trips to get them all to the classroom. We spent the next hour unloading, setting them up and installing the software. Then my husband left and there I stood, alone, waiting for my first student to arrive.

Over the next fifteen minutes, I made two trips to the bathroom, checked my hair and make-up three times, and had a small panic attack. What the heck did I think I was doing? These people were going to want their money back!

The first people walked in. I smiled, introduced myself, and checked them off my attendee list. One by one, my students wandered in and took their seats. I did my best to pretend I was busy getting set up, turning to smile nervously at the class a few times. Once everyone was present, I passed out the course sheets and began. Within minutes I was relaxed, guiding them through, answering all their questions. The hours passed quickly.

When my husband came to help me break down the computers, I ran to him excitedly. "They loved the class! They asked if I was doing others so that their co-workers could attend."

"Great!" he said, a little dazed. I'm not sure that he thought I would succeed, but he had remained supportive.

Over the next months, I did several more classes. I discovered metered mail, set up a business phone line, and got a business license. I made enough money to cover my expenses and have a little left over each time. I wasn't going to get rich, but I was helping keep us afloat, and that felt wonderful!

I will never forget the day that our new refrigerator was delivered. It was much larger than our old one. I paid for it with my training money. I could not have been more proud if I had been paying for a new car. Well, okay, that would have been a pretty big deal. Nevertheless, I had a tremendous satisfaction that I had tried and succeeded!

Eventually both my husband and I found full-time employment. My new boss told me that the two things that made my résumé stand out were my training experience and the fact that I had run my own business, indicating that I could handle projects and work self-directed. I have been with that company for sixteen years.

Whenever I am handed a seemingly overwhelming project or I have to work with something new, I still hear my mother's voice, "Can't never could until he tried." Thanks Mom!

—Debbie Acklin—

Chapter 7

In-laws and Outlaws!

My First Hanukkah

With all other foods, there's a right way and a wrong
way. With brisket, there's only "my way."
~Psychotherapist and top brisket maker Phyllis Cohen

Michael and I dated for six years before we married, so I had been to Hanukkah celebrations at his parents' house. I'd seen the beautiful table settings, the traditional linens, the special platters and the beautiful family menorah. The celebrations were wonderful events and I appreciated being a part of them. I was from a family of English and Irish origin, raised a non-denominational Christian, and in my family Christmas and St. Patrick's Day were the big celebrations. It was fun to learn about other traditions.

One month after Michael and I were married, I decided to take on the task of hosting the first night of the eight-night celebration at our house. Just like my mother-in-law, Barbara, I love entertaining. Hosting parties of any kind is right up my alley and I relished the thought of planning and hosting this new kind of party.

I enjoyed all the planning. There were decorations, little gifts to give my new family, candles, dreidels, chocolate coins and the food, including the star of the show... the brisket! We all loved Barbara's brisket and now it was my turn to make one. I was a good cook so I wasn't worried.

Next came the shopping. I made my list and, to borrow from a Christmas song, checked it twice, and decided I had all the fun stuff.

Now it was time to hit the market. Potatoes, lots of oil in which to fry the latkes, carrots, onions, horseradish, wine, applesauce and donuts. One more thing on the list... the brisket. With my shopping cart almost overflowing (our family never goes hungry), I headed to the meat aisle. I really wanted to impress my new family, so I picked out the biggest brisket I saw. It was funny how Barbara had never mentioned to me that brisket comes in a sealed bag and already has its own spices in with it. I called Michael to make sure I was getting the right thing, and he assured me there is only one type of brisket. Great. I threw it in the cart and headed for home.

The next morning, the first thing I did was put the brisket in. It needed to slow cook all day to be really tender and juicy. The spices that came with it smelled familiar, but I couldn't quite place them. No matter — I had this under control.

I busied myself for the rest of the day decorating, setting the table, wrapping the presents, placing the menorah, and even printing myself a phonetic reading of the Hanukkah prayer so I could say it with my new family as we lit the first candle. The brisket smelled delicious as it slow-cooked its way through the day. It was making me hungry. I hoped it was as good as Barbara's.

As I was frying the last of the latkes, the family arrived, ready to eat. Everyone commented on how beautiful everything looked. The table was set all in blue, white and silver, the traditional colors of Hanukkah. I even made a Hanukkah bush out of branches that I spray-painted silver, put into a vase and wrapped with blue and white twinkle lights. "It looks perfect," my mother-in-law said. Ah. I could relax. Everyone sat down at the table and I began to bring the food in, reserving a space in the center of the table for the brisket. Everyone was oohing and aahing at the dishes as I brought them in. It got a little quieter as I set the brisket down. I thought that everyone's mouth must have been watering too much to mention the brisket.

I sat, we said a prayer, made a toast and began passing the food. Everyone took a lot of everything. With the very first taste of my brisket, I recognized the flavor. This was not traditional Hanukkah brisket at all. It was a corned beef brisket like my family ate on St. Patrick's Day!

Everyone was watching and they all saw me realize what I had done, my English-Irish heritage trumping all my plans for a traditional Jewish brisket! There was complete silence. My face was turning red. Just then Barbara declared that this was the best brisket she'd ever had... even though it was corned beef. And, as with almost all of our family gatherings, we all started laughing hysterically.

The next year, when I was brave enough to host Hanukkah again, someone mysteriously put a little leprechaun at my place setting. I think it's safe to say that my first Hanukkah was anything but forgettable.

— Crescent LoMonaco —

Backseat Driver

When your mother asks, "Do you want a piece of advice?"
it is a mere formality. It doesn't matter if you answer
yes or no. You're going to get it anyway.
~Erma Bombeck

She couldn't drive. Well, maybe that's being unfair. In reality, she never tried to drive. She was too afraid. She never even sat in the driver's seat of a car. She was always the passenger in the front seat.

But not knowing how to drive did not stop her. She was full of advice for the driver.

She was my mother-in-law. She was old school, from the old country, and she didn't trust anything much. That included cars — and me. She understood that cars were a necessary part of living in California if people wanted to go somewhere and didn't want to be stuck in their houses. But she didn't like them.

One time, she was invited to her friend's birthday luncheon. Her friend lived over an hour away, and my mother-in-law was really torn about going because it involved traveling. In a car. In the end, her desire to go to the party won out over her fear of getting there. Everyone else in the family was busy, so guess who was "volunteered" into taking her?

The day of the party came. I told her I would pick her up at 11:00 a.m. to get her to the party by 12:30 p.m. As I pulled into her driveway at 11:00, I noticed that she was already out on the front lawn pacing back and forth—hat on her head, purse over her arm and purpose to her movements.

"Where have you been? You're late. The party starts at 12:30, and I just know we'll be late."

"Don't worry. We have plenty of time to get there. Please, just get in."

Before she could get in, she had to check the tires. Check them for what, I don't know. To be sure there were four of them? That they were round? She wouldn't know if anything was wrong unless the tires were completely flat and the treads were gone. She circled the car, leaning down at each tire to assure herself that all was well. I guess they passed the test because she got in the car.

She buckled her seat belt and then unbuckled it. She buckled it again and asked if I had filled up the car with gas. Yes. Had I checked the oil? Yes, it had been checked. Does the horn work for emergencies? Honk, honk! Did I know where we were going? Yes. Did we have to go on the freeway? Yes. Finally, she announced that she was ready.

I looked over my shoulder as I backed out of the driveway. She looked over her shoulder, too. After she gave me the all clear, she told me to turn the wheel to the right and drive down the street. She told me to be sure to stop at the stop sign. She then directed me to turn right at the corner and to make another right at the next corner. Wouldn't it have been easier to go in the other direction instead of going around the block? Oh, I forgot… She didn't like left turns!

As we entered the freeway on-ramp, the fun really began. Now, in all fairness, I must admit that I like to drive fast—not faster than is safe, but I don't drive in the slow lane either. And maybe, just maybe, having my mother-in-law in the car made me drive even a little faster just to annoy her. After entering the freeway, I put on my blinker to change lanes, and you would have thought my mother-in-law was watching a tennis match. Her head moved from side to side, back and forth, checking the traffic in the next lane over, both behind and in front of me. Then she gave me the all-clear message. Thank goodness she was alert and guiding me. How would I have known when it was safe to change lanes without her help?

The traffic slowed, and I braked. So did she. Although she had no brake pedal on her side, she stomped her foot down hard on the floorboard as if applying the brake. How helpful. She clutched her purse and held it tightly to her chest. I'm not sure what that was supposed to do, but I guess if she were ejected from the car, she would have her purse with her ID in it when they recovered her body from the ditch she was sure to be found in.

And then there were the noises she made. There was the sharp intake of breath at every bend in the road, the little grunts and gasps and whistles as we passed another car or another car passed us, and the shrill *Eeeeeek!* as we came close to and passed any semi-trucks. She didn't like semis and never wanted me to pass them. I had to explain that it was the law to keep up with the traffic, and I couldn't just stay slower than a semi. But she didn't want me to stay behind a semi either — that just wasn't safe. She knew that the semi would suddenly switch into reverse, crash and roll over us, and we would be dead. That was a given. Semis were murderous machines.

I am happy to report that we did make it to her friend's birthday luncheon — and on time. (And back home, too.) We were not hurt, did not crash, and were not dead. I am positive that the only reason we made it there and back safely was because of her assistance. I never could have driven there without it.

— Barbara LoMonaco —

Kiss the Cook

Trapped by reality, freed by imagination.
~Nicolas Manetta

"**H**ow are we ever going to buy Christmas gifts this year?" I asked, with tears in my eyes.

Mark, my husband of ten years, cupped my face in his hands and silently mouthed the words, "We're not."

It was our first Christmas back in the States after spending six years in Italy where our older son was born. We returned just in time for our second son to be born in Walnut Creek, California. Afterward, our little family settled in Brentwood and rented from my parents. We lived on a pauper's income that year — $900 a month, which had to cover rent, health insurance, food, gas, and utilities.

I planted zucchini in the back yard. After three months, we had what we called "zucchini world": zucchini bread, zucchini soup, and zucchini pasta for three "square" meals a day. Mark rode his bike to work, and I homeschooled our older son, Jeremy, so we only needed to use the car for shopping and going to church.

It would be a slim Christmas, and I was overwhelmed with things to do. Mark's family celebrated Christmas in a big way. There were so many gifts under the tree that they spilled out into the entryway and dining room. My family was more modest with gift-giving; it wasn't a priority.

After ten years of marriage, I had come to dislike Christmas because it was always the same story. "What are we going to buy your family for Christmas?" I'd ask. It was stressful to worry about stretching our budget to accommodate their kind of Christmas.

That night, after I got the boys to bed, I went through all my cross-stitch materials and found the perfect pattern. There were two hearts, one on each side, with the words "Kiss the Cook" in the middle. It could be framed in an embroidery hoop with a ruffle made from material or lace. I would need to make ten hoops in all. It was already the middle of October, so I had a little over two months to complete the task. Thankfully, I had enough fabric in my stash to match the colors in everyone's kitchen. And, of course, I'd make zucchini bread to go along with it.

The only time I had to work on the gifts was after the boys went to bed. I made sure everything was done during the day, including lesson plans for Jeremy, dishes washed, and laundry folded and put away. If I worked a few hours every night, I'd have them finished by Christmas Eve.

What I hadn't planned on was both boys getting sick with earaches and strep throat, which meant doctor visits and medicine. When one got better, the other one got worse. It was a vicious cycle. At 3:00 one Saturday morning in late November, I realized that the "Kiss the Cook" project might have to be abandoned, and zucchini bread might have to suffice. I knew my family wouldn't mind, but Mark's family was a different story. I simply couldn't arrive empty-handed on Christmas Eve for the big Italian tradition of eating dinner, opening gifts, and attending Mass.

I persevered, even though I barely slept during the last week leading up to Christmas. On the eve of Christmas Eve, I stayed up all night finishing up the ruffles that adorned each hoop, wrapped them in boxes, and added zucchini bread in red and green bags.

As Mark loaded up the "sleigh" with the kids and gifts, I made sure that I had extra zucchini bread — with the recipe written on the front — just in case I had forgotten someone. The drive across the Bay Bridge to Mark's childhood home in San Mateo was bumper-to-bumper. But all was forgotten when we pulled into the driveway and smelled the makings of a Pombo Family Christmas. It was all fish, of course, starting with shrimp cocktail, oysters on the half-shell, crab cioppino soup, crab and prawns. Mark's mom made sure she put in her order at Petrini's Italian Market months in advance to ensure everything was the very best.

When I saw all the gifts under the tree and spilling into the entryway, I started to panic. What if my best wasn't good enough? Maybe we could leave right after dinner and spare the disappointment on everyone's faces.

Too late.

After dinner, we all gathered in the living room, and the gift-giving began in a time-honored tradition: reading out the name (to and from) and waiting until that person opened the gift and said "thank you" before going on to the next person. It went on for hours. Since I placed our gifts near the wall, away from the tree, maybe ours would be overlooked.

No such luck.

"To Mom and Dad — Love Connie, Mark and Boys!" Dad Pombo read aloud from the gift tag. Mom Pombo smiled warmly and asked, "What have we here?"

I glanced over at Mark, with my heart racing, and gave him a weak smile as all eyes were on Mom Pombo.

I wrapped Mom and Dad's gift in the nicest paper I could find with a handmade card. It was the boys' handprints sprinkled with red and green glitter. And I made Mom's hoop in blue — to match her kitchen colors. I grabbed Mark's hand and squeezed tightly as Mom opened the box and peeled away the tissue paper. Mom clutched her hand over her heart, with tears filling her eyes, as she held up "Kiss the Cook."

"You made this?" she asked tentatively.

I nodded my head and felt a sense of relief wash over me. Mom Pombo got up from her chair, walked across the living room, and kissed me on the cheek. "I know exactly where I'm going to put this," she said, as her face filled with a bright smile. When she got back to her chair, she carefully put "Kiss the Cook" back in the box — as if it was a piece of fine china. My heart swelled as I wiped away tears.

I hardly noticed the stack of cashmere sweaters, pearls, and glass figurines next to her.

Years after that first Christmas back in the States — even after we moved to Pennsylvania — I enjoyed coming back to Mom Pombo's kitchen and seeing "Kiss the Cook" over the stove where she attached blue ribbons with a gold fork and spoon on either side. It was the only decoration in her kitchen, and it stayed there for three more decades until we kissed the "cook" goodbye.

— Connie K. Pombo —

63

Bad Tidings to You

*I once bought my kids a set of batteries for Christmas
with a note on it saying, toys not included.*
~Bernard Manning

Many years ago, when I was engaged to Eleanor's son, Eleanor said something that I considered very odd. "Don't worry, honey," she said out of the blue. "I don't play games."

I had no idea what she was talking about. Parcheesi? Bridge?

"Head games," Eleanor clarified, seeing my confusion.

That didn't clear it up for me. I come from a family that could easily be called honest to a fault. Head games? I was perplexed and a little uneasy.

Turns out that Eleanor's family — and it is most definitely Eleanor's family — does indeed play head games. And what's more, the object of the game is to do whatever The Head dictates at all times or suffer the punishments. This great reigning toad of a woman can wield anything from a cold shoulder to a rude e-mail, but my favorite without a doubt is what I call "Punishment by Christmas Present."

It started after I had been married to Eleanor's son for a couple of years, when Eleanor's other son married Natalie. Eleanor didn't like the new bride, so everyone in the family dutifully shunned her. Everyone but me. I'd never met Natalie. How could I know if I liked her or not?

This did not sit well with Eleanor. On Christmas morning, she fixed me with her shrewish eyes as I opened my gift. It was… a cloth thing of some sort. I was twenty-seven years old and a size four, and it looked like a billowing tent made from yards and yards of gray fleece. It easily could have housed a family of three and some small pets. At the top was something that looked like a three-foot-tall, knitted chimney in candy cane stripes. That turned out to be a turtleneck. It rolled down and down until it looked just like a cross between a striped goiter warmer and a neck brace. Eleanor's gift was a muumuu that practically mooed.

Did her eyes twinkle, or did I only imagine it?

And then, the proverbial fly on the poop: "I thought it looked just like you!" she grinned. The horror!

As bad as my Punishment Gifts were, they were nothing compared to Natalie's. Every year, Eleanor sent each of her sons' families the ceramic pieces to a Christmas village. One year, Natalie's birthday gift was the five-dollar garbage cans that went with the set. Natalie cried.

Eleanor is not simply a bad gift-giver. She never buys bad gifts for herself or her daughter, but only for those who refuse to agree with her or stroke her ever-wounded ego. If Eleanor is pleased, the gifts are downright lavish. Whenever anyone does something that she considers a slight, they can count on getting the Punishment Gift at the next holiday. Or worse, their children will get bad gifts. If Eleanor is really angry, the gifts will be about three days late.

Ironically, Natalie and I became friends because of the way Eleanor divided her family. As a result, my gifts got worse… or better, depending on how one looks at it, since I've grown to enjoy the surprises.

One year, I couldn't figure out what the gift actually was. It was a small plastic square with a snow scene on it. Cap to something? Coaster? Tiny wall hanging of some sort? I had fun secretly polling friends. No one else knew, either. And I was somewhat proud of the way I got around the topic in my thank you note. Since I lived in a temperate climate at the time, I told Eleanor that her gift reminded me of the years I had spent in the cold.

Natalie took a different tack. "I will certainly think of you every time I see these!" she exclaimed of the garbage cans.

We figure Natalie will never get another gift from Eleanor again. She is not heartbroken.

— T. Powell Pryce —

64

Mom's Sneaky Tree

Blessed is the season which engages the
whole world in a conspiracy of love.
~Hamilton Wright Mabie

Both my parents grew up Jewish, but by the time I was about ten, I could already tell that only my dad's side of the family actively practiced. My parents were divorced, and I lived with my mom, but for Jewish holidays I went to services with my dad and his mother, whom I called "Bubbie."

Bubbie was the perfect grandmother. She knitted blankets and sweaters. She told stories and sang lullabies. She taught us to play double solitaire and *Rummikub*, and she could get the right answers before every contestant on every game show. She cooked beef brisket (I was never allowed to reveal that her secret ingredient was orange juice), and made applesauce with the apples and plums from the trees in her back yard.

Bubbie was a founding member of her synagogue. She kept kosher at home and observed the Sabbath. She spoke Yiddish and said her Hebrew the old way: *Shabbes* instead of *Shabbat*.

My mother was never observant or religious, but she liked strings of lights. She liked trees. She liked, for a few weeks every winter, having a tree adorned with strings of lights in the living room.

It wasn't a Hanukkah bush; it was an unapologetic Christmas tree. It had lights, tinsel, and shiny glass balls, along with the rough glitter-and-glue ornaments I'd made in preschool arts and crafts.

One winter, after a nice Hanukkah weekend at Bubbie's house, when Dad got ready to drive me home, he invited Bubbie to come along for the ride. To my surprise, Bubbie said, "Yes."

Playing it casual, Dad said, "Why don't you call your mom and let her know we're all leaving soon?"

Bubbie's phones were all the big, heavy black rotary phones. I loved the weight of them, even though I sometimes lost my place in a phone number while I was dialing because the higher numbers took so long.

Mom answered.

"Hi, Mom. We're heading home, and Bubbie's coming with us. What do we do?"

Mom didn't answer to her former mother-in-law, but she still liked her and respected her. She knew that any fallout from having a Christmas tree in the house would land squarely on me, the unfortunate victim of her heretical parenting.

"Don't worry," Mom said. "I'll take care of it."

I didn't know what "taking care of it" looked like, and I didn't know how to make myself not worry. Mom sounded casual, and Dad was playing it casual, so I tried to be casual, too. It was twilight when we set out, and though we mostly took the big highways, we could see the lights outlining the windows and roofs of the houses we passed.

"I like the twinkly lights. They're like fireflies," I said, testing Bubbie's reaction. She told me about the fireflies she used to see at the lake when she was my age. She didn't say anything about liking, or being tolerant of, Christmas lights, and even at such a young age, I knew better than to press or she might get suspicious.

Traffic was light, and in about thirty minutes we were pulling into the parking lot at my mom's apartment building. I took a long time getting my backpack out of the trunk, double-checking as if something might have spilled out between the teeth of the closed zipper.

Dad finally cleared his throat, and I had to act as if I'd found whatever it was and put it back. I straightened, smiling weakly. Bubbie was going to see the tree and have a fit. She would say that it was bad for my Jewish upbringing, and maybe even that my mom shouldn't be the parent to raise me. Worry lumped up in my stomach and made my feet as heavy as lead.

"Come on. Your grandmother's standing out here in the cold," Dad called, and I followed, trudging up the steps and leading the way inside.

Mom opened the door, gave me a hug, and stepped aside to invite Dad and Bubbie in. I looked around the living room.

The tree — the big, brushing-the-ceiling, light-strewn and tinsel-dripped tree — was gone, without even a shred of silver strands or a speck of glitter to show that it had ever been there.

Dad and Bubbie stayed long enough to each use the bathroom before their return drive, and to listen to me play a couple of songs on the piano. They gave me warm hugs when they left and said, "Happy Hanukkah." They said they'd see me in two weeks, but that I should call Bubbie in between. I said I would.

When the door closed behind them, their footsteps padded out of earshot, and the car finally pulled away, Mom and I looked at each other.

"But… the tree!" I said. "How did you make an entire tree disappear in half an hour?"

She winked at me and led me out the sliding-glass doors to the apartment's balcony. There, sitting dark and clandestine like a thief in the shadows, was the tree. She flipped a switch, and the lights came on, twinkling in slow patterns and shining brilliant colors on the glass ornaments.

"You moved it out here all by yourself?" I asked her. Trees were heavy, and my mom was not very tall.

"Sure," she said. "It wasn't that hard. If Bubbie wants to visit again, just let me know, and I'll move the tree again. I know it would upset her to know that we had one, and the whole point of having the tree is that it makes people happy."

"It wouldn't have made Bubbie happy," I agreed. "I'm glad you moved it. But since she's gone now, can we move it back? It's really cold out here."

— Gabrielle Harbowy —

65

Outspoken and Outright Outrageous

The day two girls or women can genuinely be
friends to each other, we will see then no war,
camouflaged or open, between the wife
and her mother-in-law in any house.
~Anuj Somany

They could make an entire TV show with my mother-in-law, Agnes, as the main character. She was born in South Fork, Alabama, graduated at the top of her class of twelve, and has truly made her mark on this world.

She wasn't sure I should marry her son. In fact, I'll say it like it was. I wasn't her first choice. I wasn't even in the running! Yet, Marty and I did marry, and we made our home on the opposite side of the United States.

Marty was quite content with living in California, keeping his mom at a distance. I, on the other hand, wanted our future children to have two sets of grandparents who were involved in their lives.

Before we got married, I tried to look past his mom taking my seat at our rehearsal dinner. I even pretended not to hear her when she said, "I just don't understand why God is takin' Marty away from me and givin' him to you" — right as we left for our honeymoon! I fought the temptation to get mad. Instead, I thought about the wonderful man she had mothered and wanted somehow to reach her heart.

At first, we began with weekly phone calls. They were expensive back then, but I believed it was money well spent. Week after week, we called "home," with Marty and I each on a line. Eventually, we invited her out for a visit, paying for her plane ticket. Sometime within that first year, I won her over. She was now proud to have me as a daughter-in-law. But this did not change the fact that Agnes was outspoken — and at times outright outrageous.

Years went by, and we learned to live with the unexpected from her. But my husband and I, and eventually our three children, were smothered in love. We made it a policy to laugh our way through the shock over the crazy things she would say and do.

I'll never forget the cold December day when Agnes and I took my three kids, ages six and under, to the mall to see Santa. We were there for several hours, window-shopping, picking up a few presents, and eating lunch. Then the kids sat on Santa's lap, whispering in his ear exactly what they wanted for Christmas. By the time we were finally ready to leave, I'm sure we'd have worn out even the best of shoppers.

Just as we got in the van with the three tired kids, a downpour hit — and the whining began. The kids had been angels all day. Not a single reminder to behave while at the mall, even after they had seen Santa and given him their Christmas list.

"Jason," I said now, "quit kicking the back of Jenna's seat, please."

And then, "Jenna, quit screaming! Now the baby is crying."

And again, "Jason, I've asked you more than once! Stop it!"

I could barely think as the noise and commotion took over the van. It seemed the more I asked the kids to sit quietly, the louder they got. Even the rain now pelting the windows didn't drown out their dissatisfaction.

Finally, I'd had it. "If you guys don't stop when I count to three, I'm going to stop the van and come back there! Okay, one, two, three!"

But they still totally ignored me!

Furious, I turned down a side street and parked the car. In the pouring rain, I got out of the van and walked around the front. When I got to the passenger's window, I saw my mother-in-law sitting there perplexed.

Our eyes met. And just as I reached to open the slider door, my mother-in-law made the move — locking me out of my own van!

Total hysteria broke out in the van. Crying and complaining suddenly turned into laughter and cheers for Grandma. I, on the other hand, stood in the rain staring at Agnes. With her head bowed in prayer-like fashion, she was actually shaking from laughter!

The longer I stood there in the pouring rain, the wetter I became. Without any sign of laughter or thinking this was funny, I walked back around the van and stood at my door. With the kids finally voting to let me in, Agnes unlocked it.

The kids were silent as I crawled into the van. Water was still dripping off my hair when I drove into the garage. Then I got out of the van, leaving everyone still strapped in, and walked inside.

There, my husband met me in the hall.

"Wow! What happened to you?"

Gritting my teeth, I growled, "Your mother!"

Yeah, his mother! But then I began to think about her.

She was the one who flew in to help me when my children were hospitalized, prayed for my family daily, called me with recipes and made me laugh more than most. She had truly become my friend. And today she had purposely tried to take the heat off the moment, not letting anything ruin an otherwise great day by, yes, again doing the outrageous.

I shouldn't have expected less. Thanks, Agnes!

— Janet Lynn Mitchell —

66

The Tide-Turning Whisper

Forgiveness is the fragrance that the violet sheds
on the heel that has crushed it.
~Mark Twain

From day one, I made my ill feelings toward my mother-in-law crystal clear to my new husband. "Joe, why does the photographer keep inviting your mother into every photo?"

"What? He's not."

"Sure he is. All I keep hearing is, Mrs. Beck, we need you for a photo."

"Annie, he's talking to you. YOU are the Mrs. Beck he wants in the photos."

"Oh," I said, a bit chagrined. I was so certain that the photographer had her in mind as the star of the day instead of me, the bride. And thus it started. My silent declaration of war against my mother-in-law.

Oh Mary Beck was pleasant enough, but she had ulterior motives. I'd been observing her and Joe's relationship for three years. Her slightest whim, once stated, became Joe's main mission. Whatever we had planned always took a back seat to Mary's wants and needs. Or so it seemed to me.

She also incessantly dropped little innuendoes about "her Joe" and always within earshot of me. She knew it got on my nerves. Well, we were married now. Clearly Joe belonged to me and I had the paperwork to prove it.

After our wedding in January of 1984, Joe flew back to Centerville Beach Naval Facility in California. I was not expected to join him until June, after which we would be mother-in-law-free for two whole years. Yay!

About mid-February, Mary invited me to lunch. She wanted to share some wedding photos. Ha! Did she expect me to sit there and act interested in photos she took of "her Joe"? Forget it.

I could have called her to say "no thank you" with a suitable excuse. Instead, I had the audacity to write a letter and explain that I simply wasn't a social person, which shouldn't upset her. In other words, "don't expect to see too much of me, lady."

In June, Joe came home to Philadelphia to collect me and say goodbye to his family. Then we would be off to California. When the day came to say goodbye to his mom, I declined the opportunity. After all, she wasn't my mother. Joe could just go over and say goodbye himself. And so he did, without ever being cross or asking why.

Paradise waited on the other side of the map, where Joe would be mine — all mine. Once settled, Joe called his mom once a week and every time I discretely made my way to the front door and slipped out for a nice long walk.

Two years went by, and before long, we were packing to go home. My sulking started right at the Pennsylvania border. I'd just spent two years avoiding all contact with Mary Beck and now I'd have to face her again.

Joe's mom lived in the city, and as soon as we arrived home, I insisted we get an apartment in the suburbs. When holidays came along, I dutifully purchased a gift and handed it over with a forced smile. Of course I never missed an opportunity to grumble a snarky remark or two, especially if she invited us to come for dinner or worse, suggest that we all go to the movies or a show.

As the months passed and I made no attempt to improve my attitude toward Mary Beck, my relationship with Joe spiraled downward. I repeatedly made mountains out of molehills where she was concerned. Though Joe said nothing about that issue, we grumbled at each other about everything else. As time went on, Joe and I stopped communicating all together and he began sleeping on the couch. That went on for months.

One Saturday I decided I'd had it with him too. I wanted him and everything he owned out the door and out of my life. I was tired of him lying on the couch and ignoring me, and saw no way out other than to split. I told him to pack his things and leave. He changed position on the couch and ignored me some more.

I'll fix him, I thought. So I called his mother and told her flat out that I was through with her son and she'd better get his brothers over to our apartment to collect him and his belongings. She didn't agree to it. She just asked me to give the phone to Joe. When he hung up he said his mother wanted to see us right away.

"Good," I snapped back. "Let's go over and get this move organized. The sooner you're gone the happier I'll be."

Mary opened the door and let us in. Joe headed toward the couch, but before he had a chance to flop down, Mary barked at him in a tone I'd never heard before.

"Oh no, mister, you get right back over here. I want to talk to you."

Joe sheepishly turned and stood beside me.

"Joe, I don't care one bit what this is about. I'm telling you right now, Annie is right and you are wrong. She is the woman who is going to take care of you for the rest of your life. You'll never find anyone who loves you more. Now, listen to me — stop being an idiot and make up."

Then she hugged me and whispered in my ear, "Annie, I learned a long time ago a man will never treat his wife any better than he treats his mother. That's a good thing to remember. Joe will behave himself now he knows I mean business."

And there you have it — the tide-turning, life-changing moment.

Snippets of my past outrageous behavior flashed in my mind as I looked at Joe and saw him smile, and I started to cry.

After years of pushing nothing but snide remarks and selfish behavior in Mary's face, she instantly forgave every transgression and stood up for me. Never was a person less deserving of forgiveness or more grateful for it than I.

Unfortunately we only had about fifteen years to share before Mary passed away, but she and I made the most of it. She loved me as strong and true as any mother could love a daughter, and I returned that love with the same sincerity.

At the very end as Joe and I were at her bedside, I held her hand as she tried to sing something in a whisper, but I couldn't make it out.

Later that evening I asked Joe if he knew what she was trying to sing.

"She was singing, 'So Long, It's Been Good to Know You.'"

What an understatement.

—Annmarie B. Tait—

67

My Geriatric Vacation

Let us be grateful to people who make us happy,
they are the charming gardeners who make
our souls blossom.
~Marcel Proust

"I've got a great idea for your mom's birthday present,"
I told my husband, Eric. "Her friend, Sue, moved to
Florida last year, and she really misses her. We should
send her down there for her birthday gift."

But Eric shook his head. "She wouldn't go. She'd be too nervous
to travel by herself."

"I know, and that's why I'm going with her." I shrugged. "I love
your mom, and I love Sue, too. It would be really fun."

Sue was my mother-in-law's friend first, but she and I became
fast friends as well. Despite a twenty-five-year age difference, Sue and
I clicked. We are both writers, and we both met our husbands on the
dating website eHarmony. A few years ago, Sue and I attended a writers'
conference together, and we had a blast. Sadly, her husband passed
away in 2011, and she moved to Florida to be closer to her children.
My mother-in-law had been talking about visiting her ever since.

When we told Judy about the birthday trip, she was thrilled. She
even suggested inviting her sister, Barb, who was also recently widowed.

So, it was decided. The three of us would fly down to Florida to
visit Sue. Several people told me that it was sweet of me to accompany
the ladies on their trip, and I jokingly dubbed it "my geriatric vacation."

At age forty-one I was going to cruise around Florida with three senior citizens. I expected it to be fun, but in a quiet, relaxing sort of way.

I was wrong. It was fun in the *best* sort of way.

Sue picked us up at the airport, and although we hadn't seen one another in more than two years, our friendship picked up right where we'd left off. We talked into the wee hours that first night.

The next day, we walked downtown and shopped — not for clothes or souvenirs, but for attractive older men for our two single ladies.

"Look at him," I'd say. "He's a nice-looking guy."

"Him? He's too old for either of us," they'd say.

"But he looks about seventy," I'd say. "How old do you want him to be?"

"We don't care how old he is," they'd say. "We care how old he *acts*."

I nodded, but I didn't really understand. But as the days went on, it became clear to me. These ladies might have been pushing seventy, but they weren't old.

We took an airboat ride and spotted several gators and dozens of bird species. We laughed at one another's wind-blown hair after the ride.

We had a seafood lunch and went shopping — for clothes this time. I bought a dress that was so-not-me because these ladies told me to. I even bought the matching shoes.

That night, we took a walk around the lake at Sue's condominium complex. It was a beautiful trail, and the walk gave us more time to talk about things that really matter. Things like love, and self-image, and finding purpose in life. Important things, no matter how old you are.

It was refreshing in a way that touched my soul and brought tears to my eyes. It reminded me how rare and precious true friendship is, and how blessed we are when we find it — even when many years or many miles separate us.

The next day, we took another boat ride, this time to an island to hunt for shells. On the way to the island, a pod of dolphins played just feet from our boat. We found tons of beautiful shells and sand dollars. As I walked on that island, I thought it would be the best part of the trip.

Again, I was wrong.

On the last day of my stay, we went to a manatee park. I love manatees, and it was really neat to see them, but it still wasn't the best part of my trip.

We did fun things and ate yummy food. We relaxed and enjoyed nature. It was an amazing trip. But the most amazing part wasn't what we did; it was the lessons those ladies taught me.

I went on a trip with three women, each old enough to be my mother, but it wasn't that way. They gave me advice, but as friends, not maternal figures. We enjoyed girl talk, and I never felt like anything but "one of the girls."

We were four friends on a trip together. I had a blast, and I couldn't have enjoyed myself anymore had I gone with women my own age.

The trip wasn't what I'd expected. I learned how much fun it is to do things we don't normally do, even things that seem a little scary at first. I learned that stretching our expectations of ourselves is a good thing at any age.

And although it's a cliché, I learned that age really *is* just a number, and we truly *are* as young as we feel.

— Diane Stark —

Chapter 8

Mother-Daughter Adventures

68

A Heart Full of Memories

*I am not the same, having seen the moon shine
on the other side of the world.*
~Mary Anne Radmacher

"There is no way I can live out of a suitcase!" I thought as we packed up our home in Venice, Italy. At fourteen years old, I couldn't imagine leaving my friends, school, and all my "stuff" behind to travel the world full-time with my family.

At the time, we were all going in different directions — my sister and I were stressed and focused on school and were rarely home and my parents were focused on work. I was focused on my friends, the latest gadget, and the current fashions — always wanting to buy new clothes that "fit in." Between doing my homework, texting, seeing my friends, and going to my activities, I rarely had time to spend with my family. It felt like we never saw each other even though we lived under the same roof.

That was when my mom had the idea of dropping everything to travel the world and reconnect as a family. One day she sat us down at the kitchen table and proposed the idea, which at the time seemed so crazy. Although I absolutely loved the idea of traveling the world freely, I couldn't imagine leaving my life behind. After several months of planning, packing, and saying goodbye to our old lives, off we went to explore the world with no end date in sight!

That was over two years, thirty-eight countries, and four continents ago! During that time, we have realized how little we really need to be happy. We have learned how the most important moments in life aren't when we get new gifts or things, but when we live happy moments with our family and friends. We know now that experiences are the best treasures.

As we travel, we barely carry anything with us except the essential things like clothes, a laptop, notebooks, and toiletries. We each carry a backpack and all five of us share two suitcases for clothes. After buying new trinkets or new clothes, we give some of our old outfits away to people in need and it makes us so happy to be able to give back wherever we can.

The small amount of baggage we have makes it easy to travel from country to country on planes, trains, buses, ferries, tuk tuks, etc. By traveling so light, we get to do more with less. We are free to explore countries easily and move around as much as we like. Many times we even make spontaneous travel plans and it is so easy to pack up our stuff and go!

At the beginning, it was difficult for us to get used to never having a closet, constantly changing hotel rooms, and never fully unpacking before we were back on the road. But over time we have learned to appreciate the value of having less — the freedom to live for experiences and the joy of traveling "light" in mind, body, and spirit.

Meeting new people and getting to know their cultures has been the best part of traveling for me. Instead of focusing on things, we love to focus on the people and connect with them. Wherever we go, we try to make as many friends as we can and feel like we have "family" in countries all over the world!

Many of the wonderful new friends we have made on our journey have opened our eyes to how lucky we are. We have met families in many parts of the world who live in small homes with no running water or on the streets escaping war and violence, yet they always have huge smiles and are willing to share with us.

Without all the distractions that we used to have, we have become connected as a family! I can honestly say that travel is the best way for a family to become close again, since it takes away all the distractions and reminds us of what is really important. We now know that experiences and memories are the most valuable things in life and that they can only be acquired when we let go of our need for possessions and focus on what really matters in life — enjoying our lives each day with the people we love.

So I would now say to my fourteen-year-old self, "I will gladly give up a home full of stuff to live out of a suitcase with a heart full of memories!"

— Kaitlin Murray, age 17 —

The Great Family Cook-Off

Life is uncertain. Eat dessert first.
~Ernestine Ulmer

"**D**o you think they see us?" I whispered as I peeked over some sweet-smelling cantaloupes. My almost-grown daughter, Sarah and I hid in the produce section of our local grocery store.

"No. They're too busy inspecting chicken breasts. I thought you said we only had fifteen dollars to spend. What if they go over?"

"They forfeit, and we win!" We high fived each other.

Thus began The Great Family Cook-Off.

We drew names. Fate paired the men against the women. Though I lacked the killer competitiveness prevalent in other family members, and the only prize was "bragging rights," I could literally taste victory.

The rules were simple. Each team would create a dish from a fifteen-dollar budget and any extra ingredients on hand in our kitchen. We traveled home from the store in our family van, tight-lipped about our purchases, joking about our upcoming victories.

Our opponents secured their position near the refrigerator. Sarah and I set up adjacent to the pantry. After much consultation, Sarah and I opted for chicken quesadillas since we had all the ingredients. It was colorful so it would plate well, and who doesn't like quesadillas? Plus, we had an extra culinary surprise up our salsa-spotted sleeves.

Mother-Daughter Adventures | 227

My husband is a master in the kitchen. While I tend to "throw" together various items from the fridge, Tom crafts his entrées. He carefully chooses and inspects for visual appeal and freshness. After his meticulous choices, he begins to create. A pinch of this is added to a smidgeon of that. He tastes and stirs. When he is satisfied, he plates the food. Tom can serve buttered toast that makes you gasp with delight.

My daughter described our cooking differences to a friend like this: "Mom makes four things at once from whatever is in the fridge, and I usually like one of them. My dad concentrates on one item, and it's fabulous."

Even with my seeming handicap, I persevered. The reputation of womanhood throughout history hinged on the outcome of our contest.

Our male counterparts cut, sliced, and diced. The aroma of sun-dried tomatoes and garlic permeated the kitchen. I almost panicked.

"Micah, get sweet onions out of the fridge," Tom instructed our son.

I started to sweat.

We sautéed and simmered. Both sides sneaked sideways glances at each other.

It was time. The men served sautéed lemon chicken with capers, cilantro and sun-dried tomatoes. They plated the food on a large white serving dish with two sprigs of asparagus shooting off from a cut lemon placed strategically in the center. Paprika adorned the edges, composing a perfect balance of colors, complete with a heavenly aroma.

We spread the quesadillas artistically around an Italian ceramic platter painted with whimsical flowers. We added a sweet corn and tomato relish over each piece of chicken. Colorful peppers and sliced limes dotted the dish. A bowl containing sour cream, salsa, and two small yellow peppers that surrounded a lone peapod sat in the center of our creation.

Time for the taste test. We adjourned to our dining room, placed cloth napkins on our laps, and asked the Lord for a blessing — as I silently petitioned Him for a victory.

Both were tasty, almost dead even. Tom and Micah's masterpiece was pretty and moist, but lacked Tom's usual panache. Ours was attractive, and yummy, but your run-of-the-mill quesadilla. Still, we hadn't decided.

After we finished the main course, Sarah and I pulled out our secret weapon. Dessert.

We had enough money in our budget to purchase store-bought cookie dough. We spread rocky-road ice cream between the warm cookies for an amazing culinary delight.

Time for the vote. Tom mumbled something about cheating and declined. Sarah and I registered our vote for all women everywhere. Micah remained silent.

"So what do you think, Micah?" Sarah asked.

There was a long pause and then Micah looked up, hands covered in chocolate and vanilla ice cream. "I don't know. All I can think about right now is this cookie."

Yes, victory is sweet.

The best fifteen dollars we ever spent.

— Pauline Hylton —

70

Sidewalks

Strong people stand up for themselves,
but stronger people stand up for others.
~Suzy Kassem

A s dawn breaks in the cool air of late September, I stand on the sidewalk in front of Frontier Trail Middle School in Olathe, Kansas. I hold a white poster board with "Love Wins" painted in large red letters. Beside me, my daughter Becky and fourth-grade granddaughter Rachel hold their own "love signs."

More than five hundred kids, parents, grandparents, ministers, and more join us. Some wave rainbow-colored flags and umbrellas. Our purpose is to welcome a particular student on his way to school.

On the corner stand four representatives of the Westboro Baptist Church in Topeka, Kansas. Their slogans spout, "God Still Hates Fags," "Repent or Perish," and "Parents Are to Blame." The Westboro Church announced this "street preaching event" on their godhatesfags.com website after an article in *The Kansas City Star* profiled the "boy with two moms," who attends Frontier Trail.

Word of Westboro's plans spreads through our community, and proponents of LGBTQ rights, as well as others simply against hate in general, planned this "love line" for the same day, time, and place. Signs on our sidewalk espouse sentiments like "Kindness Is Awesome" and "In a World Where You Can Be Anything, Be Kind." One message in a child's scrawl says, "We Love You, Kid with Two Moms."

People driving by honk and give us thumbs-ups.

We wave back.

Demonstrating for a cause is not new to me. I'm a child of the 1960s. I strode the sidewalks for civil rights. My friends marched for the Equal Rights Amendment and protested the Vietnam War.

A man about my age walks past me holding his own "We Love Our Kids" poster. I smile at him and say, "The Sixties live!"

He nods and smiles back. "Yes, they do."

Today is also not the first time I've stood with Becky to support a cause. When she was about Rachel's age, our city council proposed a cut in the police department's budget that would eliminate funding for school crossing guards. Becky and I attended a PTA meeting at her elementary school to discuss the child-safety issue.

"What can we do?" one mother asked.

"Why don't we picket City Hall?" I asked.

The others looked at each other.

"Can we do that?" one asked, wringing her hands.

I held my arms wide and shrugged. "Ever hear of the First Amendment?"

The group agreed with the idea, and our school's parents contacted PTAs at other schools. The day of the city council meeting, dozens of parents and kids with homemade signs joined Becky and me as we marched along the sidewalk in front of City Hall. One Girl Scout troop delayed departure for an overnight campout so they could participate. We chanted, "Save our crossing guards! Save our children!" as council members arrived for their meeting.

Like today, people honked in support as they drove by. Local television stations covered the march on the ten o'clock news, and council members voted unanimously to restore the crossing guard line item to the police budget. Becky learned that she could make a difference by standing up for something important.

Today, as I gaze at the sidewalk full of my neighbors expressing themselves, I'm reminded of news reports that have shown police in other countries using water guns, tear gas, and even live ammunition to quell protestors demanding freedom.

I turn to Rachel. "You know, some countries don't allow demonstrations like this."

She widens her eyes. "What?"

"That's right," Becky says. "We have free speech in America, and so do people who disagree with us like the ones down on the corner."

Rachel tilts her head. "They do?"

Becky and I nod. Rachel stands silent.

I imagine Rachel someday marching with her future daughters and granddaughters (or sons and grandsons) on other sidewalks for other reasons. I hope I can join them. If not, I will be with them in spirit, knowing that the love of freedom and justice will pass down to a long line of strong, loving citizens with the ability and willingness to stand up for their beliefs.

— Mary-Lane Kamberg —

71

Surfing at Sixty

Courage doesn't mean you don't get afraid.
Courage means you don't let fear stop you.
~Bethany Hamilton

I've never had great balance. Nor am I crazy about dipping into the frigid Pacific. So when my daughter Emily suggests we head to British Columbia's west coast for some surf time, I'm pretty sure she's flipped her lid. In all my sixty years of living, I've never set foot (or body) on a board—and I'm not sure now is the time to try. But I don't want to let her down. Over the past few months, she's been slammed with work and family demands. And I feel honored that she's chosen me to escape with.

"Check out the wave scale, Mom," she says with a die-hard glee that makes me nervous. "It's extreme!" Sure enough, the arrow on Tofino's rating board is nearly off the chart. For Emily, this is a dream come true. For me, it affirms another goal—to somehow switch my surf lesson to a spa treatment.

After a previous stay at the Wickaninnish Inn, I know both of our wishes will come true. This resort promises "Rustic Elegance on Nature's Edge." As well as being a popular summer haunt, during these winter days, when southeast gales produce mammoth waves, it lures surfers by the drove. My heart does a drum-roll when I think about being included in this mix.

Wanting to get better acquainted with this angry sea before plummeting into it, we stroll along the scalloped beachfront that is sandwiched between an old growth forest of wind-sculpted evergreens and untamed waves. The breakers have tossed up driftwood timbers as though they're as light as toothpicks and have left them strewn all along our sandy path. They've also left behind hundreds of tidal pools that are teeming with sea life. While checking them out and yakking about everything from work challenges to kid issues we're kissed by a fine ocean mist.

It's truly a magical setting and understandably a magnet for many; storm watching aficionados, true-blue romanticists, adventure-seeking families and yes, the crazy surfer crowd who are clad from head to toe in neoprene.

"Are you ready for your big surfing debut, Mom?" Emily says, as I squeeze into my water repellent garb the next morning. "Chill out. You're going to love it."

I'd done some reading to prepare for this wild ride. Wipeouts go with the territory and everyone falls (a lot) when they are newbies. Even concussions are a common hazard. And unlike other sports, surfing has the added danger of drowning if knocked unconscious. The only thing between me and the tumultuous wave action is my five-millimetre-thick wetsuit. I'm praying this protective cloaking also knows how to float. Although feeling more like an oversized seal than a surfer in my second skin, we meet with a dozen much younger and fitter boarder wannabes at Pacific Surf School.

"Paddle like the dickens, and then do the 'pop up' on your board," we're told by our experienced guide. "And don't lose sight of us. The next landmark is Japan!" The common senior quote, "I've fallen and I can't get up," comes to mind. Hopefully I master the pop up and not the pop off!

Our nearby resort is now calling out my name more than ever. But I can't turn back now. With board in tow and Emily by my side, we attack the thunderous waves like whales in mating season. Raging rollers are formed in the distance, their curls navigable only by the pros. Within seconds, they're upon us. One quickly after another. It reminds me a bit of Double Dutch skipping from my youth. When do I make the move? Either I catch a wave or get pummeled by its whitewater wake.

After a few royal washes, my round sixty-year-old neoprene belly melds with the board, and by the end of the lesson, I'm gliding on all fours and going with the flow.

"Next time, you'll figure out the pop-up," Emily later reassures me while we enjoy some pampering at the spa. Beneath a sheltered alcove that fronts the Pacific, we soak our worn and weathered feet, then trail off to our separate sanctuaries for more sublime action. For my daughter, it's a hot-stone massage. For me, it's the Hishuk Ish Tsawalk Awakening Treatment, a whole-meal deal that infuses the elements of life with indigenous traditional techniques.

Under the capable hands of a masseur, my salt-filled pores are exfoliated, cleansed, steamed and rubbed. He says a chant, declaring we are all connected. And while breathing in the heady scent of cedar and listening to the drone of distant waves, I drift off and dream about my next encounter with the surf.

—Jane Cassie—

72

Birthday Balloon

Courage is being scared to death,
but saddling up anyway.
~John Wayne

"W e're going where!" It was more of an excla-
mation than a question. "We're going to
do what?" Now that was a real question,
because I wasn't sure I had heard right.

And so my daughter repeated it. "We're taking you to Colorado
to celebrate your eightieth birthday. And we're all going on a hot-air-
balloon ride."

I almost started hyperventilating; my thoughts were spinning. I
took a moment to let it sink in. "A hot-air-balloon ride?"

"Mom, don't you want to go? I remember you wanting to on
your fiftieth birthday. And I want to help you fulfill your bucket list."

"Honey, eighty is a long way from fifty."

"You're not afraid, are you?"

I didn't want to admit it, but that was the reason I hadn't gone
decades ago.

She continued excitedly, "We've got a lodge reserved for your
birthday week in July."

Now I was backed in a corner. "Who's the 'we'?"

"It's going to be all girls: me, your three daughters-in-law, and your
six granddaughters. I've contacted each of them, and they're all in."

My mind was whirling. My three daughters-in-law! One was

local, one in Tennessee, and another in Hawaii.

And my granddaughters—they were scattered even farther, in Arkansas, North Carolina, Tennessee, Alabama, Illinois, and far away Australia.

"Did you say *all*?"

"Yes, all."

The tickets were purchased. The flights were scheduled. The lodge was booked.

To allay any fears, she sent me a link to watch a reporter taking her first ride with the company. I watched as they checked the wind, explained how the balloon was prepared, and finally her experience on the liftoff.

I can do this, I thought. It was time to start making my to-do list:

Pray
Mani/pedi
Lose weight
Pray

— Phyllis Nordstrom —

Saturdays with Jill

*There is a bit of insanity in dancing that does
everybody a great deal of good.*
~Edwin Denby

With the stay-at-home orders that accompanied COVID-19, our lives changed in what seemed like the blink of an eye. I decided to embrace the opportunity to dig into projects, enjoying the satisfaction of seeing organized closets and tidy drawers. I rediscovered my love of cooking and the aroma that wafted throughout the house. I even finished cleaning the entire garage — an undertaking I began five years earlier and doubted I would ever complete.

But I soon discovered that, while I felt really good about my accomplishments, I began to feel a sadness deep within. My husband had died fourteen months prior, but I was blessed to have family and friends who stepped up. Gradually, I was developing a new normal — returning to my dance group, working out at the gym, and having lunch with friends. But, of course, this abruptly stopped in March 2020 when the pandemic entered our lives.

During this time, my younger daughter, Jill, who is a professional belly dancer, was coming for visits. The two of us have always loved dancing together, so on a whim, we choreographed a number in my driveway to the music of *All That Jazz* using trash cans as props. We filmed it and posted it on Facebook to give people a smile. The response astounded us. The general consensus was that we were inspiring others and making them smile — mission accomplished. This brought us palpable joy, and suddenly we found ourselves on a roll.

In the ensuing weeks, we developed a pattern that was happily anticipated every Saturday. Upon Jill's arrival, we would decide which genre we would tackle. Once we selected the music, the choreography began, with Jill's creativity shining through. Whichever one of us was the "head choreographer" that day would teach the other, and we would practice until we were "camera ready." At age eighty-one, I prayed that I would remember the steps, but thankfully she would softly cue me as we danced. I learned that the world would not come to an end if I made a mistake, which I frequently did, and we ended up getting some good laughs from the "bloopers."

The trash cans became a favorite prop, with us sometimes peeking out from behind one or dancing around them. In our ballet number, they functioned as our ballet barre. For the jazz piece, rakes became canes. And, of course, "Singing in the Rain" wouldn't have been complete without umbrellas.

For the first two months, we were brimming with ideas — tap dancing to "Sweet Georgia Brown," a line-dance number to "Boot Scootin' Boogie," jitterbugging to "Honey Hush," and a few other styles. Then, thankfully, people started posting ideas and requests. Our repertoire now includes reggaeton, which I like to refer to as "Latin belly dance," disco, Gangnam Style and, of course, some hot Latin numbers. We even added some yoga, which included the crow pose, and we challenged each other to a "plank off" as the weather began to creep into triple digits.

Although dancing together was the core of our visits, it included other meaningful moments. After filming our dance, we would rest for a few minutes, then take a long walk, giving us the opportunity for some meaningful, powerful conversations, which were so needed, especially at this time in our lives. Sometimes, we would treat ourselves to a tasty lunch, which would be delivered to my garage. The garage also became the site of Jill's June 24th birthday celebration. As I opened the garage door, she was greeted by birthday decorations and a surprise guest, our dear longtime family friend Samantha. We had a delicious lunch and flowing champagne; it was a birthday that won't likely be forgotten.

As the weeks turned into months, one thing was always constant — Jill's presence. As busy as she was, she never missed a visit, and when she left to go home each week, my spirits were lifted in such a way that could only be provided by this treasured time with her.

How grateful I am to finally have taken the time to clean out that garage.

—Bobbi Silva—

The Gift that Keeps on Giving

Food is our common ground, a universal experience.
~James Beard

What do you give the woman who has everything? Every year our family has such a difficult time finding just the right gift for my mother.

My mother is eighty-two years young. There is nothing she wants that she doesn't buy for herself throughout the year. So, what do we do for the holidays, her birthday, and Mother's Day? What do we give to one of the most giving people on earth?

My mom begins asking all of us for our holiday wish lists in September. She has just so many days to shop and needs to get started early. She will not be in the malls in December during the flu season. When we ask what she would like, her standard answer is always "Nothing!"

We used to show up bearing the usual trinkets that had no place in her home or the piece of clothing that didn't fit and had to be returned. The grandchildren finally hit on the perfect gift — family photos, especially of the great-grandchildren and younger members of the family — but no frames, as she has enough to recycle. My sister and brother miraculously found that her garden was an untapped arena for gifts. They have purchased signs, statues, fountains, and of course, plants. They will all be able to milk these ideas for years to come. But what about me? I wanted something different!

One day, I asked my mom what she had been doing all day. She told me she was watching the cooking channel. Mom had always been a good cook and we loved to exchange recipes. In the past I had purchased special cookbooks for her from my travels. She would read them cover to cover like novels and then pass them on to other family members. Food was something she truly appreciated and, as I realized, a connection we shared.

For the next gift-giving occasion I gave my mom a certificate to a cooking class that she and I would attend together. It was a hit. I finally found the gift that keeps on giving. My mom and I have enjoyed many hours with special chefs and have now included my oldest daughter in our excursions.

During these classes we share techniques and ideas, making me realize that sometimes her old tried and true ways could have been lost to me, had I not initiated these classes. It has also made me aware that many of my mom's family specialties have never been written down. I have encouraged her to write down these recipes for all of us. So many of her best dishes were always "a little of this and a little of that." I couldn't risk that my "little" and hers would be different, so I had her include preparation instructions for perfect results in these recipes. Everything from her chopped chicken liver to something as simple as her deviled eggs — usually eaten before they were ever even brought to the table — could have been lost to us if we had not ventured down this path of cooking classes together.

We may not actually cook together, but through classes, recipes, menus, and diets, food has become a special bond we look forward to sharing.

— Kristine Byron —

75

Better than Prince Charming

Love one another and you will be happy.
It's as simple and as difficult as that.
~Michael Leunig

In April 2007, my mother got a second chance at her happy ending when she met Jody. They are now planning their June 2011 wedding.

My mother hasn't always had the best of luck with men. She and my biological father broke up soon after she announced her pregnancy with me. When I was four, she split up with my younger brother's father, and he left the province soon after my eighth birthday.

She dated a few men over the years, but they didn't last very long. I dreaded the day when she told us that she had a new boyfriend. I hated them because none of them were good enough for the one person who had dedicated her life to being a wonderful mother, who sacrificed everything for the happiness of her children. My mom had always been there for me, and all I wanted was someone who would always be there for her. She deserved her Prince Charming more than anyone I knew.

Then along came Jody. He was perfect for her. He wasn't like the others. From the moment I met him, I felt comfortable around him.

One spring night, I sat down with my mother and asked her what made her fall in love with Jody. "I love him because he's considerate, thoughtful, and down-to-earth," my mother had told me. "And I can just be myself around him."

They fell in love almost instantly, and the relationship moved quickly. By October 2007, they had moved in together.

Two years later, in October 2009, he proposed.

Earlier in the year, Jody had asked our permission to propose to our mother, and my brother and I eagerly agreed. He was better than Prince Charming. He treated us like a proper father should, and we were thrilled that he wanted to spend the rest of his life with our mother.

The day before we were going to the Rockton Fair, where he was planning on proposing, my brother and I made up excuses to leave the house for a few hours because Jody was picking us up down the street. He had asked for our help and his daughter's help in orchestrating the proposal.

"I'm going to my friend's house, Mom," I said, praying I wouldn't smile and give it all away.

"And I'm going to the mall with some friends," Ethan said more casually.

"Do you want a ride? It's raining outside," Mom replied.

"No!" I had to restrain myself from saying it too loudly. "We need the exercise, but thanks for the offer."

Ethan and I quickly left the house before she suspected something was amiss. We walked through the rain toward the silver van that was waiting for us down the street.

We drove to my aunt's house where we spent hours setting up the message, "DENISE, WILL U MARRY ME?" which spanned the entire length of her enormous green lawn. I left, satisfied that the next day would be one that we would not soon forget.

The next day, after having a fun-filled day at the fair, we headed over to the helicopter area. Two of my aunts and their husbands were there after already having their helicopter ride.

As my mom and Jody were lifted into the air, I became excited. It suddenly became more real. The next time we saw them, they would be an engaged couple! Words cannot describe how happy I was at that moment. I was bursting at the seams with joy.

"We're going to be stepsisters!" Jordan and I laughed and hugged each other happily.

When we saw the helicopter appear in the sky, coming back toward us, we started jumping up and down.

My mom jumped out of the helicopter first. She held up her hand, showing the sparkler Jody had placed on her finger only moments before. She ran across the field. I hugged her and told her how thrilled I was for her. Then I told her where we really went the night before.

"I was actually planning on driving to New Hamburg to see you yesterday," my mom admitted to her new fiancé.

It was a good thing she never did because the entire proposal might have been ruined had she decided to make the drive to New Hamburg that night. I like to believe it's because it was meant to be.

My mother had found her soul mate at forty-one years old. She had found the man who knew all of her flaws and loved her even more because of them. She had found the man who wanted to stand up in front of everyone they knew and swear to love her forever. And she had found the man who wanted to take on the responsibility of being a father to me and my brother.

My mom's very own love story shows that true love is out there for every person. It goes to show that no matter how old you are or what your past holds, there is someone out there who will love you with every fiber of their being for everything that you are. Love is going to find you when you least expect it, and it's going to sweep you off your feet, no matter if you're twenty-five or sixty-nine. You can find love at any age.

— Stephanie McKellar, age 17 —

76

Starbuck

A journey is best measured in friends,
rather than miles.
~Tim Cahill

I t had been several months since I had seen my friend Lauren. We had worked together at a local farm for several years and had shared more than a few unexpected and unconventional times.

I spent the better half of my day making chicken Parmigiana, garlic and oil pasta, a tossed salad and garlic bread. For dessert, a lovely cheesecake. It had been way too long since I had seen my friend.

Minutes before she was due to arrive I quickly set the table and opened the wine — always a staple at our dinners. My husband Jack and daughter Emma would be joining us. When we all got together there was never any shortage of laughter, or wine!

The doorbell rang and in came Lauren with yet another bottle. She was greeted by our nine-year-old, 135-pound Mastiff, Max, who approached her with the outward appearance of a junkyard dog but the inner gentleness of a nine-month-old pup. After accepting the customary kisses from Max, she came to me for our long overdue embrace.

Emma and Jack came down from the upstairs office and the three of them gathered in the living room while I transferred the food from the kitchen to the dining room. It was already almost nine so we sat down to eat right away.

Halfway through our meal I noticed that Lauren had not touched her wine.

"Lauren, would you rather have white?" I asked.

"No, I won't be drinking this evening."

I blurted out the first thing that came to mind.

"Are you pregnant?"

"No, no, no," she answered, with a surprised smile. "No! It's just that after dinner I have to drive and pick up something for the farm," she explained.

"What do you have to pick up at ten at night?"

"A goat."

"A goat? Where do you pick up a goat in suburban Connecticut?"

"He's not in Connecticut. He's in Virginia."

I waited, trying to process what my crazy friend had just said.

"So let me get this straight. You are going to leave here after ten and drive to Virginia? With whom?"

"Just me," she replied matter-of-factly.

At the same moment Emma and I looked at each other and both screamed, "Road trip!"

I looked over at my husband, who enthusiastically said, "Go for it!"

Like two little kids just invited for an impromptu sleepover, we left the table, ran upstairs, packed a quick overnight bag and met back downstairs within minutes. Jack was in the kitchen preparing a snack bag because, after all, no road trip is complete without Twizzlers, Cracker Jacks and other assorted munchies.

Before I knew it we were in the truck, Emma in the backseat and me as sidekick. Despite being direction-challenged, I would serve as navigator. I estimated it would take us approximately five hours to get to the little town in Virginia, an hour south of Washington, D.C.

Adrenaline flowed throughout the ride. Emma was home for summer break. She had countless tales of classes and roommates. She shared her dreams of saving the world. For her, the world was a blank canvas and she was going to use as many colors as she could.

Lauren and I chimed in with our thoughts and before you knew it, we were thinking of things that could help Emma as well as ourselves accomplish things that had been on our to-do lists.

Soon the conversation turned towards Lauren. She had just broken up with someone after many years. Actually, as the conversation developed, we learned that her boyfriend had abruptly broken it off. Emma and I were shocked. As upbeat as Lauren was, as she described the breakup, Emma and I knew she was broken-hearted. As the conversation developed, Emma and I started the customary bashing of the ex-beau and before you knew it we were all laughing through her tears.

It was good for Lauren to be able to talk to us about this unexpected turn in her life. And to help her realize that in all actuality she had outgrown that relationship a long time ago. Her life had been heading in a different direction for some time and now she could explore her own dreams.

Along the way we learned that the goat farm that Lauren ran was looking to expand their herd and needed an additional buck to mate with the current does. We were on a mating mission! We laughed at that thought as Emma and I made mental notes of guys we knew who would be a good fit with our newly single girlfriend.

Before we knew it, four hours had passed. We decided to stop for the night at a small motel about an hour away from the farm where we were to pick up the buck the next morning.

We awoke well rested to a crystal clear sky. There was a small diner renowned for its pies down the road, so we all had pie for breakfast. To make it well balanced we ordered our pies à la mode.

The last leg of our trip had us traveling down a long winding road towards the farm. I was so in awe of the landscape, with miles and miles of undeveloped land. It was breathtaking. At the end of the road we found ourselves in front of the most majestic farmhouse.

We sat reflecting for a few minutes and then I broke the silence. "Great trip, Lauren! Thanks for letting us invite ourselves."

She just smiled that gorgeous, dimpled smile back at me.

Getting out of the truck, we all took time to stretch. I was happy to see that a nineteen-year-old, a thirty-year-old and a forty-nine-year-old shared the same symptoms after sitting in a car for so long.

A woman in her early forties appeared from the house and asked if we had any problems finding them and whether she could get us anything.

"We're fine. Thanks."

Her young son, who had been hidden from view, suddenly jumped out from behind her. "Please Mom, can I take them to the stall? Please?"

"Go ahead, Joe. You can say your goodbyes to Starbuck and help the ladies get him in the truck."

"Starbuck?" I repeated. "Is that the name of your goat?"

"Yes," the little boy answered. "He is a star! He is so handsome and all the does love him."

Joe located Starbuck in his stall, attached a lead to him and guided him into Lauren's truck. Then, quite nonchalantly, he said goodbye, sending Starbuck on his way to Connecticut.

Driving with Starbuck in the back cab, we noticed a strange, unpleasant odor. Emma and I asked Lauren what it was. With a sly smile, she announced that Starbuck was ready to meet the does of Connecticut. He was in heat.

Five hours and several stops later we were back in Connecticut. We pulled into the farm, taking the service road to the goat pens.

Through the darkness we heard the restless sounds of the female goats pacing in their stalls. We realized that Starbuck's arrival had been confirmed. The does were looking forward to their visitor.

Starbuck settled into his new home. Emma and I got back in the truck and Lauren drove us back to our house. When we arrived, Lauren looked at us with a devilish smile.

"Now that we got Starbuck a few dates," she said, "you wouldn't have anyone in mind for me, would you?"

Emma and I laughed. "Of course!"

We were ready for another mating mission.

— Jeanne Blandford —

77

Hair Raising

Everything is funny as long as it is
happening to someone else.
~Will Rogers

It was time to start a vegetable garden. My kids were twelve and nine years old, and I wanted them to have the experience of growing their own food.

I like to think that I'm pretty handy. I love putting a good power drill to work, so I knew that buying a DIY raised vegetable garden wouldn't be too much for me to handle.

After reading online reviews and perusing a few gardening catalogs, I picked a kit and watched two YouTube videos about how to put it together. It looked straightforward, so I ordered it.

Our new raised garden arrived a few days later. I pulled out a wrench and my power drill, which also worked as a screwdriver, and set to work.

After about half an hour, I almost had the whole thing done. I was just leaning over to align the tip of the screwdriver into the X in the top of one last screw when I felt a pull on my scalp and smelled something burning.

I tried to move the drill as the blood drained from my face. My long hair was wrapped around the drill bit and being sucked into the drill.

Not needing to look, my hand felt its way around the drill and pushed the "reverse" button. But the drill only took in more hair, and the smell of burning was even stronger.

Terror flooded my mind. Quickly, I moved to unplug the drill's cord from the electrical outlet. I knew that with another touch of a button, I could possibly scalp myself.

Cord unplugged, I tugged at the drill. It pulled on a large clump of the hair attached to my scalp. I felt around with my other hand. There seemed to be only about an inch of hair between the drill and my scalp. I tugged harder. There was no movement — and the pulling really hurt.

I now had a power tool attached to the side of my head — possibly forever.

My first instinct was to call 911. This was certainly an emergency. But what would the EMTs think when they zoomed up the driveway to find a blond lady with a drill attached to the side of her head? Plus, rewind, what would I say to the 911 operator? No, that wouldn't work.

My twelve-year-old daughter, Gigi, was inside, doing homework upstairs, but I couldn't let her see me in such an idiotic position, not to mention my frantic mental state. I was the mom. I was supposed to know what I was doing.

Suddenly, it dawned on me that the pool guy was here. Maybe he could help. But that could be worse. I'd be famous all over town — but not in a good way.

I decided to call my husband. There wasn't much he could do from his workplace an hour's drive away, but at least he could guide me with a clear head.

Using the one hand that wasn't holding the heavy drill, it took a few times to dial the cordless phone since its rounded back kept sliding across the kitchen counter. Finally, it rang and rang, and the call went to voicemail.

As I listened to the familiar recording, I wondered what message I could possibly leave. None. I hung up. I waited for approximately three seconds, with my drill-holding arm aching more and more, and tried again. Voicemail.

With the drill-arm aching, I walked to look at the situation in a mirror. How bad was it really?

Really bad. I took one look at my distressed face, above which I saw a large, heavy, orange-and-black power drill snared in my locks.

I pulled again, hard. Searing pain, but no movement. Guided by looking in the mirror, I tried to untangle the hair with my opposite hand, but any jarring physical movement made my scalp scream.

Finally, I realized that I couldn't handle this on my own. Gigi was my only hope. I was going to have to humiliate myself to become free. I would get down on my knees in front of my daughter and beg for help.

"Gigi!" I screamed.

"Mom, are you okay?" I heard her yell from upstairs as she ran quickly from her room down to the kitchen. I guess she could tell from my voice that something was really wrong.

She took one look at me and laughed — hard. But she stopped when she saw me crying. Twelve-year-old girls know how important hair is.

The drill and I walked to the dining room table, and she followed. I desperately needed to sit down and rest my aching arm, and I explained how I had gotten myself into this horrible position.

Trying not to let me see her smile, Gigi got straight to work.

"Ouch!" I screamed. I heard my hair ripping, and it hurt. "Be gentle!" I shrieked.

Within a few minutes, Gigi had freed me from the drill. I stood up and hugged my baby girl, relief flooding my core. I pulled away from her, looked her deep in the eyes, and said, "You know you can't tell anybody about this, ever, right?"

"I promise," Gigi said.

If only her mom had any of her good sense.

— Jennifer Quasha Deinard —

Running on Empty

Don't forget to cheer for yourself
when you reach the finish line.
~Charmaine J. Forde

For the past three years, I have been working full-time, attending school, and raising a family. To say I am tired is an understatement. My teenage daughter has signed up to run a 5K this Saturday morning, and I intend to return to bed once I drop her off.

I drink my coffee and scurry around to pick whatever I can find to wear off the floor of my bedroom. I put on the wrinkled clothing, pull my hair back in a sloppy ponytail and rush out the door with her. When we arrive and I see the crowd, it occurs to me that I am going to miss her first race. I am overwhelmed with the feeling that I should run with her, even though I believe that I cannot do it. I have never run a race before. In fact, I haven't been physically active at all during the last three years. In addition to the obvious fact that I am not conditioned for a race, I am not dressed for it, nor have I had the proper nutrition and hydration. Despite these barriers, I find myself registering for the race as if I am under the influence of some power other than my own will. "I'll just walk it," I reason to myself. I don't even know what the rules are, if there are any.

I tie my sweat jacket around my waist and stuff my keys in my jeans pocket. Standing in a crowd of people dressed in running clothes, I hear the gun go off to signify the start of the race. Everyone else is running, so I run too. I am dead last. The crowd pulls ahead quickly, and I no longer see my daughter. The sea of runners vanishes over a hill, and I am left with only one other woman.

It isn't long before I begin to walk, and the other woman has done the same. I can tell she is older than me by roughly 20 years. She begins to run again. I cannot let her beat me, so I begin to run too. We continue this series of running and walking, and I pass her. I see a group of women running with a small child. They cannot go any faster because the child is running at a child's pace, which involves a lot of complaining by the child. I pass them. I come upon my daughter's pregnant teacher, and I tell myself that I cannot let a pregnant woman beat me. I run and walk and run and walk until I pass her.

I keep running and walking until I see one of my daughter's classmates. I pass her in my steady run-walk pace, and then I do the same with another one of her classmates. I come upon an area that is set up for the runners to get water, and I take a paper cup. It is impossible to run and drink, so I wet my mouth and throw out the rest. The course is set in Amish country, and the smell of farms is stifling. If I didn't need to breathe, I would just hold my breath.

Amish children line up to watch the race in their lawn chairs. I tell myself that I won't be able to make it up the last hill before the finish, but I keep picking goals such as a telephone pole or a mailbox to run or walk to. I have figured out that if I make my strides long when I walk, I cover more ground. I crest the top of the hill and see a truck parked in the road to stop traffic for the runners. I run through the intersection and to the finish line to find my daughter waiting for me.

I finish in 42 minutes, which is less than my age. My face is burning red and my hip hurts, but I made it. My daughter and I pose for a selfie wearing our numbers. I am so proud of both of us.

Sometimes, life teaches us lessons when we least expect it. I learned that I can complete a 5K without training. Just imagine what I could do if I had actually trained. I learned that, in the end, my daughter will be there for me. I learned that nobody cares if I run in jeans. I learned that it's okay not to know the rules; sometimes we have to figure it out as we go. I learned that running requires focus, which takes one's mind off other things. In this way, running is a healthy alternative to other unhealthy coping means. I learned that people will watch out for me and help me if I need it. I thought I was running for my daughter, but I got so much more than I gave.

—Heidi Kling-Newnam—

But I Can't Touch Bottom

Courage is like a muscle. We strengthen it by use.
~Ruth Gordon

When I visited Israel at age eighty-one, all I really wanted to do was support my daughter Crystal and her husband during a difficult crisis in their lives. However, Crystal wanted me to have some fun, so she took me to Eilat, the oasis in the desert at Israel's southern tip. We visited a bird sanctuary and an aquarium, and lounged on the beach.

"I want to take you snorkeling along the coral reef," she told me. "You'll love seeing the tropical fish and having them swim around you."

I wasn't so sure. I swim, but only in a pool where my feet can touch the bottom. On my one trip to Hawaii, I'd tried snorkeling and panicked in the deep water. Though I was perfectly capable of swimming, the fear paralyzed me. I thrashed about in the water until someone helped me back to the boat.

"You'll be fine," Crystal assured me. "We'll take a foam noodle for you. It will keep you afloat, and I'll stay right by you."

I really wanted to go, so we put on all the equipment. Crystal secured the noodle around my middle, and looking like women from space, we walked down the beach to the pier. When we started along the long pier, my mouth felt dry. The farther we walked, the more nervous I became, and the slower my feet moved. Near the end of the pier, I stopped. "I'm not sure I want to do this," I whispered, almost shaking with fear.

Again, Crystal assured me I'd be okay. I looked at the rope that stretched from the end of the pier to the next one about 1,000 feet away. "I can hold onto the rope, right?" I asked.

"Yes, yes, of course," she assured me.

Slowly, I descended the steps at the pier's end. "Oooh. It's very cold," I said, as shivers like icicles went up my legs. "I don't know if I can handle this."

"You'll get used to it," Crystal assured me, so I kept going. When I reached the last step, I took a deep breath, reached for the rope and stepped tentatively into the deep water. With my face underwater, I took another breath and discovered that the snorkel really did work. Only then did I look around me. I saw red, yellow, blue, purple and black fish of all sizes, and some with multiple colors, too. Some fish sported polka dots, while others had stripes. In and out of the coral they darted, totally unconcerned about me.

After a few moments, I began edging along the rope. As I moved along, I noticed the coral, as well as the fish. The different colors and shapes fascinated me. What wonderful hiding places the porous openings provided for the fish.

When I was about halfway to the next pier, Crystal looked at me and said, "Your goggles are taking on water." We stopped, and she helped me dump it out. A little farther, I realized the water was filling into the nose area of my goggles. I ignored it as long as I could, but soon we had to dump it out again. I looked at the next pier. It seemed a long way off. I looked at the one I had come from. It was even farther.

I breathed a prayer and slowly edged ahead, holding onto the rope. A couple of times, I almost lost my foam noodle, but Crystal tightened it around me again.

I was getting tired, but the pier ahead appeared larger each time I looked. At last, I was beside it. I took a final look at the brightly colored fish, grasped the pier, and let go of the rope.

"You did it, Mom! Look how far you came," Crystal exclaimed.

"I thought you would stay by the first pier, but you kept on going. I'm proud of you."

I looked back along the beach to the first pier. I knew I wasn't much of a swimmer, but with the help of my daughter, a rope and a snorkel, I'd accomplished something I never would have guessed I could do.

I may be getting older, but I hope I'll never stop accepting the challenge of a new adventure.

—Geneva Cobb Iijima—

Chapter
9

Like Mother, Like Daughter

80

Should Today Be a Pajama Day?

The heart wants what it wants, and my heart wants
jammies and me time.
~Kat Helgeson, *Say No to the Bro*

"Feels like the flu," my husband Gary said as he woke me up one pre-sunrise morning. We'd been here before. I threw on my clothes and dropped him off at the hospital emergency entrance before parking. When you're on chemo and flu-like symptoms present themselves, it can add up to scary infections.

After five hours of antibiotic infusion, I brought my husband home, prepared something for him to eat, ran out to pick up his prescription and... wait for it... reported to work. I was exhausted in every imaginable way.

But if I didn't do my job, it would land on someone else's desk. Or so I reasoned.

There was no resting in this weary, disheartening, cancer-picking-up-speed season. There was only kicking against it in desperation. In Gary's declining months, I fought. I didn't listen to my body. I didn't take care of my soul and spirit. Self-care sounded so self-centered.

My co-workers would have been appalled to know that I showed up at work after being out since 4:30 a.m. "Dear friend, please don't ever do that again," they would have said. "Please stay home on days like this. We've got you covered."

But they had no idea how my day had unfolded.

On that particular day, self-care would have simply meant taking the day off from the office. It would have included brewing a cup of tea and curling up on the couch in the same room with my husband — chatting with him when he was awake, taking an afternoon nap when he slept. Self-care would have meant adding to my gratitude journal and picking up my knitting or a good read as Gary dozed. And those simple things would have refueled me.

Instead, I wore my superhero cape, tattered and dragging in the mud, for entirely too long. I thought I could do it all, and I didn't want to impose on anyone.

A week before Thanksgiving, on a snowy evening, my daughter Summer and I lost Gary.

The thought of all that needed to be done unraveled me. But Summer and I did the oddest thing. We notified immediate family members, put on pajamas, popped some corn, and watched HGTV's *Love It or List It*. I suppose it was our way of coping in the moment, of leaning into the unthinkable, and pushing the details of funeral planning out of our heads. Somehow we knew what to do: fleece pajamas and salty buttered popcorn in front of the fireplace. Self-care.

The next day, we ended up doing another unplanned activity that helped refuel our bodies, souls, and spirits. Based on a meme Summer found — "I live in my pajamas unless I am going somewhere or I know someone is about to come over to my house; even then it's iffy" — we wrote three rules for that first full day without husband and father:

1. Stay in pajamas all day.
2. Don't get off the couch except for coffee and tea breaks… oh, and food and bathroom breaks… and to answer the door.
3. No one was allowed in unless they were wearing pajamas (although we did make a couple of exceptions to this rule).

Ironically, in between the remembering, laughing and crying, Summer and I got quite a bit done from the couch, making lists of everything we needed to accomplish.

By the next day, Summer and I were rested and ready to tackle the items on the lists we'd drafted.

Self-care. It isn't merely something we do for ourselves. We replenish body, soul, and spirit to have a full vessel. To better serve. To be more present in our serving. To be glad and not resentful in the service.

When Gary was on chemo, he was cold all the time. I'd warm a fleece blanket in the dryer and drape it over him as he occupied the hospital bed in our living room. Every time I wrapped a freshly warmed blanket around him he would sigh blissfully.

What if we could wrap self-care around us like a fleece blanket warm out of the dryer? What if we removed our superhero capes and accepted the startling, unexpected grace of others loving on us as we travel life's challenging, noble, heart-wrenching paths?

What if we asked ourselves from time to time: Do I need to stay in my pajamas today?

— Marlys Johnson-Lawry —

81

My Dearest Friends

A daughter is a little girl who grows up to be a friend.
~Author Unknown

I've watched two of my dearest friends grow up. I've laughed and cried at their antics. I caught them when they stumbled, taught them that rolling their eyes was rude, and shared my love of books with them.

My daughters, Lacey and Carina, have become my daughter-friends. This new relationship wasn't planned. It's blossomed over the years.

I think it started during a shopping trip. I edged out of the dressing room, tugging uncomfortably at a shirt that should have fit me. Carina, my eighteen-year-old fashionista, wasn't very subtle. She yawned.

Lacey, three years older and more sensitive, said, "Mom, it looks like everything else you own. Why not try something different?"

Carina put her hands on her hips. Her Old Navy checked shorts and coordinated top were perfect. "Mom. Definitely not. Next."

I slunk back into the dressing room. I heard Lace whispering something to her sister. I caught the words "be gentle."

They rejected all of my choices and picked a much more trendy outfit than I was used to wearing. The message was clear. Mom's taste was boring. Theirs wasn't.

That was the beginning of the change.

From clothes to relationships, the girls aired their opinions, advised me about dating, and stepped all into my business. Our roles had expanded. Friendship means being honest, loving, and loyal. My girls embodied all those characteristics and more.

One fall, my best friend, Sharon, and her husband invited me to Ohio for a long weekend, but all I could think of were bills. We were all caught up, but single moms always worry. I didn't think we could afford it.

Lacey watched me mope around the apartment all day. She and Carina disappeared into their small bedroom. I wanted to call Sharon, but I couldn't bear her disappointment. Tomorrow, I'd call.

"Mom," Lacey stood in my doorway. Arms crossed in front of her, mustering her fiercest frown. "Tomorrow morning, you're going to be on the 8:00 a.m. bus. You'll be in Pittsburg by 2:30. Rina's packing your bag. No arguments."

"Honey, what are you talking about?" I put down the book that I'd been pretending to read. "I told you that I wasn't going. We can't afford it. Who's going keep an eye on you?"

Rina nudged her sister aside. She rarely wasted time arguing. She operated with the motto, "Make your point and move on."

"Mom. Tough love time. You deserve a break, and you're getting one. Bus tickets are cheap, so we bought you one. We asked Dad to help. He owes you big time 'cause we turned out so well." Her grin softened the words.

"Yeah," Lacey said. "We're over eighteen. We're grown-ups, even if we still act like kids sometimes. So, we'll be alright by ourselves."

She and Carina exchanged that mysterious sister look that I'd intercepted over the years.

It meant they had a plan.

"Listen, this is very sweet, but you're college students. You need to save your money for books and things." I couldn't believe they'd engineered all this. I was the mom. I decided who got vacations and how money was spent, right?

"Since you've always given us rules to live by, we made a list of rules for you." The two giggled, just like they were little kids about to get into mischief.

Lace cleared her throat: "Rules for Mom's *How Stella Got Her Groove Back* Weekend. One. Call us when you get there and when you're about to leave, just like we have to."

Rina read the next rule. "Two. Don't do anything you'll regret in the morning. Remember, you'll have to tell us everything, 'cause we'll find out the truth."

"Three. No bringing back a guy as young as us. You're not really Stella."

"Four. Have fun. When was the last time you had fun, Mom?" That question floored me. Maybe I'd thought they wouldn't notice my lack of social life.

To say that I was in awe would be an understatement. I hugged these two young women whom I'd raised and worried over, realizing that they were worried about me. I loved them more every single day.

I visited Sharon, lived by the rules, and had a great time. My daughters continue to fascinate and delight me, and their friendship means everything.

Having daughter-friends is an unexpected perk to being a mom. I'm very fortunate.

—Karla Brown—

Mom's New Home

A little girl, asked where her home was,
replied, "where mother is."
~Keith L. Brooks

I remember being so excited to move into my own place at age twenty. I was nervous and couldn't wait to take on the challenge of managing my own life. I thought it a bit of an overreaction when it took my mother months to come see my new place. When I'd asked her for the hundredth time to come over, she looked at me seriously, holding back tears and said, "Give me some time to come to terms with the fact that you don't live at home anymore. I can't imagine you living somewhere else right now." I'd laughed, thinking she was overreacting, but later it resonated with me.

Ten years later, I found myself in her shoes. I was newly married but lived only a short drive from my mother and her new husband. All my sisters had moved out by then, but we would still descend on my mother's house on the weekends and cook and talk and live for a few hours as if we'd never left. We all still had stuff there, our old rooms were there, our memories, but most of all, our mother was there, the same as she'd always been.

Then, as if overnight, she decided to retire and move to Florida. It was as if she'd decided to leave the planet. At first, I was excited for her and behaved as if she were going on vacation. Florida had been her constant vacation spot throughout the years and she'd always had a good time. She always spoke of it with fondness but never did I think she'd move there permanently.

I came over to help her pack, and we talked about how excited she was and how she would enjoy the more hospitable weather. It hit me while wrapping my baby pictures in bubble wrap that something greater was happening. I looked through a box or two while my mother went to get more things from another room. My handprint mold from kindergarten, a framed picture of a childhood vacation with all of our faces painted at a downtown festival, my mother's large can of random buttons that she would keep in her sewing room. We'd learned to count with those buttons, used them to decorate our Barbie doll clothes we'd made from scraps of fabric she had, and finally sifted through them to fasten our own clothes she'd taught us to make when we got older. Suddenly it seemed as if she wasn't going on an extended vacation. She was moving our home away, with her in it, to some strange, faraway place that I didn't know.

I tried to talk her out of it, but just as that hadn't worked with me when I moved out, it didn't work with her as she enthusiastically moved into the next phase of her life. After she moved, I'd visit her periodically but her new house never really seemed like home. My sisters and I had never written on the walls or had our own room. We'd never sat down as a family to dinner after a long day at school, or snuck in the back door past curfew. We hadn't argued and fought over the use of the bathroom or done our hair and make-up in the one mirror. It was my mother's house, not the family's.

For a long while, it was like visiting a stranger. I had to ask where things were, if I could go in certain areas, what certain things were for. I actually noticed when something was new and I noticed how many pictures of me were around and when they were moved or replaced.

My mother was different too at first. She reveled in revealing personal things about herself, now that she had a new home in a new city — it was like a new chapter in her life. I found out that she loved flowers everywhere — paintings of them, figurines, silk ones and fresh ones. She arranged her house to reflect her interests and desires — not to raise a family. Her sewing room was in the center of the house and everything else was arranged around that.

It was difficult at first, and on more than one occasion I told her that I did not like her house or visiting her. Every time I left to return home, I cried. But eventually, over the years, her home became more familiar. Maybe it was because I started leaving some of my things there. Or that as my sisters and I visited more often, we were sometimes together and then had to share a room or fight over the bathroom. Whatever the case, we began to have memories in my mother's new house and at the center of those new memories was the same person — my mother. She was older, and more rounded as a person to us, and a bit more self-centered than we remembered as children, but she was the same loving, magnetic, energetic person we rallied behind to grow up into fine, adult women. And eventually I realized that wherever she was, was home.

— Audra Easley —

83

She Tricked Me!

Mirror, mirror on the wall,
I am my mother after all.
~Author Unknown

My mother tricked me. And not just me. She tricked my sister and brother as well. In the midst of three children and an additional half dozen or so in an at-home daycare, she had the nerve — the audacity — to absolutely fool us into leading healthy lives.

Sure, we were allowed two cookies after dinner. But she had us convinced that we didn't need the Sugar-Frosted Chocolate Krispie Gems calling out to us from the cereal aisle. We had something better.

We had "fruit plates."

Arranged on a brightly colored plastic plate would be a yogurt, an apple and a peach, sliced and rationed among the troops, and a handful of crackers or pretzels. Sometimes there'd be toast or half of a sandwich. And man, were we thrilled.

Fruit plates offered a brief respite from the "well-balanced" healthy meals we were forced to enjoy as a family at roughly 5:12 p.m. every single day. Fruit plates could be enjoyed at 4:30 p.m. when an elementary school open house beckoned at 5:30 p.m., or even after 6:30 p.m. on the days when soccer ran late. Fruit plates were the rebellion against the norm.

It wasn't until I tried to pass off a bagel, a handful of raspberries, and an apple as dinner for my ravenous husband that it hit me like a brick wall.

Fruit plates were the result of a woman who, once in a blue moon, didn't have time to cook a full meal in the midst of running a household, running a daycare, and running after three kids. One last-ditch effort to pull together a meal that satisfied the food pyramid.

And that woman made us think it was a treat.

Sneaky.

She probably even made us go to bed before ten so we'd be awake in school and stay on the honor roll. I wouldn't put it past her.

My mother probably knew what was best for me all along, and what's worse, she probably did what was best for me every day.

And here I am now, making fruit plates. And turning into my mom in other ways too. When I remind my sister to write down all her credit card numbers and phone numbers in case her wallet's stolen, I get it. After telling my collegiate brother to be careful at a party, the response taunts me: "Thanks, Mom."

Anyone who has ever met my mother has been let in on the secret mantra, which they then joyfully recite for their own entertainment: "You are your mother's daughter."

It's worse, though, and I don't know if anyone but me and my all-knowing mother know the extent of just how bad it is.

I am my mother.

I already type up lists of emergency phone numbers — and laminate those lists before posting them on the refrigerator. I can't stand crossing out dates on the calendar and instead take the extra seventeen minutes to locate the Wite-Out. I worry when my husband or siblings are out late and forget to call. Christmas isn't complete without a tree in every single room.

And the prognosis? Incurable. My affliction will only get worse.

Someday, I'll hang every hand-drawn picture on the fridge, and a framed drawing of a stick-people family will sit on my mantle long after the artist has gone off to college. I'll feel the need to sit in the bleachers at every basketball game and hang up posters for every school play.

Someday, I'll trick innocent young children into believing that crackers, a cut-up apple, and a peach yogurt is a treat.

Someday, I'll be the sneaky mom I was blessed to have.

—Caitlin Q. Bailey O'Neill—

84

How I Survived

Life doesn't come with a manual;
it comes with a mother.
~Author Unknown

When a teacher called with her concerns about my daughter's pallor and lack of energy, her comments failed to set off alarm bells. Like her two older siblings, Jill didn't always eat right or get enough rest. When she came home from school, I asked, "Have you been feeling okay? Your teacher thinks you need to see a doctor."

Jill let out an exaggerated sigh. "She's crazy. There's nothing wrong with me."

Although I sided with my daughter, I pushed fruits and vegetables her way and grounded her from late-night phone calls.

Her teacher contacted me a week later and asked if I'd followed up with a doctor's visit. There went my Mother of the Year Award. When she said Jill had been dozing off at her desk, I worried she'd fall asleep at the wheel.

After school, I quizzed Jill, but she slammed her book bag on the counter and yelled, "I'm NOT sick!"

Despite her protests, I called her primary physician. Suspecting mononucleosis, he ordered blood work. Results showed a low platelet count. He suggested we consult a hematologist. Although I feared the worst, I assured her it was probably nothing.

After searching the Internet for the probable causes of low platelets,

Jill came to me, sobbing and said, "Mom, I have leukemia."

I hugged her tightly and suggested other possibilities that weren't life threatening. Tilting her chin so she could look me in the eyes, I said, "Sweetheart, I'd gladly trade you places if I could. Let's wait and see what the experts have to say."

The hematologist ordered a bone marrow biopsy along with X-rays to rule out an enlarged spleen. Directing her anger at me, Jill stomped out of the clinic and raced to the car. Apparently this was all my fault.

At her follow-up visit, the hematologist greeted us with good news. Jill's test results came back negative for leukemia and her spleen was normal as well. I felt a huge weight lift off my shoulders. But when the physician revealed my daughter had a blood disease — idiopathic thrombopenia purpura, ITP, I felt as though I'd been hit by a wrecking ball. The doctor prescribed steroids and said Jill would need her platelets monitored on a regular basis. It could be worse, I thought. We can deal with this. Too bad the doctor hadn't kept the part about prednisone causing weight gain and insomnia to herself.

On the way home, Jill freaked. "Mom, I'm not gonna take a drug that makes me fat."

Getting her to take her pills became a daily battle. Going to the clinic for blood work was even worse.

During my routine mammogram six weeks later, a suspicious cluster of calcified cells sent me for a biopsy that revealed advanced stage III breast cancer. While the news devastated my entire family, Jill took it the hardest.

Late one night, I heard her sobbing in her room. I walked in, sat down on her bed and asked, "What's wrong?"

"Mom, remember when you said you wished you could trade places with me?"

Hoping to convince her it wasn't her fault, I tried humor. "Honey, I also promised to shave my head if your hair fell out from chemo."

Her eyes opened wide at the thought of parting with her long, blond locks, but then she saw my smile. A bald forty-year-old was one thing — a teenager another story.

Already worried I might not survive a life-threatening illness, I spotted the paperwork for Jill's high school class ring on the kitchen counter. I sat down, put my chin in my hands and released a deluge of tears as I wondered if her future would include me. My children weren't babies like they were when I had my previous scare, but my teenagers still needed their mother. And I needed them.

Since I had the utmost confidence in my oncologist and his entire top-notch staff, I called his office to schedule an appointment for my daughter but was told he didn't accept patients under eighteen.

At my next visit, I decided to ask the doctor myself. "Would you be willing to treat my sixteen-year-old daughter who has ITP?"

Reluctantly, he asked, "Is she mature?"

Deciding honesty was the best policy, I confessed, "If you don't count that she rebelliously flushed her prednisone tablets down the toilet because she'd gained a little weight."

He chuckled, but agreed to see her.

On her first visit, when Jill sat down in my chair to have blood drawn, I felt a terrible sadness. As much as I dreaded the procedure, I'd have gladly pushed her aside and rolled up my sleeve. She reminded me needles didn't upset her like they did me. I didn't bother trying to explain. She'd understand some day when she was a mother herself.

Jill pouted about having her platelet count checked weekly. But when the oncologist said she'd need to continue taking steroids until her numbers reached an acceptable level, she cried out, "That's not fair!"

The two of us already knew life wasn't fair.

On the way home, she pinched her puffy cheeks and said, "Mom, I look horrible!"

I glanced over and teased, "Chipmunk!"

She volleyed, "Baldy!"

My turn. "Don't forget. You have an interview at JJ's Restaurant tomorrow." Unable to resist, I added, "With your steroid appetite, if you do get the job, you'll most likely be fired for eating up the profits."

"You're right, Mom. They should hire you instead so customers won't have to worry about finding hair in their food."

All's fair in love and pettiness. She threatened to stock up on my favorite candy bars the week after chemo when food remained off limits for me.

Family and friends constantly praised my wonderful attitude. What they couldn't possibly understand was how thankful I was that it was me undergoing chemotherapy and radiation, not my daughter.

Most teenagers bonded with their mothers on shopping trips. Jill and I bonded at the cancer center where we spent the better part of a year getting blood drawn almost weekly. By the time I'd completed chemotherapy and radiation, Jill's platelets teetered on normal. She needed her counts monitored periodically, and I had checkups occasionally as well, but our lives slowly returned to normal.

Almost two decades later, I'm still cancer-free, and Jill remains in remission. Blessed to have been there for my children's graduations, weddings and the births of my precious grandchildren — two belong to Jill — I gladly share my story with newly diagnosed relatives, friends, and acquaintances. I tell them not to focus on the sorry hand they've been dealt, but on loved ones who need them. That's what helped me survive a potentially devastating late-stage breast cancer diagnosis, and that's what will enable them to survive as well.

— Alice Muschany —

85

A Magical Conversation

Unless we make Christmas an occasion to share our
blessings, all the snow in Alaska won't make it white.
~Bing Crosby

t was two weeks before Christmas and I was not ready. Not
ready with food, not ready with gifts and decorations and,
most of all, not ready in spirit. Outside, the grass was still
green. This Christmas, of all Christmases, I needed snow to
cheer me. I am Canadian after all.

It had been a tough year of financial loss from the stock market
crash and a failing business that promised to drain us further still. We
had been forced to move from a lovingly renovated home in the historic
section of Oakville, Ontario, into a house that needed a lot of work.
Worse still, we had to cram our business into what should have been
the basement family room. I had put my interior design business on
hold to help my husband with his company. I loved my design work;
I did not love accounting or administration and, with each passing
day, life was leaching from me.

This Christmas was not going to be the same as all the others. I
had already scaled back on decorating and baking and there would
be no entertaining, just our Christmas Eve fondue, and the potluck
Christmas dinner with extended family. No Martha Stewart Christmas
this year. Though their lists weren't long, our three teenaged daughters

weren't going to get everything they'd asked for. There had been no time to make a Christmas playlist to put me in the mood. I had balance sheets and packing slips on my mind where there should have been visions of sugarplums dancing. And there was no white Christmas.

And then I was offered a last-minute free ticket to see the musical *Jesus Christ Superstar* with my friend who had worked on it as a scenic artist. With my husband out of town, I was free to go. It seemed an odd show for Christmastime, but I was determined to take this break and get my mind off my troubles.

Coincidentally, a fierce storm rolled in that evening. As I drove across the city through blinding snow, I reminded myself I had hoped for snow every day for the last two weeks. "Be careful what you wish for," I scolded myself as I gripped the steering wheel with both hands.

Once inside the theatre, it occurred to me how apt this musical actually was for Christmas, sort of like reading the last chapter of a book before you begin at the beginning. It was an outstanding performance, and I felt faint stirrings of the Christmas spirit. By the time we left the theatre the wind had died down, and snow fell softly in enormous flakes. My friend and I raised our faces to the sky and laughed as we welcomed the cool kiss on our cheeks.

Driving home, it struck me that the sky was almost as bright as day. The snow had stopped and now the ground was a blanket of white and the night sky seemed to be filled with an ethereal milky whiteness, and a silent stillness. When I pulled into our driveway it was after midnight, yet two of my daughters wanted to go for a walk in the magical glow they'd been viewing from their windows.

We piled on our coats and scarves and hats and mittens and walked for forty-five minutes with the pristine snow crunching under our feet. It was truly enchanting. Then, somehow, the conversation turned to our Christmas traditions and I felt the twinge of guilt and disappointment at how different this Christmas would be. But the list they were making wasn't about the material things I knew we would be lacking this year.

"Getting our tree at Drysdale's," recounted Whitney, the mist of her breath accompanying her words. We went every year with their cousins, the tractor-drawn wagon moving past rows of pines and spruces and balsams to the Fraser firs that we preferred. Those fine needles and thin boughs were the perfect backdrop for the hundreds of tiny white lights we would wrap around the trunk and branches before we hung the garlands and ornaments. We would choose the perfect tree together and cut it down ourselves.

"Baking chocolate peanut butter pinwheels," said Morgan.

"No, caramel treasures," rebutted her sister. I smiled. Each of my daughters had her favourite Christmas cookie, and that was the cookie she helped me bake. Though our baking endeavours had been reduced this year, we had still made these favourites.

The list went on — *It's a Wonderful Life*, *A Christmas Carol*, *White Christmas*. The trip to Niagara-on-the-Lake to see the Trisha Romance-style decorations. Warm apple cider from Chudleigh's Apple Farm. Gramma's "nuts and bolts."

The last one got us reminiscing about food, especially about our unique Christmas Eve tradition of fondue and Yorkshire pudding. For a long time, I made Christmas Eve dinner of roast beef and Yorkshires for just the five of us because, although we were all together at all the big family functions, the season seemed to pass without our little family sitting focused on each other in a truly significant way. When we got together with family, the kids would rush in the door to play with their cousins, the adults would catch up with each other, and I barely saw my own children. So I made Christmas Eve our time to steal away from the chaos that we all loved and share an intimate evening with each other. I chose roast beef and Yorkshire pudding because it was the furthest thing from the turkey we would consume on Christmas Day, but one year I switched it to fondue. The girls liked that even better, but they didn't want to give up the Yorkshire pudding, so an unlikely Christmas tradition was born.

I smiled again as they went on about those dinners. As they had grown older we had stopped going to Christmas Eve church service. Instead, somewhere over the course of the evening as we set our skewered cubes of meat into the hot oil, we took turns recounting how God had shown up in our lives since the Christmas before. We learned so much about each other from those conversations.

We walked on and they added to the list—opening one gift before bed, Whitney reading the Luke 2 passage before we opened our stockings and gifts on Christmas morning. These were our traditions, the ones they talked about with enthusiasm. There was no mention of the gifts they wanted, no mention of the things I didn't have time to do this year. What they cherished were the things I had tried to instill in them all along, little things that had nothing to do with money or all the Christmas "bells and whistles."

As we headed back home in the magic whiteness, Morgan announced, "This is better than a sleepover!" With that, my cares and concerns of the previous weeks melted into gratitude. The snow was here and my kids understood what was important—perhaps better than I had this year. And I knew we would be all right.

—Marie MacNeill—

86

The Potato Salad Rule

*Tradition simply means that we need to end what
began well and continue what is worth continuing.*
~José Bergamin

When I was a young girl, my family attended a church that frequently hosted potluck suppers. Each family brought a large dish of food they were happy to share. There were carrot and raisin salads, chicken casseroles, homemade breads, Jell-O molds with fruit suspended in them, cherry pies, a cake with cat hair in the frosting. And of course, many dishes of potato salad.

My mother took a large bowl of potato salad to every church potluck. She was proud of her potato salad. She diced potatoes, eggs, onions, sweet pickles, dill pickles, and celery. She mixed in pickle juice, salt, pepper, and paprika. Her recipe seemed to go on and on. As a child, I thought these things belonged in potato salad. It was a rule.

When all the ingredients were mixed in, my mother would take a clean spoon from the drawer and taste a bite.

"It's not tart enough," she would declare. "I need to add some pickle juice." Then she would take another clean spoon and taste it again and again until she had it just right.

"Will there be any left for the potluck tonight?" my older brother, Steve, would tease.

When it was time to leave for the potluck, my mother would spoon the chilled potato salad into a pretty serving bowl. She never served it in the same bowl she mixed it in because the edges would look sloppy. She did not decorate her salad with sliced eggs. She did not sprinkle the top with paprika. She never garnished it in any way, as some ladies did. My mother's potato salad spoke for itself.

When she placed it on the table next to the potato salads of the other ladies who attended the church, she did so with a pride nearing sin. Then my mother would put a small spoon of the other potato salads on her paper plate, just to taste and compare.

"Why do you want to eat more potato salad after you just ate all that at home?" I asked her.

"You need to know what other people are up to," she said. "Remember that. It's good advice."

Then we would sit down together, and I would listen to her running commentary on all the other potato salads. Sister Hillard didn't bother to taste hers before she brought it. It didn't have enough salt. Sister Lynch didn't use the right kind of onions. There wasn't enough bite. Sister Guthrie didn't use pickle juice. Hers was too dry. Sister Shelton cooked her eggs too long, and they turned gray. Church potlucks were fraught with complications such as this.

When I grew up and started buying my own groceries, store-bought potato salad just seemed easier. A little tub, a couple of dollars, and a spoon. But I always felt like I was cheating, and it never tasted quite right.

I developed my own running commentary. This store put a funny tasting preservative in theirs. That store's potatoes were too rubbery. Another store allowed human hair as an ingredient. I started making my own, using my mother's recipe.

I didn't like onions, but no one would know. It was my potato salad, so I left them out. Pretty soon I was leaving out a lot of things. And I really liked dill, so I added a lot of that. But, somehow I felt like I had broken a rule. It was terrible what I had done to my mother's recipe. I kept it a secret for a long time.

Over the years, with my husband's taste in food as a good excuse, I got over the guilty feelings and just started making and taking my potato salad to family gatherings as needed.

My mother never said anything critical, never suggested I add anything. She never reminded me what really went in a potato salad. Still, I knew what I made was very different than the dish she had taken such pride in all those years. What I made could hardly even be called potato salad by her standards.

In my memory, my mother had been so vocal about those church ladies. Where were her comments to me? I had nearly braced myself for "Where are your onions?" but it never came.

It began to irritate me that my recipe was not important enough for her to comment on.

That summer, my irritation was replaced by anxiety over my mother's heart attack. When she recovered from a quadruple bypass, I began to sense a handing down of the crown. My mother was making me the keeper of important things.

"I thought you might like my big mixing bowls," she said. "I don't need them anymore, and you'll use them." She gave me her rolling pin, because she knew I always loved it and would keep it in the family. Shoeboxes full of family photos began appearing at my house, for safekeeping. She did not give me her recipe box.

That autumn, my brother Steve's house burned down.

"How can I help?" my mother asked him.

"You don't need to. We already have a bunch of friends coming tomorrow to salvage things and start the clean-up," Steve said.

Newly recovered from open-heart surgery, my mother could not clean up a burned and gutted house. But she could make potato salad to feed the crew.

My mother bought all the ingredients herself, and then she asked me to bring her mixing bowls back. Side by side, we chopped and mixed everything. Onions and pickles, perfectly cooked eggs. It was the rule.

I helped her taste and taste until it was just right. The sharp oniony taste of childhood was a relief after the recent events.

She bought ten pretty plastic serving bowls to spoon it into, and she did not garnish it. Her potato salad still spoke for itself. It fed a huge clean-up crew, and everyone there loved it. Of course, everyone there was dirty and tired, and a lot of people were crying, but she was sure they were comforted by her recipe.

Just recently, my mother came to my house for dinner, and I served my version of the dish. Without hesitation, she took a big bite and said, "You always have made the best potato salad I have ever tasted. I don't know why I didn't make mine just like this all those years."

Every time she hands down the crown, a little more of my heart breaks.

"You can't stop making yours, Mom," I said to her. "What would we do without you and our family traditions?"

"Family traditions? My potato salad is not my mother's recipe," she said. "It's something I figured out on my own, just like you did. That's the rule."

Mom's Potluck Potato Salad

6 medium potatoes, peeled and quartered
6 hard-boiled eggs, diced
1/2 cup minced yellow onion
1 cup minced celery
1/2 cup diced dill pickles
1 cup diced sweet pickles
1 tablespoon sweet pickle juice
1/2 cup mayonnaise
1 teaspoon yellow mustard
1 1/2 teaspoon salt
1/2 teaspoon paprika
1/4 teaspoon pepper, optional

Boil potatoes in water until tender. Cool and dice.

In large bowl, toss together potatoes, eggs, onion, celery, dill pickles and sweet pickles.

Add sweet pickles, juice, mayonnaise, mustard, salt and paprika. Mix Well.

With clean spoon, taste. Add pepper if desired.

Chill and spoon into pretty serving bowl. No garnish needed.
Serves 6

Mom says readers can adjust any of the ingredients to their own taste — that's the rule.

— Carrie Malinowski —

87

Going Where You Look

If we are facing in the right direction,
all we have to do is keep on walking.
~Buddhist Saying

"Slow down before we reach the intersection." I clutched the steering wheel with sweaty hands as I followed the instructor's direction. The car lurched toward the side of the highway, the front tires perilously close to the edge of the pavement, where a six-inch drop-off threatened to flip us over.

"Careful." The instructor calmly reached across and straightened the steering wheel. The car returned to the center of the lane, and my teenaged classmates, belted in the back seat, let out sighs of relief.

"Sorry." I tapped the brake pedal. The driver's ed car rolled to a halt in front of the white stop line.

"Keep your eyes on the road ahead," the instructor said, while I tried not to feel incompetent. "You go in the direction you look."

I remembered the remark several years later, when my mom and I reached a crossroad in our writing careers. We'd been writing separately, pursuing different paths on the way to publication. Whenever we got together, we talked about our stories, books we enjoyed reading, and the latest trends in the publishing industry, which we gleaned from writing magazines whose subscriptions we shared. We loved writing, though we weren't making progress toward our goal of getting published.

"Romances are popular," Mom said, during one of our chats. "We should write one."

"We? As in the two of us, working together on the same book?"

She nodded. "I think it'll be fun. I'm tired of facing a blank screen every morning. If we took turns, there'd always be something to build from. We could be each other's writing imp. You know, the little pixie who sneaks into the computer late at night and magically makes words appear."

"Think so?" I said. "I'd be tempted to trim the wings off any imp who changed my stories."

Mom thought about that for a minute, then admitted, "Yeah, me, too."

Still, the idea of writing together was appealing, and we kept coming back to it. After a few months of indecision, we decided to give the imp a chance to show off her talents. We outlined a romance novel and got started. I worked as first-shift imp, writing in the morning before leaving for my day job. Mom showed up at the house just before I drove off and took over the computer keyboard.

The rough draft progressed rapidly. Mom had been right — the imp made the work much easier and a lot more fun. We both looked forward to getting to the computer each day to see what twists and turns had taken place while we were gone. We both also wanted to make sure the work we left during our respective imp-stint was as interesting as we could make it.

Re-writing and editing presented challenges. The imp was great at creating, but not so good at revising. After a few ugly arguments, we established one unbreakable rule: When in doubt, delete. If we simply could not come to a compromise, we deleted the offending word, line, paragraph, or scene, and started anew — with one change: We worked together on the new part, instead of separately. We red-penciled revisions over lemonade and cookies while sitting at the picnic table on the sunny back porch, and heated disagreements turned into what my dad called "giggle sessions." We couldn't help it — we were having fun.

We finished the first book and began sending queries. We got some good feedback from agents, and a couple of them asked to read a few chapters. Despite the initial encouraging remarks, as the months went by, rejections piled up: Too much mystery. Where's the romance? Contrived plot. Sorry, not for us.

From experience, we knew the best way to keep from dwelling on the disappointment: Start the second book while we shopped the first. Once finished, we bravely sent off our second effort — and fared no better. We began a third, grinding out a set number of words each day and turning our imp-stints into grim marathons. When romance number three reached rewrite status, the giggle sessions became relentless quests to root out every error and produce a saleable manuscript.

In the summer of our battle with manuscript three, a convention for romance writers came to town. Despite the steep fee, we needed the inspiration, so we made reservations. We spent three days attending lectures, signing up for agent conferences, and networking with other authors.

Yet instead of inspirational, we found the event dispiriting. With the exception of an elite few, most attendees were just like us: hopeful and struggling. And we learned about the terms of the writing contracts we'd be expected to sign — should our work ever be accepted — which included relinquishing almost all rights. Were we working so hard only to end up for-hire hacks?

"We're never going to break in," I said, as we drove home on the last day. "We have better odds of winning the lottery or getting struck by lightning than we do of getting a romance published."

"I agree." Mom's voice was low. "Maybe we should give up."

"Do you want to?" I looked at her, and the car drifted to the right. With the practice of years behind the wheel, I straightened it automatically, and my high-school driving instructor's words came back to me. Before Mom could answer, I said, "Maybe we ought to look where we're going."

"What do you mean?" Mom asked.

"It's like driving." I gestured at the highway. "We've taken our eyes off the reason we started writing together, and we've strayed off course. We want to be published, sure, but the main reason was to have fun doing what we both enjoy."

"You're right." Mom let out a breath. "I haven't been having fun for quite a while."

"Me neither."

"So what now?"

"I still want to be published," I said. "I just don't think we're cut out for romances."

"Actually, we stink at them," Mom said, and we laughed together for the first time in ages. She added, "I think I know why, too. We only started writing romances because they're popular, and we thought it was an easy road to publication. There's no real heart in our stories, not like some of those authors at the convention. They love romance. We don't."

"True. I'd rather have the heroine pursued by a killer than a boyfriend."

"I agree. We should have paid more attention to the rejections. Apparently, our preference was obvious to everyone but us."

"Now that we've figured it out, we could try writing a mystery. They sell well."

"Isn't that the same road we were just on?" Mom asked. "Rather than picking a genre, let's write a book we'd like to read."

"Sounds like a plan." I smiled at her. "I'm looking forward to working with the imp again."

I flipped on the directional and slowed to turn onto the exit leading us home, and we launched into a conversation outlining the plot of a new book.

The SkyHorse, our young adult novel, was published by Musa Publishing last year, using our joint pen name, HL Carpenter.

— Lorri Carpenter —

88

Resolving to Honor Memories

Leftovers in their less visible form are called memories.
Stored in the refrigerator of the mind
and the cupboard of the heart.
~Thomas Fuller

T he first time I walked into my mother's apartment after she died, I turned and bolted. The smell of her perfume, the sight of her eyeglasses, her magazines, her comb — and the absence of her — were just too much.

I couldn't go back for days.

But no matter how much I wanted to avoid it, there was the inevitable sad work of clearing out the place where Mom had lived for thirty-seven years. And nobody can prepare you for going through the personal effects of a parent you've loved and lost. If grief is an ambush, this sorting out is its handmaiden.

Ultimately, I took huge cartons, and with my husband's help, stockpiled the things I couldn't bear to part with. There was no rhyme or reason to this process — just pure instinct.

How could I leave behind the shoebox filled to the brim with every card we'd ever sent her, ordinary cards I'd picked out in a moment without even deliberating over the message? Every sappy birthday card and Mother's Day card was there, dated, and in its original envelope. Why hadn't I sent her nicer ones?

No matter where I went in the apartment there was something destined to stop me in my tracks and make me sob.

But I pushed on.

I scooped up the predictable things — my mother's china, the paintings that had been in my life since childhood, because they were part of the landscape of our house, and the scarves that still carried her scent.

Those cartons came back to our house, with my husband showing remarkable and loving patience with the excesses. And they got stashed in the basement, where I wouldn't see them often, let alone open them.

And that might have been that.

Except that one day during the spring after Mom's death, I had a reckoning: I was entertaining, and knew that a beautiful English casserole that my mother had loved would make a perfect centerpiece for our table, especially if I filled it with her recipe for Swedish meatballs.

That day, I made a promise to myself, one I wasn't at all sure I could keep: I would stop avoiding the bits and pieces of Mom's life — the tangible evidence of her world in the apartment that had claimed and framed her days. Gradually, I would integrate them into my life.

I would begin with that casserole dish, one of her prized possessions, and her recipe box that contained the careful directions for her famous Swedish meatballs.

I would love to say that I simply did it. That I kept my resolve strong. But it took me a full week to bring myself just to open the first carton and pull out that lovely oval dish. Touching it made me weep.

It was somehow easier to dig out the recipe, and to place Mom's old wooden recipe box in a kitchen cabinet, out of sight for now, but not out of mind.

Small things marked enormous progress: I now carry my mother's deep blue eyeglass case in my own pocketbook. Initially, just seeing it among my things stunned me. But then I began to love its familiarity: how many times had I seen my dear mother reach for that case? She had loved it. Now I love it, too.

My mother's pearls are often around my neck. It took a while until that stopped feeling weird. Now it feels wonderful.

On cold days, I wear my mother's blue flannel bathrobe, the one I pulled out of the Goodwill pile at the last minute. "As old as the hills," my mother used to say, "but it's warm." That was enough of a rave for me.

But perhaps nothing is woven into my days and nights as completely and joyfully as the most unexpected of items.

One Mother's Day, late in Mom's life, we gifted her with a set of red cookware — spunky and modern. At first, she insisted that we take it all back. Finally, she agreed to keep just one piece: a little red pot.

No utensil was ever more lovingly cared for. Mom polished it to a gleam, delighted to see something bright and new in what had become a weary kitchen.

That pot now sits on my stove. I use it as often as I can, and cherish it, because she did.

My resolution to keep my mother "with me" may sound foolish, even macabre.

But that little red pot stands as a symbol of what has turned out to be one of the most important resolutions of my life: to honor my mother by surrounding myself with the things she wore and touched and used.

I've learned through this resolve that there's great comfort in the mundane.

And that a little red pot can make remembering an act of love.

— Sally Friedman —

89

Eight Thousand Miles

*You cannot tailor-make the situations in life but you
can tailor-make the attitudes to fit those situations.*
~Zig Ziglar

Desert winds blew sand devils around us as we trudged behind a donkey cart loaded with our backpacks. We had arrived in Mali, West Africa, to visit our youngest child, Mary, who was serving in the Peace Corps. Since Mali was a Muslim country, I'd followed Mary's advice and left my cross necklace at home, but now I felt vulnerable without it. What if my husband's fears came true? What if we were kidnapped by terrorists and held for ransom, like those tourists we'd heard about on the news? Or what if we were lost forever in the Sahel's barren landscape? There wasn't even a road to follow. We were putting all of our faith in Mary, who had only been in the country for two years.

Suddenly, a dark slender man in army fatigues appeared. He shouldered his ancient rifle and discharged a mighty blast. Mary quickly explained. "He is just alerting everyone that you've arrived. You're the first volunteer's parents to visit."

Soon, we were surrounded by some four hundred singing and dancing villagers. They insisted that we lead what had become a parade into their village. When we arrived, the generous Malians gave us small, handmade gifts. Tears rolled down my cheeks. I felt honored and appreciated — the opposite of what I'd felt nine months earlier when I'd felt pressured to resign from my job.

For twelve years I'd worked at the hospital. One day they told me I was no longer needed. I understood that it was a cost-cutting move to replace me with someone with less experience and a lower salary. But my understanding didn't excise the wretched pain of feeling discarded and useless.

At sixty-two, what opportunities existed for someone my age? In the past, during similar budget cuts, I'd watched as other employees left, awash in bitterness. I refused to behave that way, no matter how scared I felt.

My mother often said, "Act like a lady." Despite my concerns, that is what I did. For a month, I cleaned my files and wrote detailed notes. I made it easy for my replacement to do my job. The program would continue, but I wouldn't. The most painful part of all was that no one would even notice my absence.

"Dear Lord," I prayed, "show me the way." As He so often does, He answered through someone else, a fellow health educator at another hospital. When I shared my worries about my future, she told me about a conference she had attended recently.

"I've just learned the most helpful tool," she said. "No matter what the situation is, there is an opposite, a benefit. Our typical response is to focus on the losses of job, marriage, home, or even health. Instead, the speaker told us to concentrate on finding what we gained with our loss."

At first, I resisted her advice as I grieved. I didn't care about "opposites." I wanted my job back. I missed my office, my co-workers, the routine. I missed the meaningful challenges of organizing health education classes for sick people. But as time passed, I grew tired of my dreary sorrow. Maybe I should try my friend's advice and seek some opposites.

The reverse of loneliness would be friendship. I called a neighbor and asked if she would like to take an exercise class with me. Soon, we became good friends. Although I missed my busy hours at work, I now had more personal time. I had choices. I tackled cleaning projects I'd delayed due to my long work hours. I volunteered at a mental health program.

Yet it wasn't until our trip to Africa that I understood the power of opposite thinking. We had cashed in our frequent flyer mileage and flown eight thousand miles to that village. We brought many presents—deflated soccer balls, Frisbees, pens, scarves, and inexpensive watches—believing that somehow we could improve the villagers' lives. Instead, they taught us the opposite. Our lives were the ones that needed improving.

Despite living in mud huts without modern conveniences, running water, or sanitation, the villagers appeared content. Frequently laughing and greeting each other, the beautiful Malians truly cared for their neighbors. Although we slept on the ground in our daughter's tiny courtyard, I felt a peace I hadn't known since I left my job. I admired the Southern Hemisphere's brilliant stars and thanked God for bringing us here. I had expected we would spend our time helping the poor villagers. Instead, they were teaching us that having less meant less to worry about and more time and energy for each other. These wonderful people of a different faith taught us an important lesson.

When we returned home, we decided we didn't need a large house. We sold our house, gave away or stored most of our belongings, and left town in our twenty-two-foot trailer. It felt so freeing to have less to care for and so good to have more time for family who needed us. We traveled to Illinois to attend to my mother-in-law, who suffered from dementia. After we arrived, the nursing home staff decreased the numerous medications they'd administered to control her behavior. Family and friends once again enjoyed visiting her.

After she died, we traveled. For a year we lived happily in our tiny trailer, as we looked for a new home with fewer expenses and lower state taxes. Eventually, we found a small mountain cabin in Colorado, near our grandchildren.

After my job loss, I thought my life work had been stolen from me. In seeking opposites, I discovered new opportunities that enriched my life. As I age, I still mourn when a new loss occurs, but soon, I seek its opposite. I am always rewarded.

— Carol Strazer —

90

No Silver Platter

Jumping at several small opportunities
may get us there more quickly than
waiting for one big one to come along.
~Hugh Allen

Like most teenagers, I felt I would be ready spread my wings and be on my own as soon as I graduated high school. My life would be so much different than my mom's. She was already married and had me to take care of when she got her high school diploma.

I was sure attending college was the first step in an amazing, fulfilling and exciting life. I was just as sure this first step included getting as far away as possible from my family and the small Wyoming town where I had grown up.

For a while, college was a dream that I didn't share. My mom was single with five kids and worked as a supermarket cashier. She had enough to worry about. So being the independent spirit I was, I took it upon myself to start researching colleges.

Oh! The places I could go! The pamphlets started coming in, enticing me with expansive campuses and intelligent faces in far away places. One college even spoke of the chance to spend my sophomore year in Italy! Representatives from colleges far and near showed up at my high school to persuade us to apply to their schools. The possibilities were endless. I was so excited to be the first in my immediate family to get a college degree.

When I worked the closing shift at my part-time job at a fast food restaurant, I wouldn't waste time when I was mopping the lobby, knowing that I had to get home to finish my homework. I was sure that my grades, while not perfect, would be good enough to gain access to whatever college I deemed worthy of my presence.

My first lesson about college was harsh. Academically, I was prepared. Financially, I was not.

When my mom looked over some of my dream schools, she thought for sure my head was in the clouds. Just because I wanted something so badly didn't mean it was going to be possible. Good grades were important, but it wasn't the only consideration. The tuitions were just way too high. My family had always been on a tight budget and not able to save for much of anything.

I thought about saving a lot of money over the summer. I thought about working full time while going to school. Then I thought about books, about rent, and about a social life. Math was never my strong suit, but the numbers just weren't adding up to the tuition and the good life at any of my dream schools. There had to be another way.

I dove into the scholarship battle, swimming through the paperwork and essays the best I could. For someone who liked to watch from the sidelines, it was strange to suddenly be in competition for my future. I found I wasn't the only one who wasn't getting their dream school handed to them on a silver platter.

Allowing myself to dream more realistically, I applied to good universities that were public, rather than private, and therefore much less expensive. I was accepted by all of them. But even with some help that was being offered by the schools, I was still falling short. I knew I wouldn't thrive in school if I was constantly worried about making money to pay the rent, or buy books. How was I going to gain the "Freshman 15" if I didn't have enough money for food?

I knew I didn't want to wait "one more year" as some suggested, in order to save up more money. I had seen too many people say they were going to do that very same thing, and each year passed with them saying "next year." I didn't want to take the chance. Instead, a different chance was given to me.

One afternoon, I was called to the guidance office. My counselor announced that I was eligible for a Full Ride Scholarship. There are no sweeter words to a high school senior on a tight budget! Of course, there was a catch. It was only for two years, because it was for a community college. My fantasy of large lecture halls suddenly shrunk to classrooms of standard size. And the college was in the next town, about fifteen miles away. My dreams of traveling to an exciting new city and meeting new people were replaced with thoughts of driving down a familiar highway and taking classes with some of the same people I'd known since kindergarten.

The counselor focused on the benefits, understanding my collegiate expectations. I could still take part in the whole "dorm life experience," as this college offered on-campus housing. Later, I would be able to transfer to a university as a junior. It was a great way to start a college career, he said. And I might have more individual attention than I would if I went straight to one of the larger colleges. I took a packet of the literature I had always passed up before and told him I'd think it over.

My mom's eyes brightened as I told her the news. She was excited for me. Looking through the classes, she pointed out ones that sounded interesting, envisioning a fun and intellectually stimulating schedule. I began to realize that sometimes the dream and the goal can be different things, and knowing that may be one of the first steps in growing up. What I really wanted was an education in order to grow as a person. Who's to say that couldn't start fifteen miles from where I first learned the ABCs?

Once I accepted the scholarship, other things fell into place. I had won a few local scholarships, easing even more of the burden, as well as reducing the time I would have to work while going to school. After learning more about my family, my counselor thought I might be eligible for a Pell Grant, a loan that wouldn't need to be repaid. He said my mom and I could find out about it at the financial aid office at the college.

My mom was proud of me, her eldest daughter, getting to do something she had never had the opportunity to do. We were relieved that the financial aid meant I wouldn't have to spend most of my potential study time working.

Learning about financial aid didn't just help me, though. Mom got a Pell Grant for herself, and began her own college journey, with me.

Looking back now, I'm glad that I stuck around home. I excelled in my studies at the community college and it was a great preparation for university. I even ended up meeting people from all over the world — a few of my roommates were from Paris and Tokyo!

The biggest honor, though, was getting to experience English 101 with my mom. We were cooperative yet competitive classmates, often bouncing ideas off each other after dinner. My arrival into the world may have delayed her college experience, but by staying close to her, I like to think both of us grabbed onto our dreams.

— Tina Haapala —

91

Grab Bag

*I firmly believe that respect is a lot more important,
and a lot greater, than popularity.*
~Julius Erving

Standing at her bedside, the doctor asked my seventeen-year-old daughter, "Piper, do you like school?" His crossed arms revealed his agenda to discredit her physical complaints and discharge her from the hospital. It wasn't our first experience with this line of questioning.

I knew what he was implying, and as her mom I ached to jump into the conversation to protect her, but I needed Piper to answer for herself. After all, I wouldn't be able to safeguard her from such accusations all her life. I waited for her reply. *Don't raise your voice,* I thought, *or he'll accuse you of defiance. Don't falter, or you'll appear unsteady, anxious. Don't cry, or he'll label you depressed. And, most importantly, don't give him approval through silence.*

She made eye contact with the man in the lab coat looming over her, and she said, "Of course I like school. I take advanced placement classes at a private school to challenge myself, so I can get into a top university after I graduate."

That's my girl, I thought. *Nice defense.*

But the doctor refused to back down. "Do you find yourself missing a lot of classes?"

"Are you kidding?" she said. "In AP classes, missing one day is like missing a week. I've only missed two days this entire school year.

I hate to fall behind." She looked at me, and I smiled because she remained self-assured.

She could've told him how she darted from classes throughout the day to vomit in the restroom and then quietly returned to her desk as if nothing had happened. Or she could've mentioned that before the first bell, while her friends chatted about last evening's events, she marched to the nurse's office to give herself a heparin shot in the stomach. And that during lunch, she returned to the nurse to swallow one of the many handfuls of pills she had to choke down each day that enabled her to attend school in the first place. But she knew better than to provide him ammunition. The more facts she reported to the man in white, the increased likelihood of being labeled a malingerer, a faker. She had learned to say as little as possible.

"Maybe it's just your monthly visitor," he blurted.

Stunned, I looked Piper in the eyes and saw a flicker of temporary confusion turn to disbelief.

Obviously, he thought her weak, unable to handle pain.

If only he'd witnessed Piper's disappointment when she couldn't pass the ROTC physical. How bravery and courage fueled her desire to defend our nation, but migraines, seizures, joint pain, numbness and tingling in her arms and legs, blurred vision, dizziness, shortness of breath, chronic fatigue, memory loss, and vertigo dashed any hope of donning a military uniform. Denied a future as an Army warrior, she still possessed a warrior's spirit.

I stepped in to teach my daughter yet another lesson in handling misogyny.

"Do you really think she'd go to the ER for her period? You realize she was transported here by ambulance from another hospital, right? If it were her menstrual period, the other hospital would've laughed at her and sent her home. They thought her condition severe enough to admit her here."

I waited for our punishment. How dare I question a doctor? A male doctor at that.

"Well, they were wrong. She can go home."

I flinched. "Does she get the courtesy of a proper diagnosis?"

"I think it's a flu bug," he muttered.

"She's been vomiting for months. Does the flu last that long?"

I braced myself, knowing I'd crossed a bigger line by challenging his diagnosis. But what did we have to lose?

He shook his head.

"Could you at least palpate her abdomen to see where the pain is coming from? Like I said, this has been going on for months."

He glared at me. "That won't be necessary. She can get dressed and go home."

He handed her an eviction notice.

I turned toward Piper, who was on the verge of tears, and gave her the don't-give-him-the-satisfaction-of-crying look.

And home we went: a place devoid of judgment, sarcasm, eye rolling, and degradation.

Knowing that she had a chronic disease and would have more encounters with indifferent medical doctors in months to come, Piper and I developed a plan.

"Can we just get up and leave when they're so rude?" she asked.

That thought had never occurred to me, being raised by parents and grandparents who held doctors in high esteem. With this question, I realized she did not believe that doctors were almighty and all-knowing. Why not leave? As paying customers, weren't we entitled to respect? Why would I continue to allow healthcare professionals to belittle, chastise, or question my daughter's character? Or to infer she faked an illness when she suffered every day, all day?

We devised ground rules: We would no longer entertain their talk of a school phobia, hints of gender weakness, accusations of malingering or faking, or the labeling of a mental health diagnosis without sufficient cause. The most important rule: We wouldn't be rude or disrespectful in return. We would uphold our dignity.

"I'll follow your lead," I suggested. "It's your appointment, so I want you to call it when you feel the doctor crosses a line. Your line may be different from mine."

"Let the games begin," she said.

First up, a visit to a gastroenterologist for her continued nausea and vomiting.

"It could just be related to ovulation or, perhaps, anxiety." Wow. A double whammy.

I watched for a signal. Piper reached over, grabbed her school bag and stood.

The doctor's eyes widened.

"Thank you for your time," she said. "Mom, are you ready?"

I followed her lead and plucked my purse from the ground. "The only anxiety she has is when a doctor doesn't take her pain seriously. And I don't think she's been ovulating every day for months. But thank you."

As the doctor tried to process our boldness, we walked away with confidence in our decision. We no longer rewarded disrespect. We no longer paid for incompetence. We no longer argued against an archaic establishment that continued to blame the chronically ill who sought help in hopes of alleviating their pain and suffering.

Next up, an allergist. "So, you've had Lymes disease in the past?"

Ouch, I thought, and waited for Piper's decision. She grabbed her bag, signaling the end of the appointment. "It's Lyme disease. Not Lymes. If you don't know how to say it, I don't know that you can treat it. Besides, there's no cure, so I still have it."

The doctor straightened and looked at me for a second opinion, and I nodded. Piper and I high-fived all the way to the car.

We now treat the first doctor's visit as an interview, deciding if the physician's views and knowledge of Lyme disease are compatible with Piper's needs. Based on the interview, we either hire or we fire. Our treatment for curing a doctor's arrogance and rudeness? We grab our bags and take our dollars elsewhere.

— Cathi LaMarche —

A Magical Bond

92

A Little Nudge

To live in hearts we leave behind
Is not to die.
~Thomas Campbell, "Hallowed Ground"

I t didn't seem right that the sun should be so brilliant or the sky such a deep cloudless blue. Only six months had passed. Not near enough time to blur the image of my mother's thin form lying beneath white hospital sheets, or to forget the cloying smells of antiseptic and chronic illness. Yet no one's tragedy stopped Mother's Day, a grim reminder, from arriving. At the age of fifty, I had become a motherless child. Uncertain of how to handle my changed place in the world, I decided to do what I had always done for Mom. I purchased a dozen red roses. Then I took them to the cemetery.

During the drive, I reviewed bittersweet memories. Mom walking me to school my first day of kindergarten. The pride that sparkled in her eyes when I graduated from college. Her joy as she cuddled my son, her first grandchild, soon after his birth. At every important event of my life, she'd been with me. My heart ached. I couldn't imagine a future without her. I thought I'd never again feel complete.

My thoughts stilled once I passed through the cemetery gate. I stopped the car and swallowed hard. I hadn't been here since the day of Mom's burial. Hundreds of tombstones were lined up in neat rows. Where was she? After more than thirty minutes of fruitless searching, my melancholy gave way to rising panic. I could no longer pick up the phone to call Mom. Or go to her house on Sunday afternoon to visit. And now it seemed I couldn't even find the place where we had laid her to rest only half a year before. My throat constricted. Before tears could form, I shook my head and willed myself to stop thinking negative thoughts. I needed to concentrate on the search.

I stopped the car, and then, although it was undeniably futile, I couldn't help but say, "Mom, where are you?" It was a question that haunted me on many levels.

Of course no one answered. I swallowed hard and reached toward the key to start the car and leave. I suppose it really didn't matter if I delivered roses on Mother's Day or not. Mom would never know the difference.

But before I could turn the key, movement caught my eye. Two gray doves swooped by. They drifted and circled gracefully until one, then the other, landed softly on a nearby headstone. The pair strutted across the stone, heads bobbing with each step. I watched them for a moment until my gaze drifted to the name carved on stone. My eyes widened and goose bumps rose on my arms.

The birds had landed on my mother's headstone.

I got out of the car and walked toward the grave. My hand clutched the roses so hard a thorn pierced my thumb. With a whirr of wings, the doves fluttered away. I watched them fly high into the sky until they disappeared from view. Then I dropped to one knee in the soft ground at the foot of a deep pink granite stone. My fingers brushed across her name.

A feeling of wonder and hope swelled in me for the first time since Mom's illness and death. Someone sent those birds to guide me and I knew it had to be her. I needed my mom and even death didn't keep her from responding. And if she could respond to a moment of grief in a quiet cemetery, it meant she still remained as vital a force in my life now as she had ever been. I realized that all it took to find her again was to open my eyes and look around. I could see Mom in my memories, in the faces of my children, and in the woman she had helped me become. The words I whispered came straight from my heart.

"Thanks, Mom."

I put down the flowers and rose to my feet. My body felt lighter than it had in months.

Mom found a way to reach out to me through the veil that separated this life from the next. I'd always be able to find her.

And all it took to convince me was a little nudge.

—Pat Wahler—

93

The Garden

Hundreds of dewdrops to greet the dawn,
Hundreds of bees in the purple clover,
Hundreds of butterflies on the lawn,
But only one mother the wide world over.
~George Cooper

I was still struggling with my mother's death. I still reached for the phone to call her occasionally even though she had passed almost a year ago. She was often on my mind. Nevertheless, I seldom dreamt of her, and when I did, the recollection was usually vague.

But this night, after falling asleep easily after a busy day, I had an unusually vivid dream. I awoke about three in the morning with tears trickling down my cheeks. Lying motionless, I tried to comprehend the intensity of the dream. It was so surreal that I woke my husband. The details I shared with him were quite clear. I recalled walking through a winding flower garden and smelling the sweet fragrance of roses. The garden bloomed with vibrant hues of red, yellow, and purple. The luminescent colors seemed energetic in their own way. Bluebirds perched on honeysuckle vines, softly chirped a soothing song that offered hope and cheerfulness. Though I didn't recognize where I was, the feeling that surrounded me was overwhelmingly familiar. I was embraced by a powerful unconditional love.

In my dream, I was talking to someone, and we were walking toward a wooden park bench at the end of the garden path. I turned my head toward my companion and it was my mom. She was beautiful. Her short brown hair gently framed her face. Her smile gleamed as she expressed the depth of her love and joy for her family. She seemed very content and aware of the current events in our lives. It felt like she was telling me that she was watching over us from this incredible place of beauty and happiness. At the end of our visit, she whispered "I am always with you in spirit." Though my eyes filled with tears, I felt complete as she continued down the path without me. Then my eyes opened.

Shortly after, my daughter woke up crying. "I miss Nana," she wept. She too had been dreaming about my mom. While I held her close, I listened as she described the same garden that I had seen in my dream. I pondered sharing the coincidence with her but decided to let it be. Lulling her back to sleep, I softly spoke: "Nana's love is forever, my dear."

— Kathryn A. Beres —

94

An Unbreakable Bond

We are each of us angels with only one wing,
and we can only fly by embracing one another.
~Luciano De Crescenzo

T en years ago, I decided I needed to do more than teach leadership. I needed to find a real way for my teenage students to make a difference.

We decided to help the homeless. We began by collecting food and clothing for people in need. Just days before our scheduled trip, our local newspaper ran an article about the many organizations helping the homeless along Hastings Street — an area known as Vancouver's Downtown Eastside, or Canada's poorest neighborhood. We realized that the homeless there were already receiving plenty of food and clothing during the Christmas season, so I cancelled our scheduled outing.

My students were devastated. I questioned them: *If our desire was to help, and the service was already being provided, why were we disappointed?* That question made us realize that we wanted to experience the joy of giving. This led to a deeper question: *Do the homeless ever have the chance to give to others?*

Rather than handing out food and clothing, we developed what we call Project HELLO (Helping Everyone Locate Loved Ones), and we made greeting cards so that the homeless had something to give. The idea was simple: We would take our blank, handmade greeting cards to the streets and invite people to write to those they had lost touch with.

Magic began. One by one, people who had not spoken with family for years opened up and shared their stories. The homeless wrote to their children, parents, friends and siblings, and they trusted us with their messages. We searched phone directories to connect with families and mailed messages of love from long-lost loved ones. We made hundreds of connections. I recognized that some of the stories were so raw that our five-minute visits were not enough. I began what I call "Beyond HELLO" and made the personal commitment to take a homeless person to lunch once a month to hear his or her story.

Cindy was the first lady I met. She had moved to Vancouver twenty years earlier after escaping an abusive relationship and giving her child up for adoption in Ontario. On the day we met, she was contemplating suicide, knowing she had little to live for as she was battling hepatitis, HIV, and heroin addiction. As Cindy stood on the sidewalk resisting the urge to dash in front of a city bus, I approached and offered water. She turned and snapped, "I'm starving — and all you offer is water?" With a smile, I invited her to lunch. Our friendship began.

Despite Cindy's pain, she hung onto hope — her one reason for living. Although twenty-seven years had passed, Cindy still dreamed of meeting her daughter. She asked for my help. She knew the date of birth and that her daughter's birth name was Paige. She did not have a last name.

As I drove away, I could see Cindy clinging to a parking meter with tears streaming down her face. What had I done? How could I re-open such a deep wound? How would I find someone in Ontario with only a first name? I worried I had gone too far in my effort to help.

That evening, I searched social media until the wee hours of the morning, looking at every profile I could find of women named Paige in Ontario. When I was just about to give up around 3:00 a.m., I found a profile of a woman with a matching birthdate. Unfortunately, the account was inactive, so sending a message would do little to connect. Aimlessly, I clicked through Paige's friend list on Facebook. Miraculously, I found a man named Adam and recognized we had a mutual friend in British Columbia. With a few e-mails, I was able to arrange for my friend in British Columbia to call Adam in Ontario. Adam then reached out to Paige, his friend from grade school. He was able to share that Paige was adopted and she had just begun her journey to search for her birth mom.

Within hours, Paige and I were on the phone together rejoicing that her mom was alive and a connection was possible. I asked Paige if she was ready to hear of her mom's life and warned her of the harsh realities of Hastings Street.

Paige was more than ready. She had also struggled with addiction. When she learned of my work, she insisted I read a book entitled *In the Realm of Hungry Ghosts*, written by Dr. Gabor Maté. Paige credits her own recovery to this book about the Downtown Eastside.

Paige shared that during her addiction no treatment seemed to be effective. She was pregnant with her first child and she wanted to be drug-free. When she found the book about Vancouver's homeless, she was drawn to a particular chapter entitled "Pregnancy Journal." It told the story of a woman named Celia who had journaled about her own battle with addiction during pregnancy.

That story about Celia was exactly what Paige needed to get clean. She even took time to write to the author, Dr. Gabor Maté, to thank him for this powerful story. When I told Paige that her mom was from this exact neighborhood, she pleaded for me to read the book. Ironically, the author had recently given me a copy, thanking me for my work on the streets. I had placed it on my bookshelf but had not yet cracked the cover. I flipped to the "Pregnancy Journal" chapter and read about Celia.

I headed back to the streets to find Cindy and let her know we had found her daughter. On a hot summer day, I found Cindy crouched against a barbed-wire fence. I sat down, and the smells of exhaust and tobacco surrounded us. As Cindy looked up through her addicted state, I asked if she had ever heard of Dr. Gabor Maté. With wonder, she looked up and mumbled, "*In the Realm of Hungry Ghosts?*"

"Cindy, how do you know the name of his book?" I asked.

"He's my doctor. The story is about me. In the book, my name is Celia."

Without even knowing it, Cindy had already changed her daughter's life. Cindy's daughter Paige had found peace and sobriety through her mother's story without even knowing she was reading about her birth mother.

I offered to coordinate a reunion so Cindy could meet her daughter for the first time since birth.

"Not yet." Cindy paused. "Not like this."

The next day, Cindy checked herself into rehab so she could be sober for the first time in nearly three decades. Five months later, my students and I helped Cindy and Paige reconnect. It was the moment both women had waited for their entire lives. Neither adoption nor addiction was enough to shatter their bond.

— Kristi Blakeway —

95

A Grand Visitor

Pay attention to your dreams— God's angles often speak
directly to our hearts when we are asleep.
~Eileen Elias Freeman, The Angels' Little Instruction Book

My question took my mother by surprise. We were at the Wright Brothers National Memorial in North Carolina when I asked her, "Mom, did you have a grandmother?"

My mother chuckled. "Everyone has a grandmother!"

"No. I mean, was she alive when you were born? Did you know her?"

"Yes," Mom said, distracted by the monument.

I paused, unsure whether I should continue. My mother seemed happy enough to be walking around the national monument. With her mood so troubled of late, I worried my question might destroy her good mood. But the dream had been so vivid, I had to ask: "Mom, did your grandmother seem kind of like a gypsy?"

"What do you mean?" my mother asked, still half-distracted by the monument.

"I mean when she talked, did she have a thick accent, almost the way a gypsy would sound?" I asked, thinking of old-fashioned gypsy movies I had seen. It was the only comparison I could think of.

"Yes," Mom said, "though I never thought of her accent that way. Why?"

"Did she wear longish skirts, and did she have long hair?"

My mother's eyes widened. "Yes, why?"

"Mom, I think I met her."

My mother stopped. Her face drained of color.

"Describe her again," Mom muttered.

I did.

"Her hair was long."

"Was it white and pulled up in a bun?" Mom asked.

"No," I said. "It was darker, a reddish-brown, and it flowed all the way down her back. Is that what your grandmother looked like?"

My mother put her hands to her cheeks. "By the time I was born, her hair was white. It was long and silky, and she would take it down at night. By day she kept it up in a bun. But she showed me a picture of her once. She was younger, and her hair was darker." Mom's voice trembled a little. "It was a black-and-white picture, but she told me about her hair. It was a reddish-brown, and it flowed all the way down her back."

We stared at each other.

"This is kind of scary," she said finally.

I frowned. There was more, but I wasn't sure whether I should continue. Mom was still pale. I turned away as if to study the monument.

"What did she say?" Mom asked. "What did she want?"

I kept my back to Mom for the moment. My parents had been having some problems lately. With the economic downturn, my father's office was closing, and the threat of joblessness put pressure on their marriage. They fought all the time, often over nothing at all. There was no communication, and the one time I suggested they see a counselor, they both refused. My sister and I had just moved out after college, and when we called my parents focused only on superficial topics. When we asked what was wrong, they would never open up to us. And my mother had been living as if all of life's possibilities and blessings had suddenly ended.

"What did she say!" Mom demanded, regaining her voice.

"She told me that I need to spend more time with you," I said. "She said that you have been upset recently, and the real reason for it is that you have no one to talk to."

Mom frowned.

"She said that the problems you're having aren't that serious, but it seems worse to you because you're keeping it all inside."

Tears started pooling in Mom's eyes. I figured I had better finish what I started, so I continued: "She said that it's too bad you don't have a sibling, that all you've been thinking about lately is how you wish you had a sibling so you'd always have someone to talk to."

"This is very true," Mom managed to say. "Very true."

"There's one more thing," I said. It was the most difficult part, and I wanted to get it out before I lost my nerve. "When your grandmother told me that you wished you had a sibling, she said something strange. Something that didn't make sense. She said it was too bad you didn't have a sibling. But then she took this photograph. She wouldn't let me see it, but she took it out and studied it. She said, 'well, there was the one sibling, but there was the month that pained him.' Then she looked at the picture for a bit more before tucking it away in her skirt and turning back to me."

"The month that pained — him?" my mother asked.

I nodded. "What did she mean?"

"I don't believe this!" Mom said.

"What?"

"I never told you that I had a brother. He was stillborn. They named him and buried him. There was a month that pained him. It was the month he was born." By this time, tears were flowing down my mother's cheeks.

We stood in silence, watching the other tourists at the monument. It was my mother who broke the silence.

"I wonder why she told you that. What did she want?"

"She wanted me to be the one you can talk to about everything," I said. "She wanted you to be able to confide in me. She doesn't think it's good for you to bottle up everything."

"Maybe that's why she told you about the little boy in that picture. Maybe she knew it would convince me that she was real." Mom smiled sadly at me.

It would take time for my mother to process the dream, and it would take more time for her to finally open up to me. But she had always followed her grandmother's advice, and this time would be no exception. But for now, my mother stared off into the distance, warmed by the comfort of knowing that even after death her grandmother was protecting her.

— Val Muller —

96

Heaven's Mail

*A dream which is not interpreted
is like a letter which is not read.*
~The Talmud

I dialed the phone while wondering if it was too early to call. My sister, Jennifer, was away on vacation with her family and might not like my 8 a.m. interruption.

"Hello." A groggy voice answered.

"Jennifer, it's me, Joanne."

"What's wrong?" she asked, sounding more alert.

"Nothing is wrong," I assured her. "Sorry about calling you so early, but I thought the kids might have you up by now." My little sister was used to my pushy nature. Being the oldest of our four siblings, I enjoyed teasing them and pulling the bossy-older-sister card from time to time.

"None of us are up. The girls are still in bed." She sighed and continued, "I don't know about them, but I had a hard time getting to sleep last night. Lots of things going through my head…" She trailed off.

My sister was struggling to come to terms with our mother's death months before. After a two-year battle with cancer, Mom left our world for Heaven at the age of fifty-four. We were still reeling from the shock of her illness, and the fact she wouldn't be there for us to lean on, or to watch her grandchildren grow up.

Two years had been a bittersweet gift for me. I took advantage of the time to talk with Mom about as much as possible, including her death. I could see how it helped to speak with her, about things like what songs she wanted played at her funeral and how certain possessions needed to go to specific loved ones.

Sadly, my sister had none of these conversations with her. For two years Jennifer had been in denial.

Sure, she sat by like all four of us did and watched cancer transform our beautiful homecoming queen mom into a hollow shell of a person, but sadly, she never once spoke with her about dying. Mom worried about my sister and her anxiety about the whole situation. And in sparing her second child the tough conversations, Mom stunted grief's healing process.

I went on, "I have to share a dream I had about Mom. Now that I have you on the phone, it seems quite silly."

Actually, I'd debated about calling at all. The dream was so random it was borderline ridiculous. But it had been so vivid, so real, I felt compelled to share it.

I had Jennifer's full attention. "What did you dream?"

"Okay, well…" I hesitated, feeling kind of foolish. "Mom walked up to me and was smiling. She looked beautiful. She said just one thing: 'Tell Jennifer I loved what she wrote.'"

I rattled on, "I told you it was silly. Pretty out of the blue, huh? She really seemed to want me to give you that message." I softly chuckled, and then realized there was only silence on the other end of the line.

"Hello, Jennifer, are you there?" I pressed the receiver against my ear and heard a soft hiccup and gentle sobbing. "Are you okay? I'm so sorry. I should've waited to call you later." I figured my dream touched a tender place and quickly regretted my call. "I know you miss her, Jennifer."

"It's not that…" She sniffled and hiccupped again. "You're not going to believe this, Joanne."

Now she had my full attention.

"Last night I was having such a hard time falling asleep. I was tossing and turning, thinking about Mom and how I'd never talked with her about the important things."

I stayed silent, letting her get out whatever it was that had her so upset.

She went on, her voice thick. "After Mom died, I wrote her a letter. I really poured my heart out to her and told her how sorry I was about some things. On the day of her funeral I placed that letter inside her coffin." She softly blew her nose and continued. "Last night before I fell asleep, I prayed she could somehow read the words tucked away beside her."

Tears ran down my cheeks as my dream came rushing back to me. It all made sense now — my mother's gentle smile, her pleading eyes and request that I pass on a message to my little sister. I realized my mom's words were far from random, and now it was me who was sobbing.

"Tell Jennifer I loved what she wrote."

My mother's message to her hurting child — a bittersweet gift spanning eternity and inspiring hope in both of her children.

— Joanne Kraft —

97

The Accident

The relationship between parents and children,
but especially between mothers and daughters,
is tremendously powerful, scarcely to be
comprehended in any rational way.
~Joyce Carol Oates

"**I** just want to let you know that I'm running into town to pick up a few groceries. Will talk with you when I get back home." It was not an uncommon message for Mom to leave on my recorder since she often kept me informed as to her comings and goings. So why did I feel so troubled at missing the chance to talk with her?

I grabbed the phone quickly and dialed her number, hoping to catch her before she left, but she must have hurried out the door after leaving the message.

Then I saw it in my mind as clearly as if it were happening directly in front of my eyes.

Mom made a left turn onto the main highway. She apparently hit a patch of icy pavement and slid into the guardrail on the opposite side of the road. Wham!

Mom lived just up the private gravel road from our home. My parents moved to the countryside to be closer to their five grandchildren. Sadly, Dad passed away a few years later, so we tended to keep a close eye on Mom.

Without giving it a second thought, I grabbed my purse and ran out the door. I don't know whether I thought it was a premonition and I could save Mom from the crash, or if the accident had already taken place. Regardless, she needed me, and I had to go.

It was only about a five-mile drive to the highway from our house, and I made it in record time. As I pulled up to the stop sign and looked to the left, I saw Mom's black Mercury Sable crashed into the guardrail exactly as I had seen it in my vision a few minutes earlier.

No other vehicles had stopped to help, so I must have reached her within seconds of the crash. Looking carefully both ways, I tried to remain calm so I wouldn't fall victim to the same fate. I pulled slowly out onto the highway and parked directly behind the scrunched-up vehicle.

Mom looked at me strangely when I ran up and opened her door. "How did you know what happened?" she asked, somewhat baffled. I don't think it even occurred to her that I could have simply been driving by at the same time.

Other vehicles began to stop to offer help, so I didn't have the chance to explain how I happened to be there so quickly.

Later that afternoon, after dealing with the local towing company, the auto body shop and the insurance agent, Mom and I finally got a chance to sit down and chat about the accident. When I told her about my premonition, I was shocked and somewhat disappointed that she wasn't in complete awe.

"Mom, why aren't you more excited about me knowing you were in that accident?" I inquired with a bit of attitude.

"Honey," she responded, "how do you think I always know when you need me?"

She was correct — there is an inexplicable bond between a mother and her child that transcends the toughest boundaries, and I was just beginning to grasp what she had known for years.

I felt blessed to have been privy to what had transpired that day — and so thankful that I could be there when *Mom* needed *me*.

— Connie Kaseweter Pullen —

98

A Note from Heaven

*Grandmas hold our tiny hands for just
a little while, but our hearts forever.*
~Author Unknown

I can still remember the feel of her hand the last time I held it. She lay very still in my mother's bed, her kidneys failing. My thumb lovingly stroked her thin translucent skin. Her old wrinkled hands told a lifetime of stories: of cradling her children and grandchildren, preparing hearty warm Thanksgiving and Easter meals, skillfully handling dental tools, crocheting and tatting yarn into beautiful lace and flowers, and rubbing the sore back of a frail husband. I smiled as I saw the soft apricot nail polish on her long right thumbnail. Only yesterday I had knelt at her feet, oiling her dry legs and giving her a manicure. She was so proud of that long nail, holding it up and smiling, and with a wink, warning me not to file it down too much.

It was time to go back to Boston, to say goodbye forever. "I love you Gram, more than I can say. Mom will take good care of you," I whispered into her ear. I rested my head against her shoulder, gently embracing her with my arm across her chest. How do you let go? How do you pull away when you know it will be the last time? I memorized the pattern on the bedspread tucked around her, the sound of her breathing, the feel of her touch, the smell of her Estée Lauder perfume. I wanted to keep those memories with me for a lifetime.

Two weeks later, 1,000 miles away, I received the call. "Gram is in heaven," my mother said softly. Tears filled my eyes.

As the days unfolded, my mother asked me if I would sing at Gram's funeral. I was honored, agreeing to do anything I could to help make this easier for her. I set aside my own grief to prepare the hymns, the music that would comfort all of us.

After my flight back, I walked into the house and felt drawn to the room, the bed, and the place where I had last held her hand. The same pattern on the bedspread, the same quiet now filled only with the sound of my own breathing. I knelt on the floor and gripped her pillow and breathed in, searching for a little bit of the familiar Estée Lauder perfume. But there was none and I wept.

Seeing my despair, Mom quietly came over and slipped her hand in mine, leading me into another room where a shrine of sorts had been set up in my grandmother's memory. The green marble urn containing her ashes sat on a table surrounded by her red rosary, the faceted beads worn by years of prayerful touch. There were pictures of Jesus welcoming someone to heaven and lovely images of Gram in healthier days. I stood quietly taking it in.

The funeral went as well as could be expected. I made it through the emotional hymns, keeping myself together, and doing what had to be done while my mother cried her tears of loss and gratitude. After the service, I rode in the car with my dad and uncle to the store where we shipped my grandmother's ashes to Chicago to be buried next to my grandfather. My uncle and I added a single rose next to her urn before the box was taped shut.

As I flew home I watched the palm trees and beaches shrink below me as we soared over the sparkling ocean water. I felt closer to Gram, to heaven, as we slid through the white clouds.

Walking into my house, I set my luggage down and was greeted by gentle hugs from my family. As everyone dispersed, I headed downstairs to be alone.

Suddenly in the quiet of the basement, I felt overwhelmed. I fell to my knees near a closet under the stairs where I kept boxes of old photos and mementos waiting to be sorted someday. It's the kind of place where you could not put your finger on something even if you wanted to. There is no rhyme or reason, just cards, negatives and photos thrown in random boxes for "someday."

My grief bubbled to the surface at last and all the goodbyes poured out on the floor in my tears. "I miss you so much, Gram," I sobbed out loud, bringing my hands to my face. As the pain of missing her filled my heart, I called out to God, "I know she is happy being with you in heaven, and I wouldn't want to take that away from her, but I miss her so much...." I cried as I had never cried before.

Suddenly, an unexpected wave of complete, warm peace moved through my body from head to toe like a wave. I sat up on my knees and caught my breath. My shoulders relaxed as I brushed the tears and damp hair from my cheeks. I heard a whisper: "Reach into the closet."

Still on my knees, I reached for the handle, twisting it slowly. I slid it open just wide enough to slip my hand and arm into the dark. Reaching into a box I could not see, I grasped the first thing I felt, a piece of thin paper. I slowly withdrew my hand. I was holding a fragile yellowed piece of paper I had never seen before. The edges were torn but the words were intact: "Cathy. I love you! Gram." Somehow, my dear grandmother had reached out across the universe to send a message to comfort a hurting soul.

— Cathy Stenquist —

99

The Pull of the Magnet

The love of a mother is the veil of a softer light between
the heart and the heavenly Father.
~Samuel Taylor Coleridge

When my mother was dying I told her, "Mom, you have to give me a sign. Let me know you made it, okay?" She smiled and nodded. Her mouth was too dry to speak. She'd been in hospice for weeks and was reaching the end. She was more than ready.

After she passed away, I was at her house preparing for an estate sale. Family and friends had taken keepsakes, mementos, and the cherished family heirlooms they wanted. Only the stuff of life was left — pots and pans, pillows and blankets, jigsaw puzzles and books. And a large collection of magnets Mom had collected on her travels and had gotten from family and friends.

Nearly two hundred magnets covered the white refrigerator — not that anyone could see the underlying color. I managed to make room for a sign that said "2 for 25 cents."

My sisters helped with the estate sale the next day. It was a big success because it was an unseasonably warm January day. One young man was thrilled to get Dad's claw-foot hammer and box of finishing nails for $2.00. On his way to pay, he lingered at the refrigerator, carefully selecting a single magnet — the Portuguese rooster Mom had bought in Lisbon.

He gave my sister $2.25. "The magnets are two for 25 cents," she said.

"One's good," he said. "Thank you."

Two months later, I was finishing an exhaustive search for a new house and I was touring a beautifully renovated home. It was so pretty it looked like it had been staged. It was bright and inviting with an open floor plan. It was just the right size and right price. Everything was perfectly arranged, right down to the throw pillows. Even though it was somewhat impersonal, without a sense of who had lived in this house and who had carefully restored it, I felt a pull of some kind. Maybe this was the right house.

Once I entered the kitchen, I knew. On the refrigerator was a single magnet — my mom's Portuguese rooster. She had sent me a sign. We were both home.

— Teresa Otto —

100

Thanks, Mom

Death ends a life, not a relationship.
~Jack Lemmon

One Sunday afternoon during a visit at my parents' house, my mother led me into her bedroom. "Suzanne, I have something I want to give you." She pulled open her top dresser drawer, lifted out a small box, and handed it to me.

"What is this, Mom?" I asked and tugged at the lid. The interior, lined by royal-blue velvet, held a gold wedding band. A continuous leaf pattern had been etched on the surface. I glanced at her and smiled. "Really?"

"This ring belonged to your grandmother, given to her by Grandpa in honor of their 50th anniversary. She bequeathed it to me when she passed away. Try it on and see if it fits."

"But, Mom, don't you want to wear it? There's no hurry to give it to me."

"I want to be sure you have this. I made a promise to my mother to pass it down to you."

I slipped off my diamond wedding ring and slid on the shiny band. It fit my finger perfectly. Butterflies fluttered inside my chest as I admired the new piece of jewelry. My thoughts couldn't make sense of the gift, but it held a very special meaning for me. The family connection brought tears to my eyes.

"It does fit me well," I said and smiled.

"The ring's too tight on me. I'm so glad you're able to wear it in her memory. Take a look inside. He had their initials engraved in there, too."

I slid it off, squinted and saw the tiny letters inscribed in the gold. "How unique. Thank you very much, Mom." We hugged.

Three months later, we buried my mother at age sixty-eight. She had found out she had pancreatic cancer in May, and there was nothing the doctors could do. At her funeral, I reminisced about the day she gave me that ring. She had already known her fate. She was a brave soul.

Since the moment I'd put on that ring, I'd never taken it off. It meant so much to me, and I now wore it in memory of my mother *and* grandmother.

A year later, I decided to color my gray hair. I had to remove the ring to put on the rubber gloves. That next morning, I couldn't find my precious ring anywhere. I retraced my steps. Had I set it on the bathroom sink or tossed it on my dresser? I searched each place thoroughly. I couldn't find it.

I berated myself. That ring stood for so much. How could I have been so careless?

Six months later, I still hadn't found Grandma's wedding band. How could it have just disappeared? I vowed to keep looking.

One night at 2:00 a.m., when I was sound asleep, I heard my mother's voice in a dream. She said, "Suzanne, move the dresser." My eyes opened wide, and I bolted to a sitting position. I'd know her voice anywhere. Chills traveled through me. I searched the corners of my dark bedroom. *What had just happened? Was it really her?*

Nothing was amiss. My husband snored away on his side of our king-size bed. I dropped back to my pillow. First thing tomorrow, I'd check the floor beneath the triple dresser.

After morning coffee, I borrowed a wooden yardstick from my husband's tool rack. I squeezed my body into a tight corner beside my dresser and stared. Total blackness greeted me. I rose and grabbed a flashlight, returned and peered in again. In the illuminated area, I saw a glint of something metal. I stood and crammed that yardstick in as far as I could. Then I swept the carpet toward me. Dust bunnies came out. No ring.

I swiped again and dragged out a lost earring — one of a pair that had recently been misplaced when I was in a hurry to insert it. *Was that what she meant?* I sighed. Thinking positive, I gave it one more try and raked the floor even harder. A gold item flashed as it rolled by. My heart did flip-flops. I knelt and scooped it up.

My grandmother's ring.

I'd found it. Immediately, I slipped the band back on. Joy flowed through me. I glanced up to where my mother resides now. And after she spoke to me in that dream, I know she watches over me. Thanks, Mom.

— Suzanne Baginskie —

Dragonflies

To forgive is to set a prisoner free and
discover that the prisoner was you.
~Louis B. Smedes

I t was two hours past the time that I was supposed to be moved to jail from the city cells. I was sick of Hungry-Man dinners and toast, and tired of sleeping with one itchy blanket in a cold, dark cell. I made all the calls I could, asking friends and family for bail money. No one accepted. They all had their reasons.

After three days inside, I was truly scared. When the guard came and unlocked my cell, I thought it was time for the move, so I steeled myself for whatever was going to happen next. In silence, he led me upstairs. Not knowing what to expect, I trudged along behind him, anxiety coursing through my veins. When I finally looked up, there stood my mother, the last person I expected to see.

My parents split up when I was very young, and though children of divorce are often raised by a single mom, my dad raised my brother and me. I don't think I ever forgave my mother for leaving. Because of that, among other reasons, we never saw eye-to-eye, never got along, and never enjoyed a good mother/daughter relationship. So, seeing her there left me stunned, especially since she was one of the many who had declined to bail me out.

But now she had bailed me out, and we quietly drove to my dad's in her car. I had no clue what awaited me, but as soon as I opened the door to the house, I had a pretty good idea.

And so it began — an intervention just like the ones on TV. All the people who loved me most were gathered there, but they were dead serious. They told me that I needed to change and clean up my act. They loved me, but they were not willing to stand by and watch me destroy myself. It had already been agreed before I got there that I was to move to my mother and stepdad's farm. If I refused, they would "disown" me. My dad and my brother meant everything to me, and I couldn't imagine my life without them, so there was no decision to be made. Of course, I agreed.

Mom lived just outside a tiny town of about 800 people, forty kilometers away. I started out there going through withdrawal. I slept for most of the first two weeks. I was so sick that I wanted to die. I didn't think I could get by without the drugs, the partying, and the friends, let alone live in the sticks with the woman whom I felt had once abandoned me. Everything about the situation seemed impossible.

Then came the day I still recall clearly. Mom came into my room and told me I had to get up. I had to get some fresh air. I just wanted her to go away and leave me alone, but she persisted. Muttering under my breath, I got up and went outside with her.

The sun was blindingly bright, and the breeze smelled like pasture. Believe me, that is not as pleasant as it sounds. We talked, enjoyed her flowers and admired the gathering of dragonflies. It was an especially hot summer, and they were plentiful that year. I have never seen that many since. She raised her pointer finger in the air and told me to do the same. I rolled my eyes, but complied begrudgingly. Then I watched, mesmerized, as the dragonflies landed on our fingers.

At that precise moment, I realized that I was missing the small things in life. I had a sudden awareness that there was so much to appreciate and so many experiences that I had yet to live. I had my whole life ahead of me, a life more valuable than I had ever thought possible. I realized then that the parties, drugs, and fake friends weren't really living at all. They were just a way to pass the time, a way to bury my anger, hurt and feelings of abandonment that I refused to let go. More importantly, I realized that I did have a mother. She didn't abandon me, and she was here now when I needed her most. I was still her daughter, and she hadn't given up. On that day out on the prairie, in the afternoon sunshine, she became not only my mother but my friend.

That was more than twelve years ago. Since then, my mother and I have formed a relationship I had never dreamed possible. She has become a big part of my life and that of my two wonderful children. They think the world of their granny. She has held me when I've cried, consoled me when I was in pain, celebrated my successes, and carried me through my failures.

Most of all, I admire how she held my hand through recovery, teaching by example the true meaning of life and love. It took me far too long to forgive her for not being there when I was young. And as much as I regret that, I understand. Because of her, I was able to get clean and begin a relationship with her that would be unbreakable. My children are also blessed with her unconditional love. Because she taught me how to forgive, they enjoy an amazing granny who shares with them the simple things in life, like catching dragonflies. I am forever grateful that she saved me and has shown me the depth of a true mother's love.

— Celeste Bergeron Ewan —

Meet Our Contributors

We are pleased to introduce you to the writers whose stories were compiled from our library to create this new collection. These bios were the ones that ran when the stories were originally published. They were current as of the publication dates of those books.

Debbie Acklin lives in Alabama with her husband, two children, and Duchess the cat. She enjoys outdoor activities, gardening and travel. Debbie is planning to collaborate with her daughter on a book of travel stories. E-mail her at d_acklin@hotmail.com.

Annie (not her real name, of course) is a freelance writer whose work has appeared widely both online and in print. She is happy to report that her marriage has remained strong and loving for twenty years despite her mother-in-law's antics.

Kathy Ashby is the author of *Carol: A Woman's Way* published by Dream Catcher Publishing. As quoted on the back cover, Dr. Helen Caldicott says, "A very important fictional account of the activity of women to preserve the environment. Indeed most successful movements have been and are started by women." E-mail Kathy at ashbykathy@gmail.com.

Suzanne Baginskie lives on the west coast of Florida with her husband, Al. Recently retired, she enjoys writing and has been published in various *Chicken Soup for the Soul* books. Her other interests include traveling, reading, and watching movies. She is currently working on an inspirational romantic suspense novel.

Brenda Barajas will graduate high school in 2011. She does well in all academic subjects and is proud of her 4.0 GPA. Brenda loves to play volleyball and spend time with family and friends. She hopes to get into a great college when she graduates.

Kathryn A. Beres resides in rural Wisconsin, and has work appearing in over fifty different publications, including *Lifewise* (Focus on the Family) and *The Miracle of Sons*. Two-time recipient of the People's Choice Award, her inspirations are her husband Mike; four children, Kaytlyn, Andrea, Mitch and Tyler; and brother, Jeff. E-mail her at kathrynberes@hotmail.com.

Kristi Blakeway is a school principal in Maple Ridge, BC. She is the founder of Beyond HELLO, a TEDx speaker, Olympic Torchbearer and winner of the YWCA Women of Distinction award. Kristi encourages everyone to engage in soulful dialogue and connect with compassion. She blogs regularly at www.beyondhello.org.

Jeanne Blandford is a writer/editor who, along with her husband Jack, is currently producing documentaries and creating children's books. When not in their Airstream looking for new material, they can be found running SafePet, a partnership between Outreach for Pets in Need (OPIN) and Domestic Violence Crisis Center (DVCC).

Lil Blosfield fell in love with writing shortly after she learned how to read. She has a vast collection of stories and poems and truly believes that every day is an opportunity for a story with a constantly changing flow of characters. E-mail her at LBlosfield40@msn.com.

Karla Brown is a writer of non-fiction short stories, fantasy adventure and children's manuscripts. She is a flight attendant with US Airways Express. Karla adores her husband and daughters who, along with her impish grandson, make her smile every day! She enjoys children, books, swimming, and gardening. E-mail her at karlab612@yahoo.com.

Jill Burns lives in the mountains of West Virginia with her wonderful family. She's a retired piano teacher and performer. She enjoys writing, music, gardening, nature, and spending time with her grandchildren.

Kristine Byron worked as a trainer for Tupperware and in later years as an interior designer. She loves to cook and entertain. Kristine also loves to travel with her husband and spend quality time with her five grandchildren.

Leslie Calderoni has just finished her first young adult novel.

She has four children and more than a few rescue animals. She loves to cook, read, and nap whenever possible. She enjoys writing in various coffee shops on the central coast of California.

Jean Salisbury Campbell, a retired school psychologist, wife and mother, graduated from the University of Florida and FIU, where she also studied creative writing. Caring for her mother during her six-year Alzheimer's decline propelled Jean to write about the priceless lessons learned that helped her cope with the loss.

Lorri Carpenter, along with her mother, writes under the pen name HL Carpenter. A mother/daughter duo, they admit to having way too much fun writing together. Their most recent book, *The SkyHorse*, is a young adult e-novel published by Musa Publishing and available on Amazon. See more of their work at www.TopDrawerInkCorp.com.

Sandy McPherson Carrubba stopped teaching first grade for full-time motherhood. She's written for children and adults. Her essays have appeared in *Voices of Alzheimer's*, *Voices of Lung Cancer* and the *Chicken Soup for the Soul* series. Her poetry chapbook, *Brush Strokes*, was published by Finishing Line Press.

Since 1996, **Jane Cassie's** articles have appeared in more than 7,000 publications as well as sharing travel stories with armchair adventurers. She frequently escapes to her cottage in British Columbia's Cariboo where more stories unfold. She is also co-owner/editor of *Travel Writers*. Learn more at travelwriterstales.com.

Madeline Clapps lives in Brooklyn, NY, and is an actor, singer, and editor at Chicken Soup for the Soul. She recently edited *Chicken Soup for the Soul: Just for Preteens* and *Chicken Soup for the Soul: Just for Teenagers*. She also designs the monthly communiqué for Chicken Soup for the Soul contributors.

Courtney Conover is a writer, YouTube content creator, and yoga teacher who resides in Michigan with her former NFL player husband, Scott, and their two young children. After abusing her hair with a flat iron for nearly thirty-eight years, she has finally learned to love her natural curls—sometimes even more than chocolate.

Tracy Crump publishes *The Write Life* e-newsletter, moderates an online critique group, and enjoys teaching other writers at conferences and through her Write Life Workshops. Now she not only has a daughter, but a sweet little granddaughter, Nellie. Visit Tracy at TracyCrump. com and WriteLifeWorkshops.com.

Judy DeCarlo is employed as a registered nuclear medicine technologist but is at heart a writer. She resides in Northeast Pennsylvania and is a married mother of two adult daughters. Judy enjoys reading, all outdoor activities, and traveling (particularly planning trips). E-mail her at superrep1@aol.com.

Jennifer Quasha Deinard is a published nonfiction author and editor, public speaker, certified life coach, and has been a contributor to over twenty-five *Chicken Soup for the Soul* books. Learn more at www.jotcoach.com.

Crystal Duffy received her bachelor's degree in 2007 and a master's in 2008 from Georgetown University. She has three daughters, including a set of twins, and teaches high school English in Texas. She is the author of *Twin to Twin* and teaches an Expectant Twins Parents class. She enjoys traveling, running and reading on the beach.

Valerie Dyer is the daughter of Neil and Linda, mama to Aubrey and Alli, stepmom to Olivia and wife to John. She is a sister, auntie, niece, coach, and friend. Valerie is a native Mainer, a writer, a dreamer, and a breast cancer survivor. Share your own stories with her at valeriewilbur37@gmail.com.

Audra Easley is a graphic designer in Atlanta, GA. She loves volunteering in her community, drawing, and writing. She is at work on her second novel.

Celeste Bergeron Ewan works full-time as a supervisor in a pipe manufacturing plant. If that isn't busy enough, she is also a proud mother of two and a newly wed wife to her husband John. Celeste enjoys spending time with her family, camping, treasure hunting, and of course, writing. She plans to write an autobiography one day.

Melissa Face teaches and writes in Virginia. She lives with her husband, son, and dog and enjoys spending time and traveling with all three of them. E-mail Melissa at writermsface@yahoo.com.

Victoria Fedden is a writer and a mom from Fort Lauderdale, FL. Her memoir, *This Is Not My Beautiful Life*, was published June 2016 by

Picador USA. She received her MFA in Creative Writing from Florida Atlantic University in 2009, and teaches college writing in South Florida.

Bonnie Jean Feldkamp is an award-winning freelance writer and columnist. She is the Communications Director for the National Society of Newspaper Columnists, member of the Cincinnati Enquirer Editorial Board, and a board member for the Cincinnati Chapter of the Society of Professional Journalists.

Jean Ferratier, a previous *Chicken Soup for the Soul* contributor, has a passion for sharing stories. She is an Archetypal Consultant, helping people link their synchronous moments to their life purpose. Jean's book is called *Reading Symbolic Signs: How to Connect the Dots of Your Spiritual Life.* E-mail her at jferratier@gmail.com.

Carole Brody Fleet is a multi-award-winning author, media contributor and five-time contributor to the *Chicken Soup for the Soul* series. An expert in grief and life-adversity recovery, Ms. Fleet has made over 1,200 radio appearances and additionally has appeared on numerous television programs as well as in worldwide print and web media.

Denise Flint is a freelance journalist living on the edge of North America in the middle of the North Atlantic. She's lived in four provinces and three countries and her interests are diverse. Denise's articles have appeared in newspapers and magazines internationally and she has received many awards for her work.

Gloria Hudson Fortner received a bachelor's degree from David Lipscomb College and a master's degree from Nova Southeastern University and earned a National Board for Professional Teaching certification. Her writing has appeared in various educational journals. After thirty years in the classroom, she now spends her time enjoying her family.

Sarah Foster is a wife, mother, and writer. She is also a daughter, granddaughter, and sister. She loves her quirky, crazy, wonderful family with all her heart.

Surrounded by pets, farm animals, and gorgeous countryside, **Vera Frances** is a retired banker who enjoys frequenting the nearby mountains for fly fishing, hiking, and painting. She is a nature enthusiast by day and writer by night.

For three decades, **Sally Friedman** of Moorestown, New Jersey, has been chronicling her life for various publications including *The New York Times, Ladies' Home Journal, Family Circle* and regional newspapers and magazines. She writes about her life as a wife, mother, grandmother and observer. Contact Sally via e-mail at pinegander@aol.com.

Heidi Gaul lives in Oregon's Willamette Valley with her husband and four-legged family. She loves travel, be it around the block or the globe. Active in Oregon Christian Writers, she is currently writing her fourth novel. Contact her through her website at www.HeidiGaul.com.

Lynn Gilliland is a retired electrical engineer from a large automotive firm. He and his wife Karen have two daughters and five grandchildren. He has been writing since his retirement twelve years ago. He leads the local Defiance, Ohio Writers Group, and belongs to the Northwest Ohio Writers Forum.

Marsha Henry Goff is an author, editor, journalist, and former newspaper humor columnist. She lives with her husband in the home they built on a rural Kansas hill. She has two sons, four grandchildren and is rich in family and friends who provide her with great copy.

Judy Lee Green is an award-winning writer and speaker whose spirit and roots reach deep into the Appalachian Mountains. Tennessee-bred and cornbread-fed, she has been published hundreds of times and received dozens of awards for her work. As her inspiration, she often writes about her large colorful family.

Tina Haapala was a member of Phi Theta Kappa Honor Society for two-year colleges. She received her Bachelor of Science, with honors, from Arizona State University in 1996. Tina has worked in sales, marketing, and operations management. She enjoys writing, reading, yoga, and belly dancing. Contact her at tinahaapala@gmail.com.

Gabrielle Harbowy is a writer, editor, and anthologist with two published novels, a dozen short stories in print, and over seventy-five published editing credits to her name. Learn more at www.gabrielleharbowy.com or on Twitter @gabrielle_h.

Melanie Adams Hardy received her Bachelor of Science in 1984 and her Juris Doctorate in 2007. Melanie enjoys cooking, writing short stories, and volunteer work in her church and local community. She plans to write a book of short stories about her unique Southern family.

Please e-mail her at rhardy212@charter.net.

Miriam Hill is a frequent contributor to the *Chicken Soup for the Soul* series and has been published in *Writer's Digest*, *The Christian Science Monitor*, *Grit*, *St. Petersburg Times*, *The Sacramento Bee*, and Poynter online. Miriam's submission received Honorable Mention for Inspirational Writing in a Writer's Digest Writing Competition.

Gina Farella Howley received her Master's in Special Education from Northern Illinois University in 1991. She has been a teacher, tutor, and freelance writer. Most importantly, with husband John, she manages the craziness produced by her three sons Martin (thirteen), Joe (eleven), and Tim (nine). She enjoys beaches, books, chocolate and wine.

Pauline Hylton is a freelance writer living in Florida. She specializes in humor or anything else you will pay her for. She loves the Lord, her family, and dark chocolate. (Not necessarily in that order.) Feel free to read her blog, send an e-mail, or mail her dark chocolate at paulinehylton.com.

Geneva Cobb Iijima lives in the Northwest of the U.S. and has four books and over 100 stories and articles in print. She is currently researching and writing a new book, *Amazing Youth of WWII*. She enjoys her children, grandchildren and friends. Visit her website at genevaiijima.com.

Linda Baten Johnson grew up in White Deer, TX, where she won awards for storytelling. She still loves telling tales. A tornado destroyed her hometown, and the faith-based action she witnessed as people rebuilt homes and lives influences her writing. Check out her historical fiction and romance at lindabatenjohnson.com.

A speaker and award-winning writer, **Marlys Johnson-Lawry** has a passion for repurposing old junk into cool new stuff and an even greater passion for showing people how to navigate life's challenges. Her free time is filled with hiking tall mountains, snowshoeing through powder, and sipping chai tea while reading through stacks of books.

Mary-Lane Kamberg has published more than thirty nonfiction books and a poetry chapbook. She roots for the Jayhawks during March Madness. She practices Tai Chi and has been kissed by a camel.

Heidi Kling-Newnam received a Doctor of Nursing Practice from West Chester University in 2017. She is employed as a nurse practitioner in Pennsylvania. Heidi enjoys writing, hiking, and camping.

Nancy Julien Kopp lives with her husband in the Flint Hills of Kansas. She writes essays, fiction for kids, memoir, poetry and more. She has stories published in twenty-one *Chicken Soup for the Soul* books. She loves to play bridge, travel, and enjoy her children and grandchildren. Read her blog at www.writergrannysworld.blogspot.com.

Joanne Kraft is the author of *Just Too Busy: Taking Your Family on a Radical Sabbatical*. A sought-after speaker, with articles appearing in numerous family/parenting magazines, she frequents California coffee shops with her husband Paul and loves being a mom to their four children. Visit her at JoanneKraft.com or GraceAndTruthLiving.com.

Samantha LaBarbera received her Bachelor of Arts degree from Franklin & Marshall College and her J.D. from Villanova University Charles Widger School of Law. An attorney in the pharmaceutical industry, she lives in Pennsylvania with her husband and two children.

Cathi LaMarche is an essayist, novelist, poet, and writing coach. Her work has appeared in over thirty anthologies. When not immersed in the written word, she is helping to spread awareness about the devastating effects of Lyme disease.

Jeannie Lancaster is a freelance writer from Loveland, CO. She is a lover of words — sharing them through her written work, weekly storytelling with a delightful group of preschoolers, and thirty-seven years of late night word games with her husband. She can be reached via e-mail at bjlancast@msn.com.

Andrea Langworthy's columns appear in the *Rosemount Town Pages* and *Minnesota Good Age* newspapers. She's been published in *Chicken Soup for the Soul: Divorce and Recovery*, the *2009 St. Paul Almanac* and various Minnesota publications. She teaches a writing workshop at Minneapolis's Loft Literary Center.

Betsy Alderman Lewis is a freelance writer with many interests, especially history. Lewis has a B.A. degree in Cultural Studies with concentrations in writing and literature. She enjoys designing quilt and embroidery patterns. You can visit her website at www.betsylewiswrites.

com or e-mail her at info@betsylewiswrites.com.

Barbara LoMonaco received her BS from the University of Southern California and has an elementary teaching credential. Barbara has worked for Chicken Soup for the Soul since February 1998. She wears many hats there, including Senior Editor.

Crescent LoMonaco used her knowledge from years of working behind the chair and owning a hair salon to write the "Ask a Stylist" column for the *Santa Barbara Independent*. She is a frequent contributor to the *Chicken Soup for the Soul* series. She lives on the Southern California coast with her husband and son.

Catherine MacKenzie writes all genres but mostly dark fiction women can relate to — stories perhaps bizarre, yet ominously real. A published author, she's also self-published several poetry and short story collections on Amazon and Smashwords. Cathy lives in Halifax, Nova Scotia, and winters in Ajijic, Mexico. E-mail her at writingwicket@gmail.com.

Marie MacNeill is an interior designer in the Toronto area. She enjoys travelling, power walking, gardening and writing, and is currently working on an authorized biography. Marie is looking forward to carrying on her Christmas traditions with her new grandchild.

Carrie Malinowski is a first grade teacher and reading tutor. She has a degree in psychology. She wrote her first story at the age of five and has been writing ever since. She loves to write picture books. Ms. Malinowski lives in Arizona with her husband, son, and dog Chester. Please visit her at www.carriemalinowski.com.

Erica McGee grew up in Knoxville, TN, and is a University of Tennessee graduate. She is a playwright and currently performs and tours in her production, *Girls Raised in the South–GRITS: The Musical* throughout the U.S. She now calls Charlotte, NC home, where she is proud to be Tara's mom and Ryan's wife!

Stephanie McKellar is a current high school student, scheduled to graduate in 2012. She plans to attend university in Fall 2012. Afterward, she would like to work as an author.

Erin Miller is a sophomore in high school. She continues to strive for academic excellence. Erin enjoys playing the violin and singing. She cherishes her family and friends. Erin's mom, Marie-Therese Miller, is an author of non-fiction books for teens and children. Please visit her website at www.marie-theresemiller.com.

Jaclyn S. Miller graduated from Taylor University with a BA in Christian Education. She later pursued her love of writing at Bethel College and earned a degree in Professional Writing as well. Currently, she is employed at an advertising agency and writes freelance. She enjoys cooking, reading (of course!), day hiking and painting.

Janet Lynn Mitchell is an author, speaker, wife, mother, grandmother, and friend. Her passion is to communicate God's love to others. Whether writing, speaking or hanging out, she hopes to encourage others. Her latest book, *A Voice Once Silenced*, is soon to be released.

Sarah E. Morin is a kid wrangler at a history museum in Indiana. She writes poems, short stories, and unruly fairy tales, including two books: *Waking Beauty* and *Rapunzel the Hairbrained*. When she grows up she wants to be a child prodigy.

Diane Morrow-Kondos writes a weekly blog about grandparenting at www.tulsakids.com/Grand-Life/. Her book, *The Long Road to Happy: A Sister's Struggle Through Her Brother's Disabilities*, will be released fall 2019. Diane is also a triathlete and open water swimmer. Learn more at www.dianemorrowkondos.com.

Val Muller's fiction has appeared in a handful of magazines and anthologies. Her first novel, *Corgi Capers*, is a middle-grade mystery. You can keep track of her at mercuryval.wordpress.com, and contact her at mercuryval@yahoo.com.

Kaitlin Murray loves to travel, write, and volunteer. She was born in Holland and has also lived in Germany, France, the USA, and Italy. For the past two years, Kaitlin has been traveling full-time and volunteering all over the world. She also founded a charity called Kids Unite 4 Hope to help children in need. Read her blog at travelinkait.com.

Alice Muschany writes about everyday life with a touch of humor. She went so far as to write her own obituary, mostly so she could get in the last word. Her family, especially her grandchildren, make wonderful subjects. Her essays have appeared in numerous anthologies and magazines. E-mail her at aliceandroland@gmail.com.

Sara Nolt is a dedicated Christian, a happy wife and a stay-at-home mom of two preschoolers. While this defines most of her world, she also takes time for short-term mission work and freelance writing for Christian publications. Recently a first-time author, she is working on her second book.

Phyllis Nordstrom spent most of her adult years in education in addition to being a pastor's wife. This is her third publication in the *Chicken Soup for the Soul* series. Currently she is working on a book of memoirs to be presented to her twelve grandchildren. To keep her mind and body fit, she swims, reads, travels, and volunteers.

Caitlin Q. Bailey O'Neill has been previously published in *Chicken Soup for the Soul: Empty Nesters* and *Chicken Soup for the Soul: Thanks Dad*. A freelance editor and writer, she can be reached at PerfectlyPunctuated@yahoo.com. This story is for Kathy Bailey — who still loves seeing her daughter's name in print.

Teresa Otto is a freelance writer, photographer, and retired pediatric anesthesiologist. She enjoys Taoist Tai Chi and loves her four-legged children. While Montana will always be home, she is passionate about travel, especially to off-the-beaten-path places. You can keep up with her adventures at thenomadsdaughter.com.

Suzanne Garner Payne, a North Carolina native and a teacher for thirty years, has always loved helping middle school students find their voices through writing. She has now found her voice by writing about her family, which includes two fine sons, Alan and David, and her true Southern Californian husband, John.

Connie K. Pombo is an inspirational speaker, freelance writer and frequent contributor to the *Chicken Soup for the Soul* series. When not speaking or writing, she enjoys combing the beaches of Florida for shells and visiting her four grandchildren in Pennsylvania. Learn more at www.conniepombo.com.

Felice Prager is a freelance writer and multisensory educational therapist from Scottsdale, AZ. Hundreds of her essays have been published locally, nationally, and internationally in print and on the Internet. She is the author of *Quiz It: Arizona*. To find out more about Felice's book or to find links to more of her work, please visit http:

www.QuizItAZ.com.

T. Powell Pryce is a single mother of two who lives near Saint Louis, MO. She teaches and writes, and has contributed to several *Chicken Soup for the Soul* books.

Connie Kaseweter Pullen lives in rural Sandy, OR, near her five children and several grandchildren. She earned her Bachelor of Arts, with honors, at the University of Portland in 2006, with a double major in Psychology and Sociology. Connie enjoys writing, photography, and exploring nature.

Johanna Richardson, always a lover of the written word, dabbles with writing for her own pleasure and is a voracious reader. Her life has been blessed by a wonderful husband and family. She is an RN, has a master's degree from the University of San Francisco, and is a Peer Volunteer for the National Alzheimer's Association.

Keeana Saxon has a B.A. from Spelman College and a J.D. from Western New England University School of Law. She is now a commissioner with the city of Boston, a piano teacher, and the Founder and Executive Producer of Kidogo Productions, a multimedia company for preschoolers. She is working on a set of children's poems.

Is there anything more wonderful than daughters who can cook? **Deborah Shouse** is a writer, speaker, caregiver's advocate, editor and creativity catalyst. Her writing has appeared in a variety of periodicals and books. She is the author of *Love in the Land of Dementia*. Visit her blog at DementiaJourney.org.

Bobbi Silva has loved to dance her entire life, becoming a dance teacher in the 1950s. She has continued to dance throughout the years, discovering clogging, a fast-moving style of dance, and becoming a member of the award-winning Country Knights Exhibition dance team in the 1990s. Currently, she enjoys dancing at One Generation Senior Center.

Alison Singer is co-founder and president of the Autism Science Foundation, a non-profit organization dedicated to funding autism research and supporting families raising children with autism. Her daughter, Jodie, is diagnosed with autism. Alison also has an older brother with autism. Learn more at www.autismsciencefoundation.org.

Haylie Smart holds a Bachelor of Arts in Liberal Arts and has worked in community journalism as a reporter since June 2013. She plans to teach English and creative writing. She enjoys cooking, reading for knowledge, serving in church and loving her nine nieces and nephews. E-mail her at haylie.smart@yahoo.com.

Diane Stark is a wife, mother of five, and freelance writer. She loves to write about the important things in life: her family and her faith. E-mail her at DianeStark19@yahoo.com.

Cathy Stenquist is a mother of three who loves to write about everyday connections with God and with each other. You can follow her creative explorations on her blog: cathystenquist.tumblr.com, where she shares her love of writing, painting and cooking. She is currently writing her first inspirational children's book.

Carol Strazer has had several of her essays appear in the *Chicken Soup for the Soul* series. She published her first novel, *Barbed Wire & Daisies*, a historical fiction based on a little known story from WWII. She and her husband help maintain their mountain community church. They enjoy their children and six grandchildren.

Annmarie B. Tait lives in Conshohocken, PA with her husband Joe Beck. She enjoys cooking and many crafts, along with singing and recording Irish and American folk music. Annmarie has contributed several stories to the *Chicken Soup for the Soul* series, *Reminisce* magazine, and numerous other anthologies. E-mail her at irishbloom@aol.com.

Jodi Renee Thomas has published stories on many subjects, from relationships to women's rights. She is a featured speaker for the women's movement and an award-winning author of *aMused*. She lives happily in Florida with her teenage daughter, husband, and three dogs that like to bother her while she writes.

Marla H. Thurman lives in Signal Mountain, Tennessee, with her dogs Oreo and Sleeper. She is currently working on draft four of her memoirs. Her dream is that one day her favorite author, Pat Conroy, will ask for her autograph.

Erika Tremper's twin girls are almost grown now, and she devotes her non-working hours to meditation, swimming, reading, traveling, and hiking. Goals, ambitions, aspirations? No, thank you. Something always presents itself. E-mail her at erikatremper@comcast.net.

Dawn Turzio is an award-winning writer whose work has been featured in many publications including *The New York Times, MSN Lifestyle, Yahoo! News,* and *Salon,* which can be found at www. dawnturzio.com.

Donna Volkenannt is a wife, mother, grandmother, and volunteer. Winner of the Erma Bombeck Humor award and the Pikes Peak NLAPW flash fiction award, she was also a finalist in the Steinbeck short story competition. Donna divides her time between suburban Saint Peters and rural Osage County, MO.

Pat Wahler is a freelance writer in St. Peters, MO. She attempts to balance a full-time job working with juvenile offenders, a family, and writing career with varying degrees of success. Pat has published stories in several anthologies and blogs all things animal at www. critteralley.blogspot.com.

Kelly Sullivan Walden is on a mission to awaken the world to the power of dreams. She is the author of ten books, including *Chicken Soup for the Soul: Dreams & Premonitions, I Had the Strangest Dream, It's All in Your Dreams,* and the *Dream Oracle Cards.* It is whispered she is the love child of Lucille Ball and Carl Jung.

Ferida Wolff is the author of seventeen books for children and three essay books for children. She writes a blog at feridasbackyard. blogspot.com that looks at the nature/human connection. She has a passion for traveling and observing the world's birds, plants, and animals. E-mail her at feridawolff@msn.com.

Lisa Wright-Dixon received her Bachelor of Arts degree in Sociology from Syracuse University. She currently resides in South Carolina with her husband Gregory and their six cats. Lisa is currently working on other short stories and plans to write a book of childhood memoirs.

Meet Amy Newmark

Amy Newmark is the bestselling author, editor-in-chief, and publisher of the *Chicken Soup for the Soul* book series. Since 2008, she has published 197 new books, most of them national bestsellers in the U.S. and Canada, more than doubling the number of Chicken Soup for the Soul titles in print today. She is also the author of *Simply Happy*, a crash course in Chicken Soup for the Soul advice and wisdom that is filled with easy-to-implement, practical tips for enjoying a better life.

Amy is credited with revitalizing the Chicken Soup for the Soul brand, which has been a publishing industry phenomenon since the first book came out in 1993. By compiling inspirational and aspirational true stories curated from ordinary people who have had extraordinary experiences, Amy has kept the thirty-one-year-old Chicken Soup for the Soul brand fresh and relevant.

Amy graduated *magna cum laude* from Harvard University where she majored in Portuguese and minored in French. She then embarked on a three-decade career as a Wall Street analyst, a hedge fund manager, and a corporate executive in the technology field. She is a Chartered Financial Analyst.

Her return to literary pursuits was inevitable, as her honors thesis in college involved traveling throughout Brazil's impoverished northeast region, collecting stories from regular people. She is delighted to have

Meet Amy Newmark | 347

come full circle in her writing career — from collecting stories "from the people" in Brazil as a twenty-year-old to, three decades later, collecting stories "from the people" for Chicken Soup for the Soul.

When Amy and her husband Bill, the CEO of Chicken Soup for the Soul, are not working, they are visiting their four grown children and their spouses, and their five grandchildren.

Follow Amy on Twitter @amynewmark. Listen to her free podcast — Chicken Soup for the Soul with Amy Newmark — on Apple, Google, or by using your favorite podcast app on your phone.

Thank You

We owe huge thanks to all our contributors and fans. Here at Chicken Soup for the Soul we want to thank our Associate Publisher D'ette Corona for reviewing our story library and presenting us with hundreds of stories to choose from for this new collection. Publisher and Editor-in-Chief Amy Newmark made the final selection of the 101 that are included here, all personal favorites, and D'ette created the manuscript. None of these stories appeared in previous *Chicken Soup for the Soul* books about mothers and daughters. They were compiled from our books on other topics.

The whole publishing team deserves a hand, including Senior Editor Barbara LoMonaco, Vice President of Marketing Maureen Peltier, Vice President of Production Victor Cataldo, and our graphic designer Daniel Zaccari, who turned our manuscript into this beautiful, entertaining book.

Sharing Happiness, Inspiration, and Hope

Real people sharing real stories, every day, all over the world. In 2007, *USA Today* named *Chicken Soup for the Soul* one of the five most memorable books in the last quarter-century. With over 110 million books sold to date in the U.S. and Canada alone, more than 300 titles in print, and translations into nearly fifty languages, "chicken soup for the soul®" is one of the world's best-known phrases.

Today, thirty-one years after we first began sharing happiness, inspiration and hope through our books, we continue to delight our readers with ten to twelve new titles each year, but have also evolved beyond the bookshelves with super premium pet food, a podcast, adult coloring books, and licensed products that include word-search puzzle books and books for babies and preschoolers. We are busy "changing your life one story at a time®." Thanks for reading!

Share with Us

We have all had Chicken Soup for the Soul moments in our lives. If you would like to share your story, go to chickensoup.com and click on Books and then Submit Your Story. You will find our writing guidelines there, along with a list of topics we're working on.

You may be able to help another reader and become a published author at the same time! Some of our past contributors have even launched writing and speaking careers from the publication of their stories in our books.

We only accept story submissions via our website. They are no longer accepted via postal mail or fax. And they are not accepted via e-mail.

To contact us regarding other matters, please send an e-mail to the webmaster@chickensoupforthesoul.com, or write us at:

Chicken Soup for the Soul
P.O. Box 700
Cos Cob, CT 06807-0700

One more note from your friends at Chicken Soup for the Soul: Occasionally, we receive an unsolicited book manuscript from one of our readers, and we would like to respectfully inform you that we do not accept unsolicited manuscripts, and we must discard the ones that are sent to us.

Paperback: 978-1-61159-110-1

eBook: 978-1-61159-345-7

More fun and entertainment

Chicken Soup for the Soul

Me and My Cat

Amy Newmark

Royalties from this book go to AMERICAN·HUMANE
FIRST TO SERVE

Paperback: 978-1-61159-111-8
eBook: 978-1-61159-346-4

with our four-legged family members

Chicken Soup for the Soul.

Think Positive, Live Happy

101 Stories about Creating Your Best Life

Amy Newmark
& Deborah Norville
Journalist and Anchor of *Inside Edition*

Paperback: 978-1-61159-992-3
eBook: 978-1-61159-293-1

Self-care, time management

101 Stories About
Self-Care and Balance

Amy Newmark

Paperback: 978-1-61159-074-6
eBook: 978-1-61159-314-3

and positive thinking for you and yours

Changing the world one story at a time®
www.chickensoup.com